MANAGING WITH

DATA

ALA Editions purchases fund advocacy, awareness, and accreditation programs
for library professionals worldwide.

MANAGING WITH
DATA
Using ACRLMetrics and PLAmetrics

PETER HERNON | ROBERT E. DUGAN | JOSEPH R. MATTHEWS

An imprint of the American Library Association
Chicago 2015

© 2015 by the American Library Association

Printed in the United States of America
19 18 17 16 15   5 4 3 2 1

Extensive effort has gone into ensuring the reliability of the information in this book;
however, the publisher makes no warranty, express or implied, with respect to the
material contained herein.

ISBN: 978-0-8389-1243-0 (paper).

Library of Congress Cataloging-in-Publication Data

Hernon, Peter.
    Managing with data : using ACRLMetrics and PLAmetrics / Peter Hernon,
Robert E. Dugan, and Joseph R. Matthews.
      pages cm
    Includes bibliographical references and index.
    ISBN 978-0-8389-1243-0 (alk. paper)
    1. Library statistics. 2. Academic libraries—Statistics. 3. Public libraries—
Statistics. 4. Library administration—Statistical methods. 5. Libraries—Evaluation—
Statistical methods. 6. Library reports. I. Dugan, Robert E., 1952- II. Matthews,
Joseph R. III. Title.
    Z669.8.H465 2015
    025.1'021—dc23   2014018643

Cover design by Kimberly Thornton.
Book composition by Alejandra Diaz in the Mercury and Futura typefaces.

♾ This paper meets the requirements of ANSI/NISO Z39.48-1992 (Permanence of Paper).

CONTENTS

FIGURES, TABLES, AND TEXT BOXES

FIGURES

TABLES

TEXT BOXES

TEXT BOXES, cont'd.

PREFACE

THE ASSOCIATION OF COLLEGE and Research Libraries (ACRL) offers ACRL*Metrics*, an online data service providing access to ACRL and National Center for Education Statistics (NCES), U.S. Department of Education, academic library statistics; and the Public Library Association (PLA) has PLA*metrics*, an online data service for the Public Library Data Service (PLDS), which captures voluntarily submitted, annual data on staffing, operating finances, output metrics, interlibrary loaning, and technology provisions from a number of public libraries throughout the United States and Canada. With the availability of both data services, library managers can identify and track trends as well as raise management-related questions that they can use a data service to address. They can also compare their library to a set of peer libraries and to best practices. The purpose of *Managing with Data: Using ACRL*Metrics and *PLA*metrics is to provide a roadmap for using these important data services so that readers gain a foundation upon which they can build. To reinforce this purpose, a companion web portal enables readers to work with actual data variables and selected data as they answer the questions included in chapter exercises (see the accompanying text box, "Companion Website on the next page"). Because the data services described in this work require some orientation, managers in academic and public libraries, and the staff they oversee, will benefit from the guidance offered.

We realize that a number of library managers have not taken a statistics course, and some of them may feel uncomfortable dealing with large sets of numbers. This guide, it is our hope, removes any anxiety as we walk readers through the data services, showing them how to perform simple and complex manipulations as well as offering different choices for displaying findings graphically.

Readers wanting a complementary work that elaborates on the concepts discussed in the chapters and additional exercises should consult our *Getting Started with Evaluation* (ALA, 2014). To engage in formal evaluation or assessment research and explore problems that the data sets cannot address, readers might review *Engaging in Evaluation and Assessment Research*, written by Peter Hernon, Robert E. Dugan, and Danuta Nitecki (Libraries Unlimited, 2011).

Data help library managers demonstrate program and service efficiency and effectiveness, as well as show what and how much they can accomplish, perhaps within a cost management framework. The goal might be to address the value of the library to its community and stakeholders. Like it or not, data are linked to accountability, and accountability is more than the financial return on investment. Accountability documents the library's role and value to the broader organization/institution and to society. As this book illustrates, academic and public libraries can use metrics and strategic planning to promote accountability. Expressed differently, we all recognize that change is constant. We also need a context for dealing with change management (a vision and a strategic plan); an awareness of stakeholder expectations; an ability to meet those expectations, in part, by using evidence; and knowledge about the most effective ways to present that evidence in a meaningful way. This book also encourages library managers to keep asking what data or evidence do they need, what the data mean, and where do they find the data. Complicating matters, so much data are available, and the amount (and types) continues to increase. However, the two data services offer excellent starting points.

COMPANION WEBSITE

Both ACRL and PLA have kindly agreed to provide access to a *complimentary* subset of ACRL*Metrics* and PLA*metrics* to the readers of this book. This subset of data represents those libraries that have consistently provided data in annual surveys over a span of years. To gain access to these data, visit the website, ManagingwithDataandMetrics.org.

You will be asked to indicate which data service, ACRL*Metrics* or PLA*metrics*, you are interested in. Next, provide brief registration information about yourself, and answer a simple question (which you will be able to do with this book in hand). You will be provided with a user name and password, which will permit you to log in. Once you have logged in, you will be able to work through the various exercises found in the book as well as explore the database of library statistics and performance metrics for your own purposes.

In addition to providing access to the ACRL*Metrics* or the PLA*metrics* datasets that you can use to follow the exercises provided in the book, the accompanying portal will let you prepare any number of tables, charts, and graphs for your library that will be of value in helping answer a variety of questions. The portal enables us to share a variety of information with you including:

- **Presentation materials.** Copies of the PowerPoint slides that we will use when making presentations about the book.
- **Workshop schedule.** We will be presenting a number of workshops in the coming months that you may find of interest. The schedule for these workshops will be kept updated here.
- **Extra exercises.** We will post a number of additional exercises (and the answers) based on questions and issues that arise during a workshop.
- **Errata.** If we notice any errors in the book, we will alert you about them here.
- **Q&A.** Should you have any questions, please do not hesitate to contact us (for e-mail addresses see below). We will share the questions (stripping away the identity of those involved) and answers for all to see.

We believe that using all available data will to improve the decision-making process in any library. Libraries spend a tremendous amount each year collecting and reporting a large number of performance metrics. The data compiled, in our opinion, can (or should) be used more for planning, accountability, and decision-making purposes.

After only a time or two of exploring and using one of the databases, you will quickly realize the power and flexibility that are accessible anytime to assist you in answering important questions that your library is asking. The kind folks at Counting Opinions are available to answer any questions that you might have (a form for submitting questions may be found on the website shown in the "Companion Website" text box).

We trust that you will find the combination of reading the book, with its step-by-step instructions, and having access to a library database a stimulating experience and will lead you and your library to use the available performance indicators as one helpful tool in managing your library.

In addition, both Robert E. Dugan (robert.dugan@gmail.com) and Joseph R. Matthews (joe@joematthews.com) will respond to any e-mail questions that you might have.

ACKNOWLEDGMENTS

WE WISH TO THANK the Association of College and Research Libraries and the Public Library Association, American Library Association, for letting us (1) have access to both data services and (2) create a guide to enable librarians and students in master's degree programs in library and information science to experiment with the data sets in those two services. We also appreciate the support provided by Counting Opinions in producing a guide that enables more libraries and librarians to engage in evidence-based management and to develop measurable targets associated with their strategic priorities (as specified in their strategic and other plans). In particular, we want to acknowledge Carl Thompson, president of Counting Opinions, who carefully reviewed the entire manuscript to ensure the accuracy and completeness of the explanations pertaining to the use of ACRL*Metrics* and PLA*metrics*.

The Context for Libraries Today and Beyond

THE NATIONAL FOCUS ON accountability extends beyond adherence to the core values of the library profession, such as those associated with intellectual freedom and financial management (e.g., managing the budget ethically). More broadly, that focus involves the alignment of the library's mission (services and programs) with strategic priorities and the mission of the institution, including stakeholder expectations, to ensure organizational effectiveness, efficiency, and the provision of high-quality services and programs. In the case of academic libraries, accountability might be viewed in terms of the library's value and relevance to institutional goals, such as the accomplishment of student learning outcomes.[1] For public libraries, accountability means achieving greater effectiveness and efficiency; adhering to the mission of the organization and stakeholder expectations, including those of funding partners and the community served; and reporting progress on accomplishing stated goals, objectives, and outcomes.[2] Accountability might also be examined from the perspectives of stakeholders, such as the federal government and state and local governments, and their expectations (e.g., those related to the achievement of a set of standards or institutional goals as set forth by accreditation organizations).

Accountability is linked to evaluation and assessment, which, in turn, are connected to planning and the accomplishment of the mission. Critical to accountability is monitoring programs, services, and library use both on-site and remotely, while making decisions about ongoing programs and services, the creation of new ones, traffic flow within the library, and customer preferences for the use of space, collections, and equipment and for interacting with library staff. Some key questions are these:

» What evidence do library managers use to demonstrate value?
» From where do they gather that evidence?
» What are the strengths and weaknesses of that evidence?
» Does the evidence apply across time and locations?
» How do library managers use and communicate that evidence?
» How is the message received?

In *Getting Started with Evaluation*, we amplify on that evidence.[3] Suffice to say, the evidence often takes the form of the following:

» Input metrics, which are generally counts of a numeric value reflecting the budget and financial allocations to the infrastructure (collections and services, facilities, staff, and technology available for customer use); or
» Output metrics, which convey the extent of library use and tend to be counts of the kinds and volume of activity.

Library managers, however, might also compile process metrics (internal efficiencies), which focus on activities that transform resources (inputs) into the services (outputs) the library delivers. Because these metrics quantify the cost or time to perform a specific task or activity, they deal with efficiency. Finally, in some instances, library managers might measure the extent to which use of the library, its resources and services, changes customers—their knowledge, abilities, mindsets, and skills—and report the extent to which the library *truly makes a difference* in the lives of its customers and community. Such changes refer to outcomes and, more broadly, to impacts, known as impact evaluation or impact assessment. Further, determining an impact may not always be reduced simply to frequency counts and reported as a metric, a percentage (key ratio) produced from a calculation of a numerator and a denominator. The impact, in other words, might be articulated in terms of qualitative evidence.

Another way to look at metrics is that they can vary from the simple to the complex. On the simple side, a library tends to have extensive budget data showing the financial allocation to the resources (input metrics) and to use data to characterize use in the library and remotely (output metrics). Use data, in part, might come from vendor reports reflecting user activities (service use). A library might also monitor some process metrics to report on efficiencies. Moving to the complex side, managers might strive to measure outcomes, associated with or without metrics, that relate the impact of services on customers. Managers must be cautious in asserting outcomes from a mere presentation of input and output metrics that reflect the library perspective and not the perspectives of customers, communities, the broader organization and institution, and other stakeholders, including governments (see chapter 8).

EVIDENCE-BASED MANAGEMENT AND PLANNING

Evidence-based management is predicated on the assumption that managerial decisions are based on the best available evidence, which, to some stakeholders, means quantitative data. The evidence might emerge while conducting formal research or gathering data for favorite metrics. In principle, whenever possible, all managers should base decision making on evidence, and they should apply the evidence to planning and the setting of targets and measuring progress toward achievement of those targets. Managers should also acknowledge the limitations of data reliability (accuracy) and validity (the data gathered measure what they are supposed to, or the extent of generalizability of the evidence). Annotations should be recorded for all anomalous data.

Management Information Systems

For years, writers within and outside library and information science (LIS) have urged libraries and many other organizations to invest in a formal or informal management methodology and to use collected data for planning and decision-making purposes. One example of such an approach is the balanced scorecard, which aligns activities and actions to the mission and strategic priorities of the organization and enables managers to compare organizational performance with strategic goals. As originally conceived, the scorecard offered a performance measurement framework that adds strategic nonfinancial performance metrics to traditional financial metrics to provide managers with a balanced view of organizational performance.[4] Today, the scorecard might focus on customers and accountability for the use of public or institutional funds. Academic and public libraries in the United States, however, have infrequently used a formal scorecard and monitored progress relative to meeting strategic priorities. More frequently, libraries have experimented with a scorecard, but have not used it on an ongoing basis. One challenge of the scorecard is that libraries must continuously capture data. Those that have not done so might label the process as too time-consuming and cumbersome. They might also view the labor involved in developing and maintaining a management methodology as excessive in comparison to the benefits they derive. Further, when the goal is to compare performance among peer libraries, there might not be any readily available data to make meaningful comparisons easily. All of this, however, is changing, as the next section illustrates.

RELEVANT DATABASES

There are two major, online data services relevant to academic or public libraries. The first, ACRL*Metrics*, provides access to academic library statistics that libraries have supplied to the Association of College and Research Libraries (ACRL) and the National Center for Education Statistics (NCES), U.S. Department of Education, since 2000. There is also a subset of data from the Integrated Postsecondary Education Data System (IPEDS) specific to academic libraries. Each year, IPEDS provides data from those colleges, universities, and technical and vocational institutions that participate in the federal student financial aid programs.[5] In 2012, the NCES's survey asked responding libraries if their institutions had enacted student learning outcomes and included information literacy among those outcomes.[6] Respondents, however, merely marked *yes* or *no*.[7] The results consequently only provide limited insights into outcomes or impacts as they do not characterize the impact of the library on students and other groups.

The second data service, PLA*metrics*, covers the annual survey of the Public Library Data Service (PLDS) from fiscal year (FY) 2002 to FY2011 and data on public libraries available from the Institute of Museum and Library Services (IMLS) since FY2000. The PLDS includes data from more than one thousand libraries in the United States and Canada and from the IMLS data set, which represents more than nine thousand public libraries in the United States. In addition, each year the PLDS survey highlights statistics on a special service area or public library topic.[8]

Counting Opinions (SQUIRE) Ltd., a Toronto, Canada, company, provides the platform currently used to access both data services. The focus of this book is on the variables in both data services (ACRL*Metrics* and PLA*metrics*) and selected data behind those variables, and not on Counting Opinions itself. As a professional service, with agreement from ACRL and PLA, the firm has graciously provided us with access to ACRL*Metrics* and PLA*metrics*. Clearly, this unique opportunity benefits actual and potential subscribers, as well as students in master's degree programs in LIS, and enables them to associate decision making and planning with quantitative data sets.[9] As well, a user of either data service can identify preferred variables and link them to demonstrating value that different stakeholders should know.

Getting Started in Using the Data Services

Example 1.1 illustrates the steps involved in getting started with both data services, while subsequent chapters indicate how to use certain functions to perform different operations. Library managers can use the interactive features of each data service to construct a profile of inputs and outputs for their library, selected libraries, all libraries, or libraries within a particular subset, such as those representing part of the Carnegie Classifications (applies only to higher education).[10] One value of both data services is that they cover multiple years and, thus, enable users to make comparisons across time. Such trend data enable them to place a particular year or use of the library infrastructure in a larger context and to set targets to monitor long-term changes and improvements. In doing so, they can determine the extent to which their library achieves short-term goals (up to two years) while engaging in benchmarking—creating a point of reference against which they can repeatedly collect measures—and looking for relevant best practices, which refers to best management practices, meaning the processes, practices, and systems identified in different organizations that performed exceptionally well and are widely recognized as improving those organizations' performance and economic efficiency in specific areas (see chapters 6 and 7). The goal is to reduce expenditures and improve operational effectiveness and efficiency.

EXAMPLE 1.1 **GETTING STARTED**

STEP 1   Visit the website, ManagingwithDataandMetrics.org, where you will be asked to indicate which data service, ACRL*Metrics* or PLA*metrics*, you are interested in. Next, provide brief registration information about yourself, and answer a simple question (which you will be able to do with the book in hand). You will receive a user name and password, which will permit you to log in. Once you have logged in, you will be able to work through the various exercises found in the book as well as explore the database of library statistics and performance metrics for your own purposes.

STEP 2   The following screen shot enables you to see the areas critical for building a report, similar to the ones discussed in the following chapters.[11] We encourage you to re-create the tables highlighted in those chapters. (Please examine note 11 as you review the screen shot.)

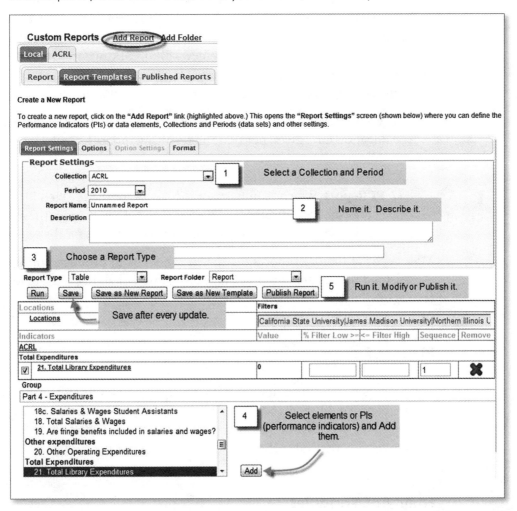

STEP 3   Review, once more, numbers 3 and 5 in the preceding screen shot. The following chapters reinforce this point.

STEP 4   Proceed to chapter 2. After reading it, review the exercises and create reports for your library based on the exercises. (Please note that if you have any questions, the home page, ManagingwithDataandMetrics .org, contains a form that you can complete and submit to Counting Opinions. They will answer questions. As an alternative, you may contact one of the authors.)

ACRL*Metrics*

Once logged onto this data service, readers can create a new report by clicking on the Add Report link, which opens the Report Settings screen (see example 1.1), where they can define the Performance Indicators (PIs) or data elements, Collections and Periods (data sets), and other settings.

Next, users can select a data set from the list of available Collections as shown in the table. Once a data set is selected, the screen refreshes with the list of available PIs for the selected Collection. To expedite the selection of specific PIs to include in the Report, users can specify a Group/Section name from the available list. They can select one or more PIs (click the PI name to highlight) and then click Add. Readers can also multi-select PIs by holding down the Control key (or Command key for Apple users) when selecting PIs. They can also add PIs from more than one data set. To do so, simply select a different Collection from the available list and then Add the PIs as appropriate.

Different types of reports might be produced, including the following:

1. **Table Report,** which "provides a summary view of the data by reporting location for a given period. The resulting report features interactive column sorting, pagination options, and feature graph icons and an Excel download."
2. **PI Report,** which "summarizes the values for the selected PI (performance indicator) and Period. The output includes the average, total, median, variances, [and] lower and upper quartiles for the selected PI(s)."

Most types of tabular reports feature graph icons to produce pop-up graphs for the selected results and downloadable Excel files, enabling readers to explore the results off-line.

PLA*metrics*

The process just outlined applies to PLA*metrics* as well. It merits mention that all reports can be published and shared with others via e-mail, text message, Twitter, or posting on a website or blog. Readers can also use the QR-Code feature to post links to reports in print materials.

Family of Variables

Through ACRL*Metrics* on this book's companion portal, the data encompass the following general variables: institutional characteristics (IPEDS data), library personnel, expenditures, hours (e.g., total public service hours per typical full-service week), collections, use (e.g., number of virtual visits, number of reference transactions, total circulation for the fiscal year, number of group presentations, and the number of participants in those groups).

Through PLA*metrics* on the portal, managers have access to data on "general information" (e.g., population of service area), "annual counts," total income, "technology" in the libraries, "Website features provided," "paid staff (FTE)," "library collections," "reference service," "library service" (e.g., visits and interlibrary loan use), and use of electronic services, as well as assorted metrics—input, output, service level (e.g., circulation per week, visits per week, and "reference transactions per visit"), website features provided, public use of technology (e.g., circulation of video game consoles and circulation of e-book readers), and cost per output. Further, for each variable, there is a definition.

DATA REPORTS

Through either of the data services, library managers and students in LIS programs can produce an array of pre-configured summary reports in online formats and ready-to-run or customizable report templates, or both. As well, PLA*metrics* subscribers can create various custom reports based on data definitions provided in both services for participating libraries for a particular year or set of multiple years. Using either data service, managers might, for instance, create a cross-tab table comparing libraries on a particular variable (e.g., percentage of professional staff to total staff), or drill down to produce a comparative chart. They can also export data to an Excel or Microsoft Word file and create special reports.[12] This guide, as well as the reports' instructions, also illustrates other ways to view and report data.

GOING BEYOND JUST LIBRARY METRICS

This guide, as already noted, focuses on the input and output metrics found in ACRL*Metrics* and PLA*metrics* that managers can use to characterize a library or compare a library to a set of its so-called peers. ACRL*Metrics*, however, offers other ways to view libraries and their contributions to the parent institution or organization. The IPEDS data set, for instance, covers institutional characteristics, including, among others, the cost of tuition, enrollment, student financial aid, degrees and certificates conferred, and student persistence. Among the data elements are

- » First-year retention rates collected since 2003;
- » Transfer-out rate, which reports the total number of students who transferred to another institution;
- » Graduation rate, which is interpreted as an indicator of institutional productivity;
- » Fall enrollment, which is the traditional metric for showing the extent of student access to higher education; and
- » Total entering class, which refers to the number of incoming students (those enrolling for the first time in a postsecondary institution and those transferring from another institution). By using this variable, institutional researchers can calculate the graduation rate cohort as a proportion of the total entering student body.

Such data elements enable libraries to view metrics from a broader perspective—that of the institution or broader organization (see chapter 8). They might also include metrics that relate the customer perspective (e.g., from Counting Opinions' LibSat) as well as that of other stakeholders, such as program and regional accreditation organizations.[13] For example, a number of state legislatures and governors, as well as private foundations (e.g., Lumina Foundation), define educational success in terms of graduation rates and the employment of graduates with high-paying jobs in the state. At the national level, President Barack Obama and members of Congress increasingly emphasize the affordability of a degree and wider availability of a college education to the American public, perhaps through community colleges.[14] Such metrics are known as *student metrics*; technically, they are output metrics, but ones applicable to the institution and to making comparisons among institutions.

Student metrics have not displaced *student learning outcomes*, which are transparent statements of the knowledge, skills, attitudes, competencies, and habits of mind that students are expected to acquire at an institution of higher education. Those learning goals might relate, for instance, to critical thinking, problem solving, global citizenry, quantitative reasoning, or information literacy. Academic programs and institutions might even be expected to develop outcomes that stakeholders can use to make comparisons about student growth across programs and institutions and to document changes in a particular institution over time.[15] Student learning outcomes, however, are often not reduced to a set of metrics. (Chapter 8 tries to link student metrics and student learning metrics to the data services and supplementary surveys that might be linked to ACRL*Metrics*.)

RELEVANT STUDIES

Some research studies view the academic library in a larger setting—that of the institution. Institutions of higher education are asking their libraries and other university departments to demonstrate their relevance and value. Studies that have investigated the impact of library use on the retention (persistence) and academic success—graduation—of undergraduate students, however, might be based on some questionable assumptions:

» They might assume all students need and use the library. In fact, use varies from low to high, and, without doubt, a number of undergraduates do not use the library, either physically or virtually.

» They might focus on grade point average (GPA), but do not factor in grade inflation. One controversial study argues that it is better to focus on the *signaling* power of grades for employment (landing prestigious jobs and higher salaries).[16] Clearly, this study relates GPA to student outcomes and accountability as articulated by state legislatures and governors; many educators, however, question the value of factoring in GPA.

» Regarding metrics based on library visits, students enter the library building for many reasons, some of which are to gain access to group study facilities, cafés, social spaces, and student services.

» The metrics used all focus on library use and do not address such issues as student satisfaction and the extent to which library variables make an *impact* at the institutional level. They also ignore student learning outcomes and the library's role as a partner in some of these outcomes.

» The data are solely based on self-reporting or self-perceptions as opposed to actual student performance or use.[17]

It would seem that future studies might add variables covering student satisfaction with the institution and the library, as well as additional data from IPEDS. Further, ACRL*Metrics* offers many variables that might be added to a regression model and an explanation of library value at the institutional level.

Using a different data set, Sharon A. Weiner focused on the ARL Membership Index, which has subsequently been replaced by the Library Investment Index, previously named Expenditures-Focused Index, and which is "less affected by changes in the collections variables."[18] Weiner examined the Index in terms of the number of reference transactions, the number of instructional presentations, and the number of attendees at group presentations, and included the following independent variables: the total professional/support staff, total library expenditures, total full-time graduate/professional student enrollment, total full-time faculty whose major regular assignment is instruction, and total full-time undergraduate/unclassified student enrollment. She created a variable for undergraduate students by subtracting the full-time graduate/professional student enrollment from the full-time student enrollment. Thus, the revised figure includes unclassified students. The Index, she found, is a reasonable predictor of some aspects of library value, as defined in terms of the variables included in that index.[19] Using the new Index, Weiner's study merits replication, but might also address satisfaction and IPEDS institutional data.

Using data collected by ARL, ACRL, and the NCES, Elizabeth M. Mezick found a significant positive effect between library expenditures and the number of library staff, and student persistence.[20] Again, the list of variables examined in future studies might address student satisfaction with the library and the institution, and IPEDS data.

Using NCES data, John J. Regazzi profiled spending, staffing, and use in academic libraries from 2008 to 2010 and compared the data to those of the previous decade. As widely recognized, the economic recession and its aftermath have led to retrenchment in academic library budgets and expenditures.[21] In many cases, retrenchment has persisted since 2010 and, to place his study in a broader context, additional research might draw on IPEDS data and report the financial decline that many small and middle-sized libraries have encountered in an institutional context: Is there a similar constriction of the budget at the institutional level?

Turning to the United Kingdom, Graham Stone and Bryony Ramsden compared e-resources use, library borrowing statistics, and library gate counts for the degrees awarded to 33,074 undergraduate students in eight universities. Relying on focus group interviews and quantitative data collection, the researchers found "a statistically significant relationship between student attainment and two of the indicators—e-resources use and book borrowing statistics—and that this relationship has been shown to be true across all eight partners in the project."[22]

And, finally, Danuta A. Nitecki and Eileen Ables created a "library value wheel," which covers satisfaction, productivity, student learning, the return on investment, social engagement, and work reward. The wheel can be viewed from the following perspectives: the library and its staff, faculty, students, administrators, and donors. The investigators tested the wheel with some faculty members who are library users and identified different reasons for their use. Nitecki and Ables concluded that "[l]ibrary value is not seen in faculty achievements but in contributing to their ability to achieve. It is not in student grades but in enhancing students' capacity to learn. It is not in scholarship, but in . . . [indulging their] curiosity."[23] Their findings question the value of focusing on grades or grade point average, and Nitecki and Ables call for research to investigate other stakeholders and to revise the model as required. As well, further research needs to figure out meaningful ways to show how libraries contribute to student outcomes and student learning outcomes at the institutional, and perhaps program, level.

In summary, the data from either data service might be used to monitor budget expenditures and use for a particular library as well as make comparisons among a set of peer libraries and all libraries (national overview). As the preceding examples illustrate, the data might also be used when investigators compare data elements and draw conclusions about issues of student retention, graduation rate, and the role of the library in an institutional context. At the same time, it is important to supplement so-called library input and output data with data representing customer satisfaction and student learning outcomes. Public libraries can substitute impact evaluation for student learning outcomes (see chapter 8), thereby adding a new component to value as being more than the return on investment.

CAUTIONS

In using nationally produced data services, it is important to read about the data-collection process and any related reliability and validity issues, as well as to review the response rate question by question. When managers engage in trend analysis, they should review the definitions of the data elements they want to use and ensure that definitions have not changed over time (at least for the years of interest to them) and that there are available explanations for outliers (anomalous data). Further, as the preceding section, "Relevant Studies," underscores, input and output data only tell a portion of the story. What data should supplement them, and how do they help to round out that story? At the same time, as new variables emerge and so much more input and output data become available, library managers can add new data elements to their managerial review. Those elements might document changes over time, within and beyond a single library, and be useful for demonstrating institutional relevance and value.

CONCLUDING THOUGHTS

Since the 1970s, there have been numerous efforts to identify performance metrics that are most useful for academic and public libraries. With the widespread availability of data on the use of digital resources, use patterns and preferences can be better documented. Nonetheless, as this chapter illustrates, there is a need and an opportunity to expand the set of metrics to include those meaningful to library and institutional stakeholders. Clearly, libraries have choices about which metrics to gather and how frequently. As they do so, they might supplement the metrics discussed in this book with LibSat and other data sets, thereby providing a richer and more varied set of data to aid managers in planning and decision making. Still, the fundamental question is, "What story does a library want to tell?" Perhaps sub-questions include: "Does a set of data actually tell the story the managers want told?" and "Is this the story meaningful to the community served and other stakeholders?"

EXERCISES

Answers to the following questions are in the "Appendix" at the back of the book. We encourage different members of a library staff to work on the exercises together and to discuss the results. Managers might also participate in that discussion.

QUESTION 1 In either ACRL*Metrics* or PLA*metrics*, do you find any variables and metrics that a library's stakeholders would value? Discuss the question from the perspective of different stakeholders.

QUESTION 2 To complement both data services, are there any additional variables you think a library or a set of libraries should gather? How should they do so?

QUESTION 3 How might libraries settle on a set of peers? How important is it to compare a library to that set? Should that set fluctuate over time?

QUESTION 4 For reference service, virtual or not, do you see any variables or data that might rise to the level of best practices? Discuss. (Note: Best practices, like benchmarking, encourage organizations to improve, look ahead, and challenge themselves to perform better rather than settle for the status quo. Benchmarking is not an end unto itself; rather, it should lead to the identification and enactment of best practices.)

Notes

1. See Association of College and Research Libraries, *The Value of Academic Libraries: A Comprehensive Research Review and Report*, prepared by Megan Oakleaf (Chicago: Association of College and Research Libraries, 2010), www.ala.org/acrl/sites/ala.org .acrl/files/content/issues/value/val_report.pdf. See also American Library Association, Association of College and Research Libraries, *Connect, Collaborate, and Communicate: A Report from the Value of Academic Libraries Summits*, prepared by Karen Brown and Kara J. Malenfant (Chicago: Association of College and Research Libraries, 2012), www.ala.org/ acrl/sites/ala.org.acrl/files/content/issues/value/val_summit.pdf.

2. See Rhea Joyce Rubin, *Demonstrating Results: Using Outcome Measurement in Your Library* (Chicago: American Library Association, 2006).

3. Peter Hernon, Robert E. Dugan, and Joseph R. Matthews, *Getting Started with Evaluation* (Chicago: American Library Association, 2014).

4. See Joseph R. Matthews, *Scorecards for Results: A Guide for Developing a Library Balanced Scorecard* (Westport, CT: Libraries Unlimited, 2008).

5. "The Higher Education Act of 1965, as amended, requires that institutions that participate in federal student aid programs report data on enrollments, program completions, graduation rates, faculty and staff, finances, institutional prices, and student financial aid. These data are made available to students and parents through the College Navigator . . . Web site [http://nces.ed.gov/collegenavigator/] and to researchers and others through the IPEDS Data Center [http://nces.ed.gov/ipeds/datacenter/]" (National Center for Education Statistics, "About IPEDS," http://nces.ed.gov/ipeds/about/).

6. NCES will no longer conduct the Academic Library Survey (ALS); it conducted its last survey with the FY2012 data. It was decided at the federal level to eliminate the ALS and transfer part of the information to two IPEDS surveys. The primary reason for this decision was that the numerous questions on the ALS created an undue data collection burden. Further, the migration of library data represents the movement toward the evolution of IPEDS into the omnibus postsecondary institutional data collection. Some library data will be moved into the winter IPEDS survey collection. Additional limited data about staff will be moved into the Human Resources IPEDS survey. The next collection will be of FY2014 data, and it will be collected annually as part of IPEDS. No FY2013 data was collected by NCES or IPEDS.

7. These are items 800 and 801 on the survey (see also chapter 8).

8. PLA discontinued printing a paper copy of its statistical report in 2011. Thereafter, the data are only available as a data set; see also chapter 8.

9. Counting Opinions has taken all of the appendixes found in *Viewing Library Metrics from Different Perspectives* by Robert E. Dugan, Peter Hernon, and Danuta A. Nitecki (Santa Barbara, CA: Libraries Unlimited, 2011) and enabled subscribers of LibSat to re-create each metric.

10. "Starting in 1970, the Carnegie Commission on Higher Education developed a classification of colleges and universities to support its program of research and policy analysis. Derived from empirical data on colleges and universities, the Carnegie Classification was originally published in 1973, and subsequently updated in 1976, 1987, 1994, 2000, 2005, and 2010 to reflect changes among colleges and universities. This framework has been widely used in the study of higher education, both as a way to represent and control for institutional differences, and also in the design of research studies to ensure adequate representation of sampled institutions, students, or faculty." See the Carnegie Classification of Institutions of Higher Education, "About Carnegie Classification," http://classifications.carnegiefoundation.org/.

11. The five critical areas illustrated in Step 2 include: (1) The Collection enables the user to select a data set (e.g., ACRL or PLA) from a drop-down box. Once a data set is chosen, the user may change the time period of the data. The Period is also influenced by the Report Type chosen (critical area 3). (2) Report name provides a text box for the user to name or otherwise describe the report to be created. It also displays the name of a report chosen from a list of locally created reports or report templates. (3) Report Type provides a drop-down menu of reports that may choose to run, including trends, tables, and graphs. (4) This drop-down box provides a list of Performance Indicators and/or data elements from which to select. The availability of indicators and elements depend on the Collection and period chosen above in criterial area 1. A user can pick one or more indicators to apply in the report. (5) The buttons in this area provide the user with actions that can be taken. The user can run the report, save the variables of the report as a new template for later use, and publish the report by creating a unique URL for those who do not have secure access to the Counting Opinions' platform.

12. For an overview of different reports and ACRL*Metrics*, see Christopher Steward, "An Overview of ACRL*Metrics*," *Journal of Academic Librarianship* 37, no. 1 (January 2011): 73–76; Christopher Steward, "An Overview of ACRL*Metrics*, Part II: Using NCES and IPEDS Data," *Journal of Academic Librarianship* 38, no. 6 (November 2012): 342–45. See also Ian Reid, "The Public Library Data Service 2012 Statistical Report: Characteristics and Trends," *Public Libraries* 51, no. 6 (2012): 36–46.

13. LibSat, produced by Counting Opinions, includes online surveys designed to capture customer satisfaction and library use data, including the actual comments of customers on a library and its infrastructure. See Peter Hernon and Ellen Altman, *Assessing Service Quality: Satisfying the Expectations of Library Customers* (Chicago: American Library Association, 2010).

14. See Peter Hernon, Robert E. Dugan, and Candy Schwartz, *Higher Education Outcomes Assessment for the Twenty-First Century* (Santa Barbara, CA: Libraries Unlimited, 2013).

15. Hernon, Dugan, and Schwartz, *Higher Education Outcomes Assessment for the Twenty-First Century.*

16. Evangeleen Pattison, Eric Grodsky, and Chandra Muller, "Is the Sky Falling? Grade Inflation and the Signaling Power of Grades," *Educational Researcher* (2013), http://edr.sagepub.com/content/early/2013/05/09/0013189X13481382.abstract.

17. See Krista M. Soria, Jan Fransen, and Shane Nackerud, "Library Use and Undergraduate Student Outcomes: New Evidence for Students' Retention and Academic Success," *portal: Libraries and the Academy* 13, no. 2 (2013): 147–64; Gaby Haddow, "Academic Library Use and Student Retention: A Quantitative Analysis," *Library & Information Science Research* 35, no. 2 (2013): 127–36; Mark Emmons and Frances C. Wilkinson, "The Academic Library Impact on Student Persistence," *College & Research Libraries* 72, no. 2 (March 2011): 128–49; Shun Han Rebekah Wong and T. D. Webb, "Uncovering Meaningful Correlation between Student Academic Performance and Library Material Usage," *College & Research Libraries* 72, no. 4 (July 2011): 361–70.

18. Association of Research Libraries, "ARL Statistics: ARL Ranking," www.arlstatistics.org/analytics.

19. Sharon A. Weiner, "Library Quality and Impact: Is There a Relationship between New Measures and Traditional Measures?" *Journal of Academic Librarianship* 31, no. 5 (September 2005): 505–28.

20. Elizabeth M. Mezick, "Return on Investment: Libraries and Student Retention," *Journal of Academic Librarianship* 33, no. 5 (September 2007): 561–66.

21. John J. Regazzi, "U.S. Academic Library Spending, Staffing, and Utilization during the Great Recession 2008–2010," *Journal of Academic Librarianship* 39, no. 3 (May 2013): 217–22.

22. Graham Stone and Bryony Ramsden, "Library Impact Data Project: Looking for the Link between Library Usage and Student Attainment," *College & Research Libraries* 74, no. 6 (November 2013): 556.

23. Danuta A. Nitecki and Eileen G. Ables, "Exploring the Cause and Effect of Library Value," *Performance Measurement and Metrics* 14, no. 1 (2013): 24.

Accountability

THE WILLINGNESS OF FUNDING decision makers to continue to invest significant sums of money in higher education or to provide funds for public services provided through local governments without question has likely come to an end. Those controlling the purse strings are asking for meaningful evidence that demonstrates the outcomes or impacts resulting from their investments (see chapter 8). The calls for accountability and transparency are happening at a time when "public libraries are grappling with a 'new normal' of flat or decreased funding, paired with increased demand for public library technology resources."[1] The situation for many academic libraries is not different; as colleges and universities have felt the need to reduce costs, many departments on campus, including the library, have been asked to accept budget cuts.

Library budgets have declined as a portion of total institutional budgets, and within the library's budget, collections account for an increased portion.[2] This downward trend in library budgets is clearly illustrated in figure 2.1, which shows the average library budget as a percentage of institutional budget from 2004 to 2010 for five groups of libraries (grouped by the size of the library's budget).[3] Figure 2.2 indicates how widely spread the data are for one group of reporting libraries. [4]

"The business of libraries" is "part of a rapidly evolving environment in which information is proliferating [at] unimagined rates," in which there is a shift in the use and preservation of print information resources to those in a digital form, and "in which the ability of academic libraries to deliver high quality information is challenged by technologies."[5] In such an environment, "libraries and the librarians who lead them now find themselves asking a series of fundamental questions:

FIGURE 2.1 **LIBRARY BUDGET AS A PERCENTAGE OF INSTITUTIONAL BUDGET, 2004 TO 2010**

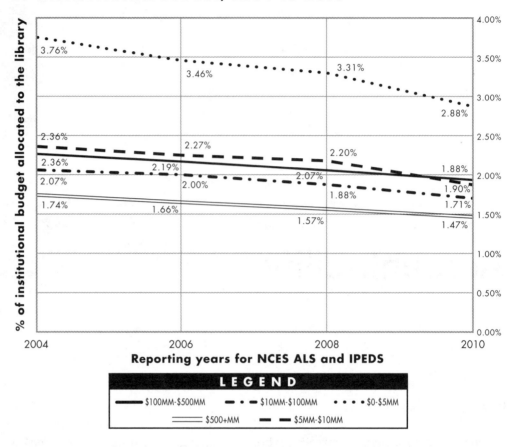

FIGURE 2.2 **LIBRARY VERSUS INSTITUTIONAL BUDGETS FOR INSTITUTIONS WITH ANNUAL REVENUE OVER $500 MILLION**

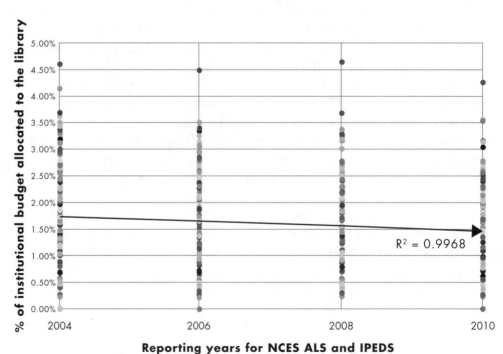

» To what extent, and in what ways, are academic libraries likely to change?

» What new roles will librarians come to have in the changing information environment?

» What aspects of the academic library will prove the most resistant or impervious to change?

» Will technology finally spur a recasting of how colleges and universities produce and disseminate knowledge? If such a merging of interests takes place, what impact will that have on academic libraries? Or conversely, if there is not a merging of these two agendas, will academic libraries be caught in the middle of an increasingly difficult competition for institutional resources?"[6]

Public libraries face a changing environment as well, including "considerable philosophical, information content provision, market place, and technology challenges that impact their ability to claim and demonstrate value."[7] As local governments wrestle with declining financial resources, primarily as a result of the nation's stagnating economy, decision makers must make budget cuts or begin to accumulate debt. Local governments, in an effort to reduce costs in a so-called painless manner, often target *nonessential* government services (e.g., libraries, parks, and recreation) for draconian budget cuts. Politicians often call for public library systems to reduce their budgets quite significantly, such as they have in Chicago, Los Angeles, New York, and Toronto.

Government policy makers demand more accountability and transparency in higher education. Institutions of higher education, in general, continue to increase tuition year after year, while families ask, "Is a college education worth it?" The cost of attending college and graduating relative to the average family income has gone up tremendously over the last couple of decades. Many critics are asking about the real value of getting a college education as students about to graduate face significant debt and are often unable to find a job, one that pays well, especially a job in the field in which they majored.

The pressure for accountability, however, is not coming solely from the federal government. Some states, including Indiana, Ohio, Tennessee, and Wisconsin, have moved from input approaches (providing funding based on number of students enrolled) to output- or outcome-based funding (degrees awarded).[8] And, some institutions, notably the University of Massachusetts (UMass), have laid out their plans to measure their progress in achieving their goals over a fifteen-year period. The performance metrics for this one university are grouped into six broad areas:

1. Student experience and success
2. Educated workforce and engaged citizenry
3. World-class research and development enterprise
4. Enhanced social well-being
5. Good stewards of resources
6. Telling and selling the UMass story[9]

WHAT IS THE RETURN ON INVESTMENT?

Many public libraries are faced with strong competitive pressure resulting in a tug-of-war for funding with other municipal agencies and the continual need to justify their funding (and, in some cases, their continued existence). For many decades, public libraries have experienced the support of their communities and funding decision makers as they were considered a *public good* with obvious positive social impacts. A public good is a service that is difficult to exclude someone from using, and one person's use does not preclude someone else from use of that good or service. Yet, there is increasing demand for a library to communicate the tangible and intangible value of the library to interested stakeholders, such as library board members, funding decision makers, and the community at large.

The traditional reason for library funding, usually a use or output metric (e.g., annual circulation), once used to demonstrate value, is no longer effective. One of the ironies of public sector funding is that the library often takes a disproportionate budget cut, as compared to other departments, just when the economic downturn prompts an increase in demand for public library services.

One of the ways that some libraries have attempted to improve the discussion of their value is to prepare a return on investment (ROI) analysis. Considering the possible economic benefits from the customer's perspective, there are three categories of library benefits:

1. **Direct Use Benefits**, which are sometimes called tangible benefits, involve the use of library collections and services that can be measured directly using output and outcomes metrics. Direct use benefits, which focus on the avoidance of cost to the individual, include:

   » Cost savings from avoiding the purchase of materials (books, CDs, DVDs, magazines, newspapers, reference materials, downloading of electronic resources, and so forth);
   » Free or low-cost access to computers, photocopiers, audio and video equipment, meeting rooms, programs, instructional classes, and so forth; and
   » Access to trained professionals for assistance in finding quality information.

2. **Indirect Use Benefits,** or economic impacts, are the intangible outputs and outcomes associated with a library's programs and services. Among such indirect benefits are leisure enjoyments; literacy encouragement for children, teens, and adults; library as place for community meetings; and attendance at a program.

3. **Nonuse Benefits,** or the nonuse value of a library, is the utility that individuals might gain from a library other than their active use of a library. Nonuse value may be of benefit to an individual at some time in the future, and the library may be of benefit to others in the community now and in the future. For example, those who do not use the library might derive satisfaction from its mere existence.

The majority of studies that calculate the library's economic value use the criterion known as "maximize the ratio of benefits over costs." This ratio is usually referred to as a cost-benefit analysis or an ROI. A report that identifies the ROI value of the library typically makes a statement such as "for every dollar supporting the library, the library sees a return on investment of X dollars" (almost always more than one dollar). The formula for calculating ROI is expressed as:

$$(\text{Total benefits} - \text{Total costs}) \div \text{Total cost} \times 100$$

Joseph Matthews, who analyzed a number of ROI studies, found the following:

» Those studies have produced ROI numbers, which are variable, but they seem to group in the range of $4 to $6 of benefits for each dollar spent by the library.

» Relying on a single measure, such as ROI, does not produce a long-term positive reaction among the library's funding decision makers year after year.

» The ROI focus is short term and quantitative in nature while a library's lasting impact is more likely to be long term and qualitative in nature.

» Such studies provide only one indicator of value, effectiveness, and efficiency.

» Determining the ROI as one of several key performance metrics might yield positive results for the library.

» Relying on an overall management framework for displaying and reporting key performance metrics is effective for many for-profit and nonprofit organizations. The library's ROI could be one of the key performance metrics within such a framework.[10]

When library managers engage in ROI, they should carefully construct the study, only use meaningful data elements, and effectively communicate the process of data collection and the meaning of the results. In *Getting Started with Evaluation*, we instruct readers about how to conduct these studies in a step-by-step manner.[11] Further, they should review library use calculators, such as the University of West Florida's Libraries Value Calculator (http://libguides.uwf.edu/content.php?pid=188487&sid=2261667), the Pasadena Public Library's Services Value Calculator (www.ci.pasadena.ca.us/library/about_the_library/value_calculator/), and the Maine State Library's Library Use Value Calculator (www.maine.gov/msl/services/calculator.htm).

AND THE VALUE IS . . .

Establishing the value of an information service (providing access to the library's physical or electronic collections or both, reference services, instructional services, and so forth) can only be done from the customer's perspective. The important question is not how much an information resource or service is used, but, rather, what impact or benefit accrues to customers when they use library collections and services or when they attend a library program. Such an approach to understanding value means that libraries must reexamine all of the activities they undertake and ask, "How does this activity add value in the customer's life?"

Endeavoring to identify the benefit of the library to its larger organizational entity is a challenging proposition. For academic libraries, the goal is to demonstrate how the library and its services contribute to student achievement, improve faculty teaching skills and productivity, and assist researchers with funded and non-funded research. The goal might also be to demonstrate how much money faculty and students can save by using the library; for students, what portion of their tuition dollars do they regain from use of the library's technologies, collections, services, programs, and facilities?

In *The Value of Academic Libraries*, Megan Oakleaf goes beyond ROI and summarizes the available research, suggesting a variety of ways in which a library can gather data to answer the value question on a specific campus.[12] In order to develop the evidence concerning value, a library must reach out and partner with other units on campus involved with evaluation and assessment. These partnerships are important if the library managers want to use student performance data for outcome-based analysis. They will also help the library to understand better how it might contribute more significantly to student success as well as improve faculty and researcher productivity.

In the public library setting, the challenge of evaluating and assessing the outcomes and impact from the use of the collections, services, and programs is also demanding. One tool that can be useful in developing outcome metrics is the logic model, which is an analytic tool developed in the late 1980s in the field of program evaluation and used successfully in the not-for-profit sector (for example, by United Way), the private sector, the public sector, and libraries. A logic model shows the relationships among the

- » resources that go into a program or service offering;
- » activities the program undertakes or the service provides; and
- » changes or benefits that result.

The model describes the sequence of events thought to bring about benefits or change over time. It should portray the chain of reasoning that links investments to results. In reality, a logic model is a systems model that shows the connection of interdependent parts that together make up the whole. The value of the model is that it helps mangers to plan, implement, evaluate, and communicate more effectively. In reality, the successful use of a logic model requires any organization to be able to fill in the blanks for the following logic model statements:

The library will do	**A**
which will result in these	**B**
so our patrons will be able to	**C**
as measured by	**D**

The model often is depicted graphically, showing the logical relationships between the resources (inputs), activities (process), outputs, and outcomes of a model, as shown in figure 2.3. When planning a program or service, it is important to start with the end in mind. That is, focus on the right-hand side of the logic model (the outcomes and desired impacts) and then move to the left. A logic model serves as a framework and provides a process for planning to bridge the gap between where the library is and where managers want it to be. The model provides a structure for understanding the situation that drives the need for the program or service, the desired end state, and how investments are linked to the targeted market segment (or group of people) in order to achieve the desired results.

FIGURE 2.3 **PROGRESSION OF METRICS**

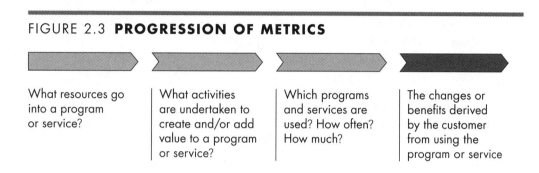

| What resources go into a program or service? | What activities are undertaken to create and/or add value to a program or service? | Which programs and services are used? How often? How much? | The changes or benefits derived by the customer from using the program or service |

If the model is viewed as a kind of time line, things on the left occur before those on the right. Moe Hosseini-Ara and Rebecca Jones issue a reminder: there are some problems that libraries must confront when using the logic model. These include:

» Not having targeted metrics
» Not beginning the conversation with stakeholders
» Not building the metrics into the design
» Confusing operating metrics with value metrics
» Not having someone manage the metrics[13]

Outcome Measurement

Many knowledgeable individuals writing about outcomes suggest that it is better to divide them into three groups: short-term impacts, medium-term impacts, and long-term impacts. Short-term outcomes occur in the individual while, at the other end of the spectrum, long-term impacts affect the organization or society at large. Changes that occur within the individual are often referred to as outcomes while the long-term impact is sometimes referred to as higher-level change. For example, undergraduate students who receive instruction report an outcome that they have a better understanding of the library, its services, and how to apply them to their studies, whereas the impact is higher grades and lower dropout rates.

Outcome measurement answers two questions: (1) "What difference did this program make to the user?" and (2) "What sorts of changes in people might it be possible to measure in some way?" These changes might be:

- » **Affective:** having to do with attitudes, perceptions, levels of confidence, and satisfaction;
- » **Behavioral:** concerning the things people do differently—for example, asking different types of questions, being more critical in assessing information and situations, being more independent;
- » **Knowledge-based:** concerning intellectual activity—for example, being able to differentiate among information sources in terms of their quality, knowing where to look for specific types of information, and so forth;
- » **Competency-based:** concerning functional abilities—for example, being more effective, learning new skills, applying new skills; or
- » **Community-based:** concerning the impact or level of involvement of the community with the library.

For example, it is possible to identify a range of traditional output metrics as well as outcome metrics for early childhood education programs offered by the library, as shown in table 2.1. Clearly, developing a set of outcome-based performance metrics requires libraries to think about outcome performance measurement in different ways, some of which may necessitate a closer relationship with parents/guardians of children (in this case), as well as partnering with the local schools to gain access to student performance data.

We insert a caution about the discussion of outcomes measurement in this chapter—namely, that the focus is on self-reporting and what people say. A higher level of outcomes assessment involves the actual, documented changes in people's understanding, abilities, habits of mind, ways of knowing, attitudes, values, and skill set (see chapter 8).[14] This topic is beyond the scope of this book.

Value Calculation

One approach to determining value, sometimes called the Short-Cut Method in the public library environment, identifies the services provided by the library as well as a price for a market substitute for each library service. The market value can be determined by examining options within the local community or by averaging costs provided by a number of suppliers (e.g., the average cost to download an electronic journal article). Combining the market substitute price with the volume of activity produces the total value for that service. Table 2.2 provides a sample form that a library could use to determine the value of each library service. Values have been included in the table to illustrate the calculations. Obviously, the library needs to determine its own services to include in this analysis because some of the provided examples might not apply. It is also suggested that the library include notes describing how the value for each service is calculated.

TABLE 2.1 **POSSIBLE EARLY CHILDHOOD EDUCATION QUANTIFIABLE PERFORMANCE METRICS***

Output Metrics	Outcome Metric
» Number of programs offered per year » Number of adult/child pairs who participate » Number/percentage of children under age 5 who participate compared to total number of children under age 5 in community » Number of children's picture books borrowed after each program » Number of parenting materials borrowed by participants each year » Number/percentage of children who participate in preschool programs outside the library setting (day care centers, community centers, church meeting rooms, etc.)	**AFFECTIVE** » Children ask their parents/guardians to read to them more frequently » Children enjoy spending time with their parents/guardians reading to them (based on self-reports of adults) » Children ask to return to the library to attend storybook reading programs **BEHAVIORAL** » Families who participate borrow more materials to read to their children (based on self-reports of adults) compared to those who do not participate » Children seem to enjoy interacting with their peers more (based on self-reports of adults) **KNOWLEDGE-BASED** » Parents/guardians report that their children's vocabulary is growing **COMPETENCY-BASED** » Adults modulate voice tones to add variety and interest to the stories they read to their children (based on self-reports of adults) **COMMUNITY-BASED** » Percentage of children ages 3–5 in the community who are read to daily by a family member » Percentage of preschool children who are judged "ready" for kindergarten based on a school readiness assessment for all children entering school

*See Joseph R. Matthews, *Measuring for Results: The Dimensions of Public Library Effectiveness* (Westport, CT: Libraries Unlimited, 2004), especially chapter 8.

TABLE 2.2 **LIBRARY RETURN ON INVESTMENT CALCULATIONS***

Library Service	Market Value (A)	Volume of Activity (B)	Total Value (A x B)
Borrowing books	$45 per book	Circulation of 200,000	$9,000,000
Borrowing ILL materials	$60 per item	26,000 items	1,560,000
Downloading e-resources	$45 per article	900,000 articles	40,500,000
Providing computer and information technology resources	$10 per hour	800,000 hours	8,000,000
Borrowing of laptop and tablet computers, iPads	$20 per hour	200,000 hours	4,000,000
Reference services (nondirectional queries)	$10 per such query	75,000 queries	750,000
TOTAL			**$63,810,000**

*For a discussion of determining the cost, see University of West Florida, Office of the Dean, "Calculate Your Personal Return on Investment," http://libguides.uwf.edu/content.php?pid=188487&sid=2261667. Please note that the chart contains an option, "How were these values calculated?"

Assuming this library has an annual budget of $14,000,000, then the ROI is ($63,810,000 / $14,000,000) = 4.56:1, or $4.56 of benefits for every dollar of the total library budget. Obviously, adding or subtracting a library service or determining that the local value is different from what is represented in this example changes the ROI calculations. This is one of the reasons why comparing the ROI from one library to that of another is problematic.

THE TWO DATA SERVICES

A library can find use data for other libraries in either ACRL*Metrics* or PLA*metrics*, but given the wide range of services offered by a library that are not reflected in the use statistics reported to the state library or federal government each year, any resulting analysis would be incomplete. Both data services have many missing data elements (see, for instance, table 2.3 for illustrative purposes). As a result, we cannot recommend either data service for conducting ROI.

TABLE 2.3 **HYPOTHETICAL ROI ANALYSIS FOR ONE PUBLIC LIBRARY USING THE PLDS 2010 DATA**

Service	Local Value	Volume of Activity	Total Value
Print circulation	$20 per item	1,258,348	$25,166,960
CD/DVD circulation	$4 per item	843,026	
Other materials circulation	$10 per item	40,110	$3,372,104
e-Book borrowing		No data	
Downloading of e-resources		No data	
Reference transactions	$5 per query	77,475	$387,375
Program attendance	$5 per person per program	55,165	$275,825
Computer use	$15 per hour	No data	
Wi-Fi access		No data	
Attendance at music programs		No data	
Attendance at movies		No data	
Group meeting rooms		No data	
TOTALS			$29,202,264*

*However, the story is incomplete.

CONCLUDING THOUGHTS

It is likely that the pressures for any library to demonstrate results in a manner that resonates with the library's stakeholders will continue relentlessly. Thus, the library needs to embrace a management philosophy that focuses on the impacts of its collections, services, and programs on its customers. People have a choice about how, when, and where they decide to fulfill an information need, and it is only if the library provides real value to them will they consider, and possibly use, the library. Library managers might also be asked to engage in ROI studies and to compare the findings with those of similar studies. They might also be asked to comment on existing studies or on a particular finding of a certain study.

EXERCISES

Answers to the following questions are in the "Appendix" at the back of the book. We encourage different members of a library staff to work on the exercises together and to discuss the results. Managers might also participate in that discussion. For more guidance in conducting ROI analyses and for additional exercises to construct such analyses, see chapter 8 as well as *Getting Started with Evaluation.*[15]

QUESTION 1 Using ACRL*Metrics*, determine the library's budget as a percentage of a college's or university's annual operating budget for the past five years.

QUESTION 2 Based on figure 2.3, what metrics could a public library match to the progression, starting with inputs, then activities, output, and outcome/impact, reportable to stakeholders about a focused children's summer reading program designed to raise an attendee's reading level by one grade at the end of the program?

Notes

1. American Library Association, "The 2012 State of America's Libraries," www.ala.org/news/mediapresscenter/americaslibraries/soal2012/public-libraries.

2. Such trends are easily documented through an examination of input data from ACRL*Metrics* and PLA*metrics*.

3. Data Sources: IPEDS and NCES ALS 2004, 2006, 2008, 2010. The figure only includes values when both the institutional IPEDS and NCES ALS data were available, so that the comparison is a complete match, The results are broken out in five categories, based on the average of their institutional expenses over the reporting periods (2004, 2006, 2008, and 2010). Several organizations (fewer than 20) were removed from the results where anomalous data indicated that the NCES ALS data might be suspect (e.g., Library Expenditure swings that could only reasonably be explained by bad data or the inclusion of capital expenditures) and/or where the IPED's data looked suspect (sudden huge swings in total expenditures that might be either bad data and/or possibly the result of some form of one-time merger/divestiture). This figure was prepared by Carl Thompson, Counting Opinions.

4. This figure was prepared by Carl Thompson, Counting Opinions.

5. American Library Association, Association of College and Research Libraries, *Changing Roles of Academic and Research Libraries* (2007), www.ala.org/acrl/issues/value/changingroles.

6. American Library Association, Association of College and Research Libraries, *Changing Roles of Academic and Research Libraries*.

7. Paul T. Jaeger, John Carlo Bertot, Christie M. Kodama, Sarah M. Katz, and Elizabeth J. DeCoster, "Describing and Measuring the Value of Public Libraries: The Growth of the Internet and the Evolution of Library Value," *First Monday* 16, no. 11 (November 7, 2011), http://firstmonday.org/ojs/index.php/fm/article/view/3765/3074.

8. See Peter Hernon, Robert E. Dugan, and Candy Schwartz, *Higher Education Outcomes Assessment for the Twenty-First Century* (Santa Barbara, CA: Libraries Unlimited, 2013).

9. University of Massachusetts, *UMass Performance: Accountable and on the Move* (2013), http://media.umassp.edu/massedu/umassperformance/umass_performance.pdf.

10. Joseph Matthews, "What's the Return on ROI? The Benefits and Challenges of Calculating Your Library's Return on Investment," *Library Leadership and Management* 25, no. 1 (2011): 1–14; Joseph Matthews, "Assessing Organizational Effectiveness: The Role of Performance Measures," *Library Quarterly* 81, no. 1 (January 2011): 83–110; examples of reports using this approach are available online—see, for instance, Martin Prosperity Institute, *So Much More: The Economic Impact of the Toronto Public Library on the City of Toronto* (2013), http://martinprosperity.org/media/TPL%20Economic%20Impact_Dec2013_LR_FINAL.pdf.

11. See also Peter Hernon, Robert E. Dugan, and Joseph R. Matthews, *Getting Started with Evaluation* (Chicago: American Library Association, 2014), chapters 8 and 9.

12. Association of College and Research Libraries, *The Value of Academic Libraries: A Comprehensive Research Review and Report*, prepared by Megan Oakleaf (Chicago: Association of College and Research Libraries, 2010), www.ala.org/acrl/sites/ala.org.acrl/files/content/issues/value/val_report.pdf.

13. Moe Hosseini-Ara and Rebecca Jones, "Overcoming Our Habits and Learning to Measure Impact," *Computers in Libraries* 33, no. 5 (June 2013): 3–7.

14. See Peggy L. Maki, *Assessing for Learning: Building a Sustainable Commitment across the Institution*, 2nd ed. (Sterling, VA: Stylus, 2010).

15. Hernon, Dugan, and Matthews, *Getting Started with Evaluation*, 154–55.

Collections

IN THIS TIME OF transition as libraries move from providing access to physical collections to providing access to digital content, the evaluation of library collections is taking on increasing importance. As academic libraries repurpose space by moving some portion (or all) of their physical collections to on- or off -campus storage facilities or to a shared print storage facility, or by using an automated storage and retrieval system (robotic system), an important question becomes, "What segments of the collection should remain and what should be moved to storage?"

It is important to gain a better understanding about what library customers find (and use) in the collection and what the library must purchase or borrow from another library. And, as Google Books and other projects digitize more books (an estimated 20 million books had been digitized as of early 2014), the need to visit the library to view or borrow an item in the collection has been significantly reduced.

This chapter considers the ways to use available data sources to evaluate a library's collections. It should be recognized that there are a number of additional methods to evaluate a library's collections that will not be covered in this chapter but have been reviewed and summarized elsewhere.[1] The content of this chapter covers the evaluation of physical and electronic collections.

EVALUATION OF THE PHYSICAL COLLECTIONS

When print dominated library collections, the primary means for evaluating a library's collections was often based on their size. This approach of creating large "just-in-case" collections led to judging quality by size—consider, for example, the Association of Research Libraries (ARL) Investment Index—and, in good times or

EXAMPLE 3.1 **COMPARISON OF AN ACADEMIC LIBRARY'S ACQUISITIONS BUDGET WITH ITS PEERS**

STEP 1   Log onto ACRL*Metrics*.

STEP 2   Click on the Local tab and the Report tab—if not already highlighted.

STEP 3   Click the Add button to create a new report.

STEP 4   Select ACRL as the Collection, type in a descriptive Report Name, and perhaps a more comprehensive description of the report as well as a Title if you would like. In conclusion, click on the Save as New Report button.

STEP 5   Because we want to run a PI Report, select "PI Report" from the pull-down menu of options adjacent to Report Type. Then go back up to Period in the Report Settings to choose the year of the data being reported—in this case, FY2012.

STEP 6   We can now select the performance indicators for this Report. Scroll through the list of available indicators and select "Carnegie Classification Code," "Total Library Expenditures," "Total Library Materials," "Total Library Materials Expenditures Per FT Students," and "Total Library Materials Expenditures per Instructional Faculty." It is always a good idea to click on the Save button periodically so you don't lose your work.

bad, libraries were held captive to this notion.[2] As Allen Pratt and Ellen Altman wryly note, the consequence of this view is that the library will live and die by the numbers.[3] In addition to total counts, there is no end of the permutations of metrics that reflect size: the number of volumes per capita, number of volumes per student (FTE), growth of the collection, counts of subdivisions of the collection (by call number range, by material type), and so forth. It is also important to acknowledge that any size of collection is going to be expensive to maintain over the years. Paul Courant and Matthew Nielsen, in a thorough analysis, identify that it costs the library $4.26 *per book per year* to provide access to a collection using open stacks, while it costs $0.86 per book per year using high-density compact shelving.[4] The largest cost components derive from the construction and annual operation of space. Interestingly, they note that the HathiTrust provides access to its digital collection of books for $0.15 per book per year.[5]

Not surprisingly, a comparison of the size of one library's collection to that of a set of peer libraries was often prepared as a justification to support the request for additional funding to *improve* a library's collection. Libraries have historically evaluated a library's collection using five approaches:

1. Materials or acquisitions expenditures
2. Size of the collection
3. Type of materials
4. Use of the collection
5. Use of other library collections (ILL)

STEP 7 Once you have selected one or more indicators, the Locations function appears. If you have saved a set of peer libraries, click Locations and select the filter you created. If you have yet to create a set of peer libraries, click on Locations and select all of the libraries you wish to include as peers. Provide a Filter Name (Peers for the ABC Library), and click on the Apply button to save this group. In this case, we have used the Filter function to limit our results to Baccalaureate Colleges—Liberal Arts using the Carnegie Classification code and further limited the results by restricting Total Library Expenditures to between $1,000,000 and $1,150,000 as seen here.

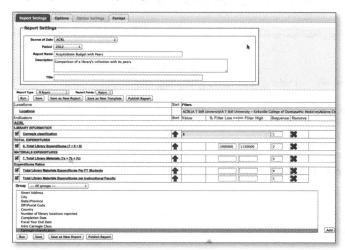

STEP 7a At this point, click on Run, and the resulting report looks like this.

STEP 7b Notice the icon for a spreadsheet. If you click on it, you can download the resulting report that you just ran. Doing a bit of cut-and-paste, you can wind up with a spreadsheet that looks like this.

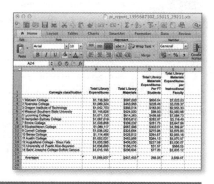

Acquisitions Expenditures

One of the most popular ways to compare one library's collections, and especially to evaluate what is being added each year, with those of other libraries is to examine and compare acquisitions expenditure data. These statistics are of value to those to whom library managers report, and the data can be presented over time.

ACADEMIC LIBRARIES

As seen in example 3.1, a library can easily determine how its collections compare to those of its peer libraries by first focusing on the acquisitions budget. The data analyzed in the example are taken from the ACRL*Metrics* data set. Some libraries, however, did not respond to the current ACRL survey with detailed library information. Managers can compare the average with the other libraries and see how their organization relates to some comparable libraries.

PUBLIC LIBRARIES

For this sample analysis, we selected libraries that serve a total population that ranges from 100,000 to 150,000 residents. The various methods that can be used to select a set of peer libraries are discussed in considerable detail in chapter 6. As can be seen in example 3.2, the average library budget for these twenty-six libraries is a little more than $4 million (and note that two libraries in this group have budgets twice as large as the average).

EXAMPLE 3.2 **COMPARISON OF A PUBLIC LIBRARY'S BUDGET WITH ITS PEERS**

STEP 1	Log on to PLA*metrics*.
STEP 2	Click on the Local tab and the Report tab—if not already highlighted.
STEP 3	Click the Add button to create a new report.
STEP 4	Select PLDS (Public Library Data Service) as the Source of Data, type in a descriptive Report Name, and perhaps a more comprehensive description of the report as well as a Title if you would like. In conclusion, click on the Save as New Report button.
STEP 5	Because we want to run a PI Report, select "PI Report" from the pull-down menu of options adjacent to Report Type. Then go back up to Period in the Report Settings to choose the year of the data being reported—in this case, FY2012.
STEP 6	We can now select the performance indicators for this Report. Scroll through the list of available indicators and select "Population of legal service area," and "Total operating expenditures (for the Library)." It is always a good idea to click periodically on the Save button so you don't lose your work.

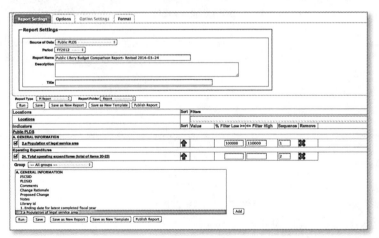

STEP 7	Once you have selected one or more indicators, the Locations function appears. If you have saved a set of peer libraries, click Locations and select the filter you created. If you have yet to create a set of peer libraries, click on Locations and select all of the libraries you wish to include as peers. Provide a Filter Name (Peers for the ABC Library), and click on the Apply button to save this group.

In this case, we have used the Filter function to limit our results to the Population of Legal Service Area between 100,000 and 150,000 as seen in the following screen shot.

Size of Collection

Another popular method for comparing library collections is to use the size of the collections as reflected in the count of items. The total size of a collection can be compared with that of other libraries, and total size can be compared for the number of items being added each year.

STEP 8   If you now click on the Run button, the program will produce a report that looks like this.

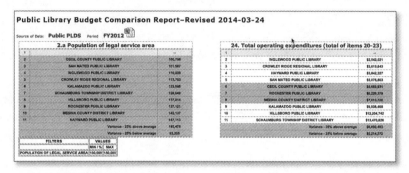

STEP 9   Alternatively, you can view the result in chart form. Changing the Report Type to Graph/PI will result in a display that looks like this.

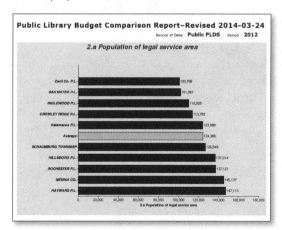
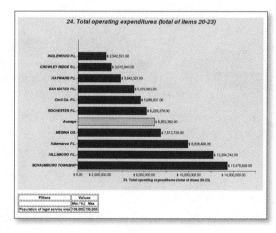

ACADEMIC LIBRARIES

In this example, a group of libraries have been selected using the Baccalaureate Colleges—Liberal Arts category from the Carnegie Classification and further limiting the results using total library expenditures between $1,000,000 and $1,115,000, as seen in example 3.3.

EXAMPLE 3.3 **COMPARISON OF AN ACADEMIC LIBRARY'S COLLECTION SIZE WITH ITS PEERS**

STEP 1 Log onto ACRL*Metrics*.

STEP 2 Click on the Local tab and the Report tab—if not already highlighted.

STEP 3 Click the Add button to create a new report.

STEP 4 Select ACRL as the Collection, type in a descriptive Report Name, and perhaps a more comprehensive description of the report as well as a Title if you would like. In conclusion, click on the Save as New Report button.

STEP 5 Because we want to run a PI Report, select "PI Report" from the pull-down menu of options adjacent to Report Type. Then go back up to Period in the Report Settings to choose the year of the data being reported—in this case, FY2012.

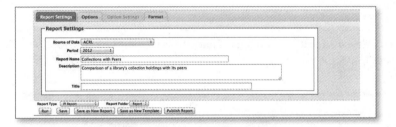

STEP 6 We can now select the performance indicators for this Report. Scroll through the list of available indicators and select "Carnegie Classification Code," "Total Library [Operating] Expenditures," "Books and Other Paper Materials Held," "E-Books Held," "Microforms Held," and "Audiovisual Materials Held." It is always a good idea to click periodically on the Save button so you don't lose your work.

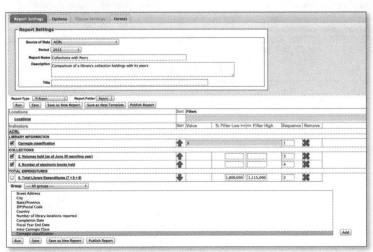

STEP 7 Once you have selected one or more indicators, the Locations function appears. If you have saved a set of peer libraries, click Locations and select the filter you created. If you have yet to create a set of peer libraries, click on Locations and select all of the libraries you wish to include as peers.

Provide a Filter Name (Peers for the ABC Library), and click on the Apply button to save this group.

In this case, we have used the Filter function to limit our results to Baccalaureate Colleges—Liberal Arts using the Carnegie Classification Code and further limited the results by restricting Total Library Expenditures to between $1,000,000 and $1,150,000, as seen here.

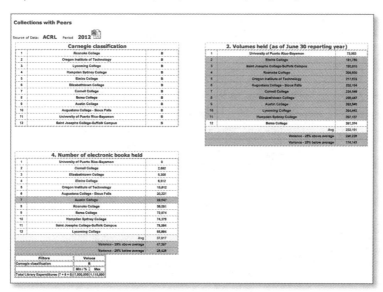

Going back to the main Report Settings page, we can change the Report Type to "PI Graph," click on Run again, and we will wind up with two bar charts as shown here.

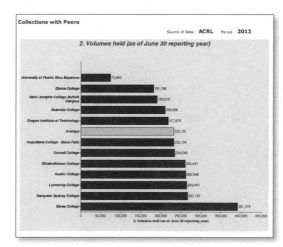

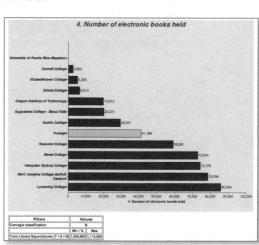

PUBLIC LIBRARIES

A public library can quickly determine how its collection size matches up with a designated set of peer libraries, or, as seen in example 3.4, the group of peer libraries has been selected from those with a legal service area population that ranges from 100,000 to 150,000. Looking at these data, we can see that the average collection size is 413,836, with a low of 226,019 and a high of 650,000.

EXAMPLE 3.4 **COMPARISON OF A PUBLIC LIBRARY'S COLLECTION SIZE WITH ITS PEERS**

STEP 1   Log on to PLA*metrics*.

STEP 2   Click on the Local tab and the Report tab, if they are not already highlighted.

STEP 3   Click the Add button to create a new report.

STEP 4   Select Public PLDS as the Source of Data, type in a descriptive Report Name, and perhaps a more complete description of the report as well as a Title, if you would like. In conclusion, click on the Save as New Report button.

STEP 5   Because we want to run a PI Report, select "PI Report" from the pull-down menu of options adjacent to Report Type. Then go back up to Period in the Report Settings to choose the year of the data being reported—in this case, FY2010.

STEP 6   We can now select the performance indicators for this Report. Scroll through the list of available indicators and select "Population of legal service area" and "Holdings." It is always a good idea to periodically click on the Save button so you don't lose your work. Your screen should look like this.

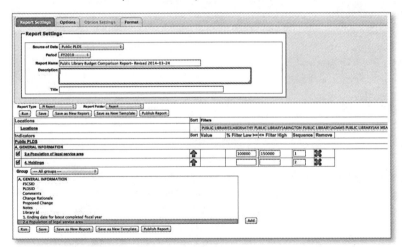

Use of Collections by Type of Material

Using data from ACRL*Metrics*, it is possible to consider the holdings of a comparative group of libraries and to see that the number of materials varies considerably based on the type of material (see example 3.3).

| STEP 7 | Once you have selected the indicators, the Locations function appears. If you have saved a set of peer libraries, click Locations and select the filter (your name for a group of peer libraries) you created. If you have yet to create a set of peer libraries, click on Locations and select all of the libraries you wish to include as peers. Provide a Filter Name (Peers for the ABC Library), and click on the Apply button to save this group. In this case, we have used the Filter function to limit our results to "Population of legal service area" of between 100,000 and 150,000, as seen in the preceding screen shot. |

| STEP 8 | At this point, click the Run button and a report should appear on your screen similar to the following one. (You can download a spreadsheet of the resulting data by clicking on the Excel icon.) |

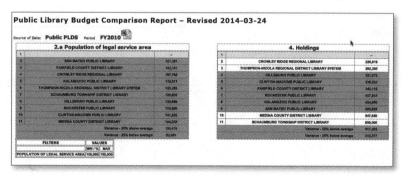

You can also see the data in graph form as shown here.

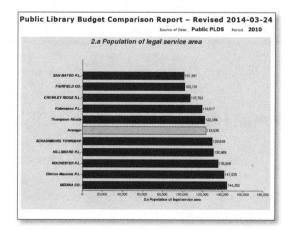
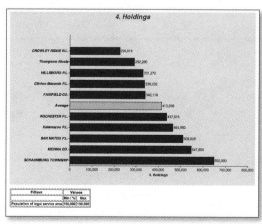

EXAMPLE 3.5 COMPARISON OF AN ACADEMIC LIBRARY'S COLLECTION USAGE WITH ITS PEERS

STEP 1 Log on to ACRL*Metrics*.

STEP 2 Click on the Local tab and the Report tab—if not already highlighted.

STEP 3 Click the Add button to create a new report.

STEP 4 Select ACRL as the Collection, type in a descriptive Report Name, and perhaps a more comprehensive description of the report as well as a Title if you would like. In conclusion, click on the Save as New Report button.

STEP 5 Because we want to run a PI Report, select "PI Report" from the pull-down menu of options adjacent to Report Type. Then go back up to Period in the Report Settings to choose the year of the data being reported—in this case, FY2012.

STEP 6 We can now select the performance indicators for this Report. Scroll through the list of available indicators and select "Carnegie Classification Code," "Total Expenditures," "Total Received" (Interlibrary loans and documents received), "General Circulation Transactions," and "Reserve Circulation Transactions." It is always a good idea to click periodically on the Save button so you don't lose your work.

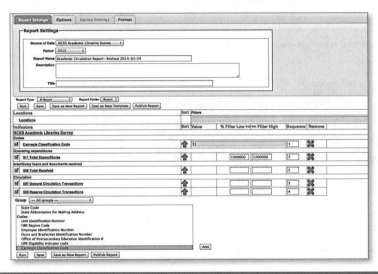

ANALYSIS OF USE OF MATERIALS

The use of a collection is the raison d'être for the creation and maintenance of a library's collections. A library can evaluate the degree to which its materials are being used in a couple of different ways. First, the library can track the amount of use as a percentage of its total collection holdings (often referred to as the turnover rate). Note that, as the size of a library's collection increases, the percentage of use compared to total holdings declines. Second, the library can track total circulation over time.

Using ACRL*Metrics*, the library can compare use of its collections as shown in example 3.5. For libraries whose institutions are members of the Association

STEP 7   Once you have selected one or more indicators, the Locations function appears. If you have saved a set of peer libraries, click Locations and select the filter you created. If you have yet to create a set of peer libraries, click on Locations and select all of the libraries you wish to include as peers. Provide a Filter Name (Peers for the ABC Library), and click on the Apply button to save this group. In this case, we have used the Filter function to limit our results to Baccalaureate Colleges—Liberal Arts using the Carnegie Classification Code and further limited the results by restricting Total Library Expenditures to between $1,000,000 and $1,200,000, as seen here.

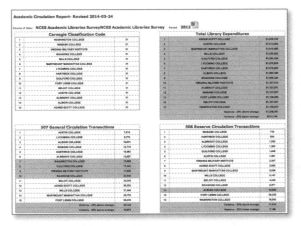

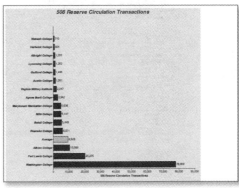

STEP 8   Alternatively, you can look at the data using a chart format. From the Report Type box, choose "Graph PI" and then click Run. The result will look like this.

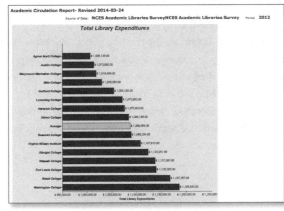

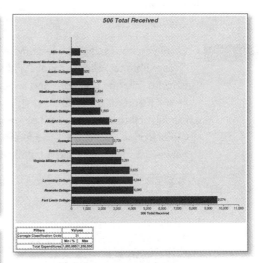

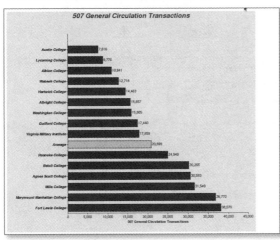

EXAMPLE 3.6 **COMPARISON OF AN ACADEMIC LIBRARY'S ILL USAGE WITH ITS PEERS**

STEP 1 Log on to ACRL*Metrics*.

STEP 2 Click on the Local tab and the Report tab—if not already highlighted.

STEP 3 Click the Add button to create a new report.

STEP 4 Select ACRL as the Collection, type in a descriptive Report Name, and perhaps a more comprehensive description of the report as well as a Title if you would like. In conclusion, click on the Save as New Report button.

STEP 5 Because we want to run a PI Report, select "PI Report" from the pull-down menu of options adjacent to Report Type. Then go back up to Period in the Report Settings to choose the year of the data being reported—in this case, FY2012.

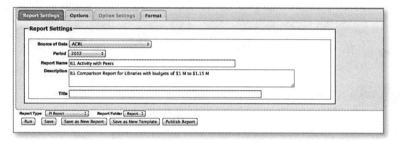

STEP 6 We can now select the performance indicators for this Report. Scroll through the list of available indicators and select "Carnegie Classification Code," "Total Library Expenditures," "Total Items Loaned (ILL)," and "Total Items Borrowed (ILL)." It is always a good idea to click periodically on the Save button so you don't lose your work.

STEP 7 Once you have selected one or more indicators, the Locations function appears. If you have saved a set of peer libraries, click Locations and select the filter you created. If you have yet to create a set of peer libraries, click on Locations and select all of the libraries you wish to include as peers. Provide a Filter Name (Peers for the ABC Library), and click on the Apply button to save this group. In this case, we have used the Filter function to limit our results to Baccalaureate Colleges—Liberal Arts using the Carnegie Classification Code (BAC) and further limited the results by restricting Total Library Expenditures to between $1,000,000 and $1,250,000, as seen here.

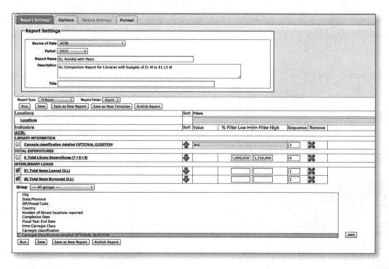

STEP 8   You then click on Locations and a Pop-up Window appears. Click on Filters and choose "All libraries" and, after all the libraries have a check mark, click on Apply. The Pop-up Window will then disappear, and all the libraries will be listed to the right of Locations. Remember to click Save.

STEP 9   At this point, click on the Run button, and the result will look like this. Data are presented for thirteen institutions (the ones that met the selection criteria).

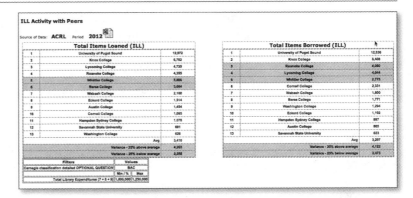

of Research Libraries, for instance, circulation and reference requests have declined for years as use patterns shift. Furthermore, historically, any print book purchased has no more than a 50 percent chance of ever being borrowed. Furthermore, as books in the collection age and do not circulate, their likelihood of circulating greatly diminishes.[6]

USE OF INTERLIBRARY LOAN SERVICES

Because no library can anticipate and build a collection that will meet all of its customers' information needs, libraries have created and nurtured interlibrary loan to facilitate the sharing of resources. A library or a document delivery supplier provides almost all journal articles as an electronic file, and customers have the choice of receiving a paper or an electronic copy. Any books that are needed are almost always borrowed from another library. Using data from ACRL*Metrics*, we have illustrated how a library can compare its use of interlibrary loan (both borrowing and sending materials) with other, comparable institutions (see example 3.6).

MATERIALS AVAILABILITY STUDIES

Many academic libraries have conducted availability studies to determine the reasons that customers are unable to find items that they are looking for when they visit the library. A review of these studies suggests that, on average, customers are successful in finding what they sought about 60 percent of the time.[7] Using a paper-based survey, a sample of customers might be asked if they found what they were looking for. If they were unsuccessful, they are asked to provide specific information about the items they were seeking (author, title, call number). Library staff then determine the reason why the searches were unsuccessful. Paul Kantor created a visual branching diagram to illustrate the reasons why customers were unsuccessful: not acquired, in circulation, library error (misplaced on the shelf, waiting to be shelved, and so forth), catalog error, and customer error.[8] In general, libraries enhance customer satisfaction by improving signage and location maps, streamlining processes associated with the return of items, and encouraging customers to suggest titles for purchase.

EVALUATION OF THE E-RESOURCE COLLECTIONS

Increasingly, libraries of all types are facing pressure to provide access to an ever-increasing number of electronic journals and other digital resources. The obvious appeal of digital resources is that the library's customers can have anywhere, anytime access to them using a variety of devices (desktop computers, laptops, tablets, and cell phones). In many cases, electronic journal articles are accessible from several sources, including the publisher as well as indexing and abstracting—full-text—databases.

In addition to providing electronic journals, libraries are providing access to e-books. In the academic environment, many publishers are only selling or licensing access to e-books and not printing the book at all. Digital collections save the library space and staff costs. The trade-off is that libraries are no longer purchasing paper copies of journals and books (and providing access to and preserving the content for future generations), but they must now license the content annually for time immemorial.

Finally, it is possible to determine the e-book holdings for a library or a group of libraries, but no data are available that track the number of downloaded e-journal articles or other metrics related to e-resource use.

CONCLUDING THOUGHTS

ACRL*Metrics* and PLA*metrics* provide a flexible yet powerful tool to gather a selected group of metrics and to analyze the resulting data in ways that are immensely useful for an individual library. Comparative data comprise a useful and powerful tool when managers advocate on behalf of the library and its budget.

EXERCISES

Answers to the following questions are in the "Appendix" at the back of the book. We encourage different members of a library staff to work on the exercises together and to discuss the results. Managers might also participate in that discussion.

QUESTION 1 An academic library wants to explore how its collections compare in size and use to a group of comparative or peer libraries. How would the managers proceed?

QUESTION 2 The managers of an academic library are concerned that it may not be moving fast enough to provide e-books to its customers (the library has received a number of complaints). What can the library do to determine what other peer libraries are doing in this area?

QUESTION 3 A public library is concerned that its total budget and per capita funding have been dropping over the last five years or so. What can the library do to find out the trends in this area by comparing itself to other, comparable libraries?

Notes

1. See Joseph R. Matthews, *The Evaluation and Measurement of Library Services* (Westport, CT: Libraries Unlimited, 2007), chapters 8 and 9.

2. See Association of Research Libraries, "Library Investment Index Summarizes Relative Size of ARL University Libraries for 2011–12," www.arl.org/news/arl-news/2884-library -investment-index-summarizes-relative-size-of-arl-university-libraries-for-2011-12.

3. Allen Pratt and Ellen Altman, "Live by the Numbers, Die by the Numbers," *Library Journal,* 122 (April 15, 1997): 48–49.

4. Paul Courant and Matthew Nielsen, "On the Cost of Keeping a Book," in *The Idea of Order: Transforming Research Collections for 21st Century Scholarship* (Washington, DC: Council on Library and Information Resources, 2010), 91.

5. The HathiTrust is a partnership of academic and research institutions; see HathiTrust Digital Library, www.hathitrust.org/.

6. See Peter Hernon, Robert E. Dugan, and Danuta A. Nitecki, *Engaging in Evaluation and Assessment Research* (Santa Barbara, CA: Libraries Unlimited, 2011), 29. Figure 2.2 on this page covers turnover of the print collection at the University of Pittsburgh Library System from 1987 to 2007.

7. See Matthews, *The Evaluation and Measurement of Library Services,* chapter 8.

8. Paul B. Kantor, "The Library as an Information Utility in the University Context: Valuation and Measurement of Service," *Journal of the American Society of Information Science,* 27 (1976): 100–112. See also Paul B. Kantor, *Objective Performance Measurement for Academic and Research Libraries* (Washington, DC: Association of Research Libraries, 1984).

Services

THE QUALITY OF SERVICES that a library provides has an immediate impact on the utility and value of those services as customers perceive them. Delivering high-quality customer service requires an understanding of customer needs, wants, and expectations.

Perhaps one of the earliest individuals to call on libraries to focus on service quality and value was Richard Orr, who believed that *quality* reflects how good the service is, while *value* reflects how much good the library does. Implicit in his perspective is that libraries need to embrace and use outcome metrics to demonstrate value, or how much good the library does.[1] It is important to remember that outcome and effectiveness metrics address the question, "Are we doing the right things?" In the case of this chapter, *right* can only be determined from the perspective of the customer.

The management and marketing literatures tend to suggest that there is a positive correlation between the quality of services provided and the levels of customer satisfaction and that the customer perspective focuses on either customer satisfaction or service quality. Although a number of writers in library and information science confuse the concepts, *satisfaction* is an emotional reaction—the degree of contentment or discontentment with a specific transaction or service encounter or overall encounters. *Service quality*, on the other hand, is a global judgment relating to the superiority of a service as viewed in the context of specific statements that the library is willing to act on if customers find them of great value.[2] In essence, both service quality and satisfaction encompass the interactive relationship between the library and the people whom it is supposed to serve.

The interactions between the customer and the service provider might be viewed in terms of the Gaps Model of Service Quality, which posits five gaps that reflect a discrepancy between:

» customers' expectations and management's perceptions of these expectations (gap 1);
» management's perception of customers' expectations and service specifications (gap 2);
» service specifications and actual service delivery (gap 3);
» actual service delivery and what is communicated to customers about it (gap 4); and
» customers' expected services and perceived service delivered (gap 5).[3]

Any of these gaps may hinder an organization in providing high-quality service; however, the fifth one serves as the basis of a customer-oriented definition of both service quality and satisfaction. Collectively the five gaps may contribute to a *service quality gap*, which occurs when there is a difference between the perceived service and the anticipated service. An *understanding gap* arises from the differences between customer service expectations and management's understanding of customer expectations. A *design gap* occurs between management's understanding of customer expectations and the design and delivery of the service, and a *delivery gap* reflects a disparity between the specification of quality service and the actual quality that is delivered. Finally, a *communications gap* may develop between what is actually delivered and what has been promised.[4]

It is possible to examine service quality through four different perspectives:

1. **Excellence** for many organizations is externally and defined by their customers over time. Focusing on excellence means that the organization only settles for being the best, even though the attributes of excellence may change over time.
2. **Value** focuses on the benefits that are received by the customer of a product or service, while *quality* is meeting or exceeding customer expectations.
3. **Conformance to specifications** means that a detailed list of customer requirements must be prepared as a set of written specifications. While it is possible to prepare specifications for a product or service, the use of specifications represents an internally focused view of the world.
4. **Meeting/exceeding expectations** is a customer-centric perspective that implies a host of challenges. Expectations are subjective, neither static nor predictable, and change over time. Customer expectations change over time due to the customer's interactions with similar services in other contexts. For this perspective, service quality is usually defined as reducing the gap that exists between the quality of service provided and customer expectations.

In reality, service quality has two components: *what* is delivered to the customer, and *how* the service is conveyed; the *how* is sometimes called service deliverables or service interactions. The service deliverable may be given some directions or instructions, coaching, or answering a question. The combination of staff and equipment impacts how customers experience the service interchange or interaction. A disproportionate share of the literature focuses on the *what* to the omission of the *how*. (We cannot overemphasize that customers are worth listening to and that they are the best judges of the quality of services they receive.)

Customer service assumes an ever-increasing importance given the expanding number of options people have when they decide where, when, and how to satisfy their information needs and expectations. For many people the library is simply not on their radar screen. Thus, it would seem that one important way that any library can distinguish itself is to provide a level of service that delights or dazzles its customers.

The firms that provide legendary customer service are well-known. At the Ritz-Carlton hotels, for instance, any staff member can spend up to $2,000 to resolve a customer complaint without prior approval. A member of the Zappos customer loyalty team will gladly stay on the telephone as long as it takes to assist a customer, and a Nordstrom employee once refunded the purchase price on a set of tires, even though the store does not sell tires. Although not every organization can (or wants to) be one of these firms, any organization can provide service that delights its customers. Given the opportunities for customers to broadcast their complaints to the world via Twitter, Facebook, Yelp, or YouTube, it is imperative that libraries provide great service and resolve complaints quickly to the satisfaction of the individual.[5]

Gregory Crawford and Glenn McGuigan suggest that the use of a Total Service Index (TSI) might be useful for one library to compare its index rating with a set of peer libraries. Using the ACRL*Metrics* service and the NCES data set, a library can create a TSI by combining the following performance indicators:

- » Total circulation (adding general circulation and reserved circulation)
- » Total ILL (adding number of items loaned and number of items borrowed)
- » Total reference transactions (in-person reference transactions plus e-mail reference plus chat reference plus SMS or text messaging reference × 30 weeks)[6]
- » Total gate count (weekly gate count × 30)
- » Total attendance at instruction sessions[7]

The TSI, therefore, is the sum of these five indicators.

The rest of this chapter deviates from coverage of the two data services, *ACRLMetrics* and PLA*metrics*, because neither of them captures the customer perspective; rather, they convey measures important from the organizational perspective. This is important to remember because, as library managers interpret the data they derive from both data services discussed in this book, they should supplement the organizational perspective by having greater insights into the customer perspective. The two data services, however, do address stakeholder perspectives, including the customer perspective, but only when managers focus on a return on investment or consideration of value.

RELEVANT METHODS OF DATA COLLECTION

Evaluating the level of customer service that is actually provided is necessary if library managers wish to improve customer service. Peter Drucker notes that "[p]erformance has to be built into the enterprise and its management; it has to be measured—or at least judged—and it has to be continually improved."[8] Rather than thinking about service quality and customer satisfaction as a report card, library managers should view them as a means for improving the quality of library services—better aligning service delivery with a strategic plan.

Library managers can explore service quality and customer satisfaction using *qualitative methods* (one-on-one interviews, focus groups, mystery shoppers, systematic analysis of all complaints received by the library, or exit interviews), *quantitative methods* (locally developed surveys or standardized surveys), or some combination of the two methods.[9] Although the perception may be that using a local survey is a less costly option for a library, the validity of the questions and the resulting data might be suspect. In addition, entering data from a paper-based survey and then preparing an analysis will occupy many staff hours. Thus, a number of libraries rely on a standardized survey. Within the library profession, there are two well-known, standardized surveys: LibQUAL+ for service quality and LibSat for customer satisfaction.

LIBQUAL+

More than 1,300 libraries have participated in LibQUAL+, a web-based survey offered by the Association of Research Libraries (ARL) for a fee. The genesis of the survey was a project sponsored by the Texas A&M University library to determine the utility of service quality measures using SERVQUAL, which was created for use in the retail industry. SERVQUAL focuses on customer-perceived quality rather than objective quality, and it compares the performance of a firm with the expectations of customers using five attributes:

1. **Tangibles,** which includes the physical appearance of the firm: its employees, equipment, merchandise displays, and communications materials (signage, handouts, and so forth).
2. **Reliability,** which addresses concerns about the consistent and reliable delivery of service. Among the five factors, this is the most important perspective for customers.
3. **Responsiveness,** which examines whether the firm's employees provide assistance in a timely and helpful manner.
4. **Assurance,** which examines employees' competence, courtesy, professionalism, and confidence in their knowledge of the product or service.
5. **Empathy,** which focuses on the cheerfulness and attentiveness of employees when interacting with customers.

LibQUAL+, which evolved over a number of years from the original five SERVQUAL dimensions, now includes twenty-two core questions that measure user perceptions of service quality along three dimensions:

1. **Affect of service,** which relates to the courtesy, knowledge, helpfulness, and reliability of library staff members
2. **Information control,** which relates to how customers prefer to interact with the library and whether necessary information is provided in the format, location, and time of their choice
3. **Library as place,** which measures the library as a place for work or study, the usefulness of the space, and the symbolic value of the library

Survey respondents indicate their minimum service level, desired service level, and perceived service performance using a Likert scale of one to nine for each question. Additional questions focus on demographic information, information literacy outcomes, library use, and, to some extent, general satisfaction; the library can also insert local questions. Although the majority of participating libraries are academic, the survey has been used in other library settings (and translated into more than twenty languages).

In general, a library asks students, staff, and faculty to participate, and the resulting convenience sample reflects the opinions of a small portion of the total campus population. Each participating library is presented with a report noting survey results. Those results include a graph known as a radar chart, which plots the values of each category along a separate axis that starts in the center of the chart and ends on the outer ring (see figure 4.1). In every case the minimum service level is exceeded, and the perceived service level is less than the desired service level; in no case is the perceived service level greater than the desired service level.

FIGURE 4.1 **LIBQUAL+ RADAR CHART**

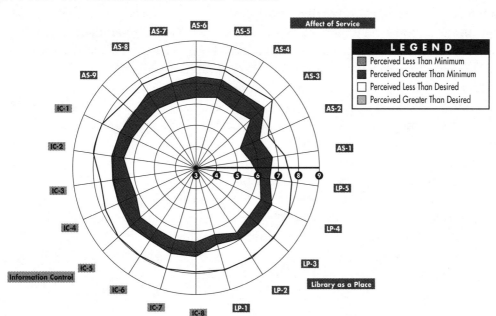

The benefit of the survey to a library is that the perception of quality of service levels can be followed over time to discern trends.[10] Data can also be segregated into various segments: undergraduates, graduate students, staff, and faculty members. The library can also prepare an analysis to discover any service gaps and gain a better awareness of its existing customer concerns through the analysis of the open-ended comments. One library used the results to help staff focus on their commitment to listen to users and to create a service plan centered on meeting users' needs.[11]

When considering the use of the survey, it is important to remember that a number of challenges exist. Among these are the following:

» **Conceptual problems.** The instrument has evolved away from the original service quality frameworks used to develop SERVQUAL.[12] Some respondents have difficulty in differentiating among minimum, desired, and perceived service levels, and the definitions of expectations and needs are confusing to others.[13]

» **Response rates.** The response rates might be very low and not representative of the demographic pattern of the total campus population, especially multicultural ones.[14]

» **Data analysis problems.** Using descriptive statistics may not be appropriate as determinants of service quality perceptions. Some groups (e.g., graduate students) may have fewer than four hundred respondents, making the resulting statistical analysis a concern.[15]

LIBSAT

LibSat is a web-based survey that assists managers in prioritizing and improving their library's quality of service. The survey, a fee-based subscription service from Counting Opinions, captures quantitative responses to survey questions but also encourages library customers to express their views using open-ended feedback. Several versions of the survey are available for both public and academic libraries: a short form (which takes about two to three minutes to complete), a regular form (which takes about seven minutes to complete), and a long form (which takes fifteen minutes to complete). The number of questions presented varies depending on what respondents say; if the response to a question is no, then one or more additional questions will be skipped.[16]

Because the LibSat survey is available 24/7, 365 days a year, the library receives continuous customer feedback about how well it is doing. This customer voice is an important perspective, one that helps librarians see things through the perspective of those actually using the library. The library has an opportunity to respond quickly to a specific issue should the need arise and to classify problems and concerns as they are reported as well as assigning responsibility for resolving/responding to the concern.

Some of the benefits accruing to a library using the LibSat service include the following:

» Continuously engaging with customers and providing them a voice in library operations
» Assisting in determining operational priorities by ranking customers' satisfaction opportunities
» Allocating resources more effectively
» Improving service delivery and customer satisfaction
» Tracking changes and monitoring outcomes better
» Assisting in creating a culture of evaluation and assessment
» Enhancing funding strategies and community advocacy

Library managers can benchmark the results and compare trends in customer satisfaction over time (e.g., a calendar year). In addition to relying on a set of standard reports, a library can create custom reports, and the data can appear in a variety of ways:

» Table—Summary data
» Performance measure report—Summary of selected variables
» Trend analysis—Summary of selected variables over time
» Graph—Performance metrics (sorting of variables is an option)
» Summary—Summary data for all selected performance metrics
» Period (gap) comparisons—Data values for the selected periods

Figure 4.2a illustrates a portion of the standard report options. For the library shown in the figure, the number of responses for calendar year 2013 was 1,825. Figure 4.2a shows the dashboard view of the data, followed by the tabular view in figure 4.2b.

FIGURE 4.2a **DASHBOARD VIEW OF THE MARKHAM PUBLIC LIBRARY USING LIBSAT DATA**

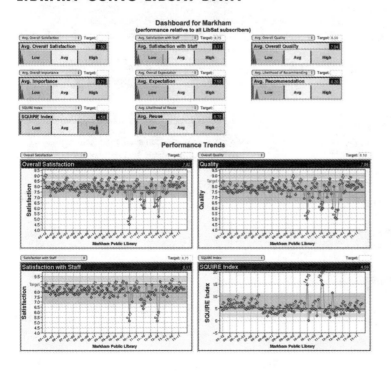

FIGURE 4.2b **TABULAR REPORT OF THE MARKHAM PUBLIC LIBRARY USING LIBSAT DATA**

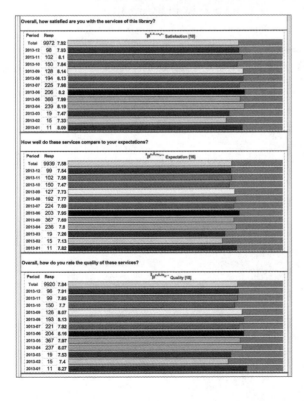

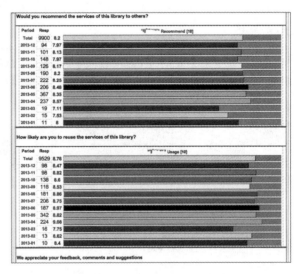

	Current Date 2014-03-24			Survey Summary Report Markham Public Library					Survey Start Date 2005-12-23		

Format: Text Report ⬍ Reload
Location: ⬍ -- All -- ⬍
Surveys: -- All --, SURVEY, In-depth, Regular
Dimension(s): All, Overall, Service, Staff
From: Jan 2013 ⬍ To: Dec 2013 ⬍

2005-12 2006-08 2007-04 2007-12 2008-08 2009-04 2009-12 2010-08 2011-04 2011-12 2012-08 2013-04 2014-0
2005   2006   2007   2008   2009   2010   2011   2012   2013   2014

Period	Responses	SQUIRE Index	Total Time	Average	Fastest	Slowest	Email	Comments	Zip/Postal	Avg Distance
Total	1825	4.61	9:01:57:11	07:21	00:00	15:58:21	345	525	874	3.96
2013-12	127	4.72	01:45	00:01	00:00	00:10	48	17	99	2.01
2013-11	120	4.94	01:57	00:01	00:00	00:16	52	21	105	2.4
2013-10	156	5.91	16:41:46	08:38	00:00	46:52	36	45	80	4.88
2013-09	131	4.1	17:27:30	07:59	00:25	07:29	18	37	55	4
2013-08	197	4.26	20:37:44	06:18	00:23	34:58	23	51	77	4.32
2013-07	228	4.02	1:21:42:10	12:01	00:39	58:21	38	77	90	4.51
2013-06	207	4.05	1:06:06:20	08:43	00:27	01:04	28	65	93	4.33
2013-05	371	5.2	2:00:02:55	07:46	00:31	31:09	60	108	158	4.21
2013-04	242	4.26	1:10:04:48	08:26	00:24	43:08	33	79	107	3.72
2013-03	19	6.2	02:16:23	07:10	01:17	20:45	6	12	2	0.72
2013-02	15	2.88	01:45:36	07:02	01:13	23:27	1	6	4	2.55
2013-01	12	4.62	01:08:17	05:41	00:34	13:19	2	7	4	2.64

Overall

Overall, how important is this library to you?

Period	Resp	Importance [10]
Total	9973	8.71
2013-12	98	8.55
2013-11	100	8.87
2013-10	150	9.01
2013-09	129	8.84
2013-08	193	8.66
2013-07	226	8.53
2013-06	206	8.92
2013-05	366	8.92
2013-04	238	9.05
2013-03	19	8.74
2013-02	15	8.93
2013-01	11	9.45

Overall, how satisfied are you with the services of this library?

Period	Resp	Satisfaction [10]
Total	9972	7.92
2013-12	98	7.93
2013-11	102	8.1
2013-10	150	7.84
2013-09	128	8.14
2013-08	194	8.13
2013-07	225	7.98
2013-06	206	8.2
2013-05	366	7.99
2013-04	239	8.19
2013-03	19	7.47
2013-02	15	7.33
2013-01	11	8.09

How well do these services compare to your expectations?

Period	Resp	Expectation [10]
Total	9939	7.58
2013-12	99	7.54
2013-11	102	7.58
2013-10	150	7.47
2013-09	127	7.73
2013-08	192	7.77
2013-07	224	7.69
2013-06	203	7.95
2013-05	367	7.69
2013-04	236	7.8
2013-03	19	7.26
2013-02	15	7.13
2013-01	11	7.82

Overall, how do you rate the quality of these services?

Period	Resp	Quality [10]
Total	9920	7.84
2013-12	96	7.91
2013-11	99	7.85
2013-10	150	7.7
2013-09	126	8.07
2013-08	193	8.13
2013-07	221	7.92
2013-06	204	8.16
2013-05	367	7.97
2013-04	237	8.07
2013-03	19	7.53
2013-02	15	7.4
2013-01	11	8.27

Would you recommend the services of this library to others?

Period	Resp	Recommend [10]
Total	9900	8.2
2013-12	94	7.97
2013-11	101	8.13
2013-10	148	7.97
2013-09	126	8.17
2013-08	190	8.2
2013-07	222	8.25
2013-06	206	8.48
2013-05	367	8.35
2013-04	237	8.57
2013-03	19	7.11
2013-02	15	7.53
2013-01	11	8

How likely are you to reuse the services of this library?

Period	Resp	Usage [10]
Total	9529	8.76
2013-12	98	8.47
2013-11	98	8.82
2013-10	138	8.6
2013-09	118	8.53
2013-08	181	8.86
2013-07	206	8.75
2013-06	187	8.97
2013-05	342	8.82
2013-04	224	9.06
2013-03	16	7.75
2013-02	13	8.62
2013-01	10	8.4

We appreciate your feedback, comments and suggestions

Subscribing libraries receive a great flexible tool called InformsUs, which allows them to develop quick, open-ended surveys or a survey focused on a specific issue, or both. A library can record all customer feedback received, regardless of the form in which the feedback is delivered: e-mail, telephone call, letter, customer feedback forms, postcards, and so forth. In addition to having all of this feedback data in a single place, the LibSat system allows the library to assign responsibility for learning more about a particular situation and, in turn, to contact the customer with a response to a customer query (if desired by the customer).

Opportunity Index

One of the helpful standard reports from LibSat is the Opportunity Index report, which provides a list of the services, from the customer's perspective, that would have the greatest impact on improving customer satisfaction.[17] The survey asks people to indicate their degree of satisfaction and to indicate the relative importance of each service. Combining the importance and satisfaction data enables the system to format a report that lists the areas for improvement (see figure 4.3), and this list can be displayed for each outlet as well as for the organization/institution as a whole.[18] For example, expanding parking and increasing the hours of operation would have an impact on improving customer satisfaction although the library is constrained by the reality that the parking lot has a maximum size and the existing budget precludes increasing hours.

FIGURE 4.3 **THE OPPORTUNITY INDEX (FOR THE MARKHAM PUBLIC LIBRARY)**

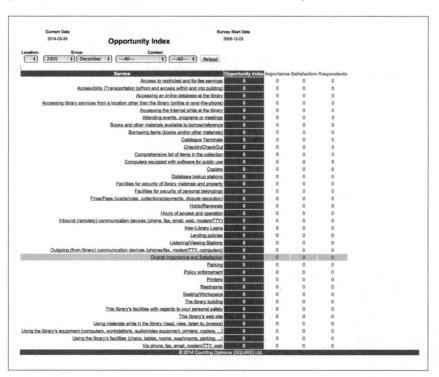

A version of the Opportunity Index data can also be depicted as a quadrant chart, as shown in figure 4.4. The *x* axis is *importance*, while the y axis of the chart is *satisfaction*. The smaller objects represent data from all respondents since the survey began, while the larger symbol represents the results for the selected period (say, the last three months). The goal for any library is to get as many symbols as possible out of the lower right-hand quadrant, where the relative importance is high, yet the relative satisfaction is low. A library will have a number of areas in which it can make improvements. For example, the greatest opportunity for improvement is indicated by a shape located in the lower right-hand quadrant.

FIGURE 4.4 **OPPORTUNITY INDEX DATA DISPLAYED AS A QUADRANT CHART**

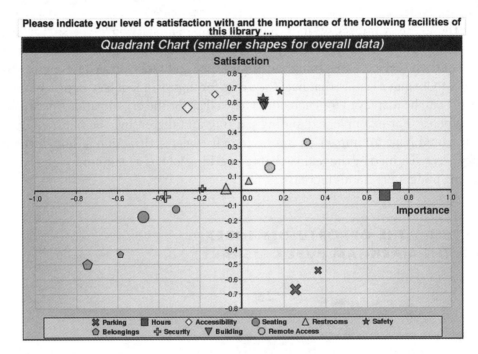

MAPHAT Reports

Some libraries ask their staff to wander or rove in order to be of assistance to customers at their point-of-need rather than being stationed behind a service desk. The public library version of the LibSat survey asks a series of questions to explore the quality of service interactions provided by staff in their frontline service capacity. Mentor Group Training has developed a shorthand acronym, called MAPHAT, as a way to remind staff of six dimensions of customer service:

1. **M**eet and greet (whether roving or at a service desk)
2. **A**sk a quick question (and Appreciate the customer)
3. **P**robe (for further information about needs and wants)

4. **H**ear (use active listening skills, watch body language, and so forth)
5. **A**ssist (including education and serving multiple customers at once)
6. **T**hank (and invite the customer to return to *her* or *his* library)

The LibSat survey allows the library to set goals for each area of the MAPHAT dimensions, and the reports clearly show how well the library is doing in comparison with its goals as well as compared to the other public libraries using the LibSat survey.

MAPHAT data can be presented in summary form as shown in figure 4.5. In addition, the data can be cast as a quadrant chart (see figure 4.6). The purposes are to show managers how the library is doing over time, to compare the performance in one branch to performance in all the other branches, or to determine how well the library is doing compared to other libraries, or any combination of these.

FIGURE 4.5 **MARKHAM PUBLIC LIBRARY MAPHAT SUMMARY DATA**

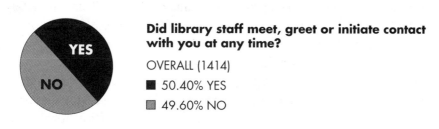

Did library staff meet, greet or initiate contact with you at any time?

OVERALL (1414)

■ 50.40% YES
■ 49.60% NO

FIGURE 4.6 **MARKHAM PUBLIC LIBRARY MAPHAT QUADRANT DATA CHART**

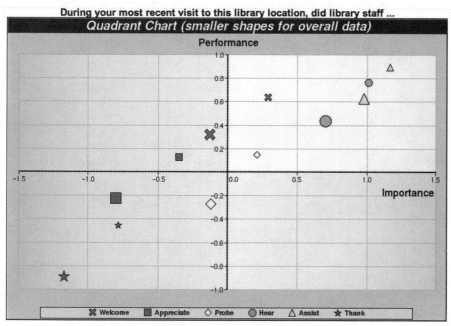

Did library staff meet, greet or initiate contact with you at any time?
Overall (1414)

The value of the MAPHAT questions is that they provide specific, up-to-date, and actionable feedback from the customers to library staff members about how they can improve (individual staff members are not singled out). Staff can see how well they are doing from the customer's perspective. The library management team can recognize and celebrate the progress made in improving the quality of services delivered as well as celebrate success. In addition, library managers can see the actual impact of a training program using before-and-after gap results and can measure any improvements over time.

CONCLUDING THOUGHTS

Unfortunately no metrics of customer satisfaction and service quality are captured and shared across all academic or public libraries. The costs of gathering meaningful data and ensuring consistently high-quality results would be too large to do this. Although a library might examine trends about the use of its services, visits, reference queries, and so forth as a proxy, the value of the resulting data analysis is questionable. The use of output metrics does not inform the library about how well services are being delivered—just that, to some extent, they are being used.

It is one thing to assert that a library provides high-quality services and that its customers are all *happy campers*. Yet, the only way to demonstrate that these statements are true is to measure customer satisfaction and service quality and to compare the results with the services provided. It is important for managers not to rely on gut feelings, but, rather, to gather, analyze, and use data about the actual quality of service that the library delivers in order that the library can continuously improve. In this age of accountability and transparency, libraries need to have actual data to demonstrate the customer perspective. Using data about service quality and customer satisfaction allows library managers to make more judicious reallocations of precious resources that will have a measurable impact on truly delighting customers.

EXERCISES

Answers to the following questions are in the "Appendix" at the back of the book. We encourage different members of a library staff to work on the exercises together and to discuss the results. Managers might also participate in that discussion.

QUESTION 1 Does your library offer a customer service experience that is equivalent to that of, for instance, Nordstrom? How would you know (gut reaction or access to objectively gathered data)? Further, how important is it for the library to be comparable to Nordstrom?

QUESTION 2 Does your library's website provide an online experience that meets or exceeds one offered by Amazon or Zappos? What has your library done recently to improve its website? Did customers have any input into that improvement?

QUESTION 3 Does your library offer a customer service experience that meets the local competition found at Starbucks, a local bookstore, or other popular retail establishment in your community? How important is it for the library to provide such an experience?

QUESTION 4 Has your library recently conducted a customer satisfaction survey? If it has, was the survey developed locally, was it downloaded from a library website (e.g., state library), or was a standardized survey used? Are the library managers generally pleased with the resulting information derived from the survey? How has the library used the results, and has it linked them to a strategic plan?

QUESTION 5 Does your library report customer satisfaction metrics to stakeholders annually, such as in a budget presentation or in an annual report? If not, why not? (As you answer this question, address the net promoter score.[19])

QUESTION 6 If your library subscribes to LibSat, have the managers set targets for the six dimensions of customer service represented in the MAPHAT acronym? How well is the library doing?

QUESTION 7 If your library participates in the LibQUAL+ survey, has it used the results to improve service? Are any improvements connected to a strategic plan? How do you mine the qualitative textual data provided by customers as they respond to the open-ended questions of the survey?

Notes

1. Richard Orr, "Measuring the Goodness of Library Services," *Journal of Documentation* 29, no. 3 (1973): 315–52.

2. Peter Hernon and Ellen Altman, *Assessing Service Quality: Satisfying the Expectations of Library Customers* (Chicago: American Library Association, 2010), 138.

3. For a graphic depiction of the Gaps Model, see Peter Hernon and Joseph R. Matthews, *Listening to the Customer* (Santa Barbara, CA: Libraries Unlimited, 2011).

4. For an elaboration of the different types of gaps, see Mik Wisniewski and Mike Donnelly, "Measuring Service Quality in the Public Sector: The Potential for SERVQUAL," *Total Quality Management* 7, no. 4 (1996): 357–65.

5. For a more thorough discussion of customer satisfaction, see Joseph R. Matthews, *The Evaluation and Measurement of Library Services* (Westport, CT: Libraries Unlimited, 2007), chapter 15; Hernon and Altman, *Assessing Service Quality*; and Hernon and Matthews, *Listening to the Customer*.

6. The number 30 equals the sum of two academic sessions of an academic year.

7. Gregory Crawford and Glenn McGuigan, "An Exploratory Quantitative Analysis of Academic Library Services: An Examination of Performance Based Metrics," *Library Leadership and Management* 25, no. 3 (2011): 1–19.

8. Peter Drucker, *The Essential Drucker: Selections from the Management Works of Peter F. Drucker* (New York: HarperCollins, 2001), 12.

9. See Hernon and Matthews, *Listening to the Customer*.

10. For more information about the survey, visit www.libqual.org/home.

11. Tom Wall, "LibQUAL+™ as Transformative Experience," *Performance Measurement and Metrics* 3, no. 2 (2002): 43–48.

12. See A. Parasuraman, Leonard Berry, and Valarie Zeithemel, "A Conceptual Model of Service Quality and Its Implications for Future Research," *Journal of Marketing* 49 (1985): 41–50.

13. Xi Shi and Sarah Levy, "A Theory-Guided Approach to Library Services Assessment," *College & Research Libraries* 66, no. 3 (2005): 266–77.

14. Claire Creaser, "One Size Does Not Fit All: User Surveys in Academic Libraries," *Performance Measurement and Metrics* 7, no. 3 (2006): 153–62.

15. William Edgar, "Questioning LibQUAL+: Expanding Its Assessment to Academic Library Effectiveness," *portal: Libraries and the Academy* 6, no. 4 (2006): 445–65.

16. The LibSat questions are available at http://co.countingopinions.com/review/. Currently there are more than five hundred customer libraries.

17. Anthony Ulwick, the originator of the Opportunity Index, used gap analysis (customer importance compared to satisfaction) to produce a rank-ordered list (high to low) of those service areas that customers perceive as needing improvement. See Anthony Ulwick, "Turn Customer Input into Innovation," *Harvard Business Review* 80, no. 1 (January 2010): 91–97.

18. For more about the index and how to produce it, see Peter Hernon, Robert Dugan, and Joseph Matthews, *Getting Started with Evaluation* (Chicago: American Library Association, 2014), chapter 6.

19. The net promoter score, a metric that divides customers into three categories (promoters, passives, and detractors), serves as a means to make comparisons across libraries and other departments in academic institutions and local government. See Hernon, Dugan, and Matthews, *Getting Started with Evaluation*, 114–15.

Staffing

LIBRARY PERSONNEL ALONG WITH collections, facilities, and technologies are the four components of every library's infrastructure. For the purposes of this chapter, one critical aspect of personnel is staff expenditures, which is defined as the sum of all expenditures for salaries, wages, and benefits. In addition to staff expenditures, operating expenditures include collections (content materials and resources regardless of format) and other expenses—for example, consumables (supplies) and telephone and equipment maintenance costs.

WHY IS IT IMPORTANT TO UNDERSTAND STAFFING?

A study of library staff expenditures from 2000 through 2009 found that salaries/wages and benefits expenditures consume as much as 70 percent of some public library operating budgets, making it the largest portion of infrastructure operating expenditures.[1] Staff costs could exceed 50 percent of operational expenditures for libraries at many small academic institutions as well when viewed from the perspective of institutional enrollment and Carnegie Classification.

Understanding staffing characteristics, including the number of staff measured as full-time equivalents, their classification (e.g., professional and credentialed or support staff), organizational alignment (e.g., public services or administration), and other related costs (e.g., benefits) helps to inform operational decision making. For example, knowing when and what type of staff are needed for coverage of a public service point will help to define core public service hours: When do the users need staff? The building may be at least at 50 percent capacity at a specific time and day of the week, but there may be few measured user interactions with library staff; the customer is doing something that does not require mediation by library staff. This information will inform decision making about how many and whom to situate to staff a public service point adequately. As another example, if staff expenditures are extremely high, it may indicate that other aspects of library operations lack adequate funding, such as collections. Conversely, if staff expenditures are extremely low compared to collections and other expenses, it may indicate a lack of professionally trained library staff or an adequate number of staff to provide high-quality services.

Because of staffing's percentage of all operating expenditures, and its relationship to the successful provision of library services, library decision makers must have a comprehensive understanding of staffing that can be documented and explained internally as well as to the satisfaction of many library stakeholders, but especially those responsible for institution-level funding decisions concerning the library.

ORGANIZING INFORMATION BEFORE STUDYING STAFFING

Before studying staff characteristics, one must collect and organize basic data. Although several organizational approaches are possible, the first is to think of the outputs that decision makers will want to know. An important first data point is the number of full-time staff equivalents employed by the library. A full-time equivalent (FTE) is based on the number of hours worked a week as defined as full-time by the funding agency, such as the library's institution. Examples of the number of hours worked over a seven-day period are 40, 37.5, 35, and 32 hours to be considered a full-time equivalent. If the full-time workweek is 40 hours, and a person employed by the library works 20, the person is .5 FTE (20 hours worked divided by the 40 hours per week defined as an FTE). A sum of all employed by the library, excluding volunteers, yields a library staff FTE.

A second data point involves the classification of the personnel employed. The most common types are "professional librarians," "other professionals," and "support staff." As typically defined by professional library associations, "professional librarians" hold a master's degree from a program accredited by the American Library Association. "Other professionals" include staff whose duties require education or training, or both, in related fields (e.g., academic disciplines, archives, media, donor relations, and computing). "Support staff" or "all other paid staff" includes technical and clerical staff who are paid annual salaries or hourly wages. A fourth staff classification that academic libraries should separate from the other three is "student assistants"; they provide library support services, but are often not employed year-round or receive any benefits. Information concerning unpaid volunteers should also be collected and separated from data about those who receive compensation. When library personnel are classified by these types, the subtotals are usually summed as staff FTE for a fiscal year.

A third data point organizes staff by library departments or functions, or both. Departments may include circulation and reference, while functions may include collection development and management, cataloging and other technical services, public services, information technology and digital development, and administration services.

Table 5.1, an example of organizing staff data from the University of West Florida libraries, casts trend data for the past decade and can illustrate similarities and differences over that period. Sharp drops should be noted and explained. Other staff information, which might be added to the table, might include

» staff qualifications by individual, such as degrees held, library experience by function(s) from previous library employment, and the number of years working in a (or that) library;

» staff development, such as the number of training hours per staff member each fiscal year, and the cumulative number of staff hours attending workshops; and

» staff skills, such as identifying the comprehension level of other languages spoken/read and expertise in graphic design or software applications.

TABLE 5.1 **STAFFING PATTERNS—UNIVERSITY OF WEST FLORIDA LIBRARIES**

	FY2004	FY2005	FY2006	FY2007	FY2008
Total library FTE including student assistants	57.60	57.07	54.42	55.75	53.00
TOTAL LIBRARY STAFF FTE WORKING WITHOUT STUDENT ASSISTANTS					
Total professional/administrative librarians, FTE	15.70	17.50	15.25	15.85	15.35
Total other professional, FTE	0.00	0.00	0.00	0.00	0.00
Total support staff librarians, FTE	31.70	29.30	28.30	28.45	26.20
Total student assistants, FTE	10.20	10.27	10.87	11.45	11.45
DEPARTMENTAL ALLOCATION BY FTE (EXCLUDES STUDENTS)					
Acquisitions	2.75	3.00	3.00	3.00	3.00
Administration	7.00	6.00	7.00	6.00	5.10
Cataloging Services	4.00	4.00	4.40	4.00	4.00
Circulation	9.10	8.90	8.35	7.85	7.70
Reference and ILL	10.45	11.50	10.05	10.80	9.45
Serials	5.35	6.00	5.00	4.75	5.00
University Archives and West Florida History Center	2.00	2.00	2.00	2.00	1.40
Technology	1.00	1.00	0.25	2.00	1.90
Curriculum/Professional Studies Library	2.00	1.40	1.00	1.90	2.00
Emerald Coast Library at Fort Walton Beach	3.75	3.00	2.50	2.00	2.00

Continued on next page.

TABLE 5.1 (continued)

	FY2009	FY2010	FY2011	FY2012	FY2013
Total Library FTE including Student Assistants	51.54	49.27	47.12	44.53	44.87
TOTAL LIBRARY STAFF FTE WORKING WITHOUT STUDENT ASSISTANTS					
Total professional/administrative librarians, FTE	13.10	13.47	12.84	10.60	11.83
Total other professional, FTE	0.00	0.00	0.00	0.00	0.00
Total support staff librarians, FTE	26.63	24.35	22.52	24.00	23.25
Total student assistants, FTE	11.81	11.45	11.77	9.93	9.79
DEPARTMENTAL ALLOCATION BY FTE (EXCLUDES STUDENTS)					
Acquisitions	3.00	2.60	1.17	0.00	0.00
Administration	3.00	3.35	4.00	4.00	4.00
Cataloging Services	3.25	3.00	4.57	5.00	3.00
Circulation	7.80	7.35	7.59	8.20	8.75
Reference and ILL	9.43	9.22	9.06	9.25	10.83
Serials	4.50	3.80	1.78	0.00	0.00
University Archives and West Florida History Center	2.00	1.80	1.58	2.50	2.25
Technology	2.75	2.60	2.25	2.25	2.25
Curriculum/Professional Studies Library	2.00	2.00	1.91	2.00	2.00
Emerald Coast Library at Fort Walton Beach	2.00	2.00	2.00	2.00	2.00

METRICS TO COLLECT CONCERNING CAPACITY

Library decision makers must understand expectations and inputs that directly and indirectly affect staffing levels and services—the organization's capacity to provide and sustain services—at the beginning of each fiscal year. Expectations concerning access that influence staffing levels include the number of hours, days, and times the library is scheduled to be open each week. A related input metric is the number of public service desks expected to be staffed and when. Although public service desks are most often aligned with service functions expected (e.g., reference and circulation) during hours open, staffing levels in a few cases may also be related to the number of library entrances/exits to ensure the security of the library's collection and equipment (e.g., a service point to inspect users' bags as they leave the building).

Another input metric measures the financial resources allocated to support staffing types and levels. This would include salaries and wages budgeted for all staff organized by full- and part-time employees expressed in FTE and then differentiated by type, such as professional librarians, other professionals, and support

BOX 5.1 **INPUTS CRITICAL TO UNDERSTANDING STAFF CAPACITY**

Expressed in terms of FTE

- » Total staff
- » Professional librarians
- » Other professionals
- » Support staff
- » Student assistants (if appropriate)

Expressed as a percentage of total library FTE to

- » Professional librarians FTE
- » Other professionals FTE
- » Support staff FTE
- » Student assistants FTE (if appropriate)

Library staff FTE per organizational function, such as

- » Public services
- » Collection development and management
- » Cataloging and other technical services
- » Information technology and digital development
- » Administration services

Number of library personnel with responsibilities on

- » Organizational committees
- » Institutional committees
- » External organizational/institutional committees

Number of FTE library staff

- » Per capita
- » Per capita by type of user, such as children under five years old, faculty member, or senior citizen
- » Per each 1,000 capita

Number of FTE library staff by staff type to

- » Per capita
- » Per capita by type of user, such as children under five years old, faculty member, or senior citizen
- » Per each 1,000 capita

Number of FTE library staff by library function (e.g., public services) and department (e.g., circulation) to

- » Per capita
- » Per capita by type of user, such as children under five years old, faculty member, or senior citizen
- » Per each 1,000 capita

staff. Student assistants, if funded through the library, would be another staff type. Each staffing type could also be stated as a ratio to the other classifications, such as support (technical and clerical) staff FTE as a percentage of total staff FTE. Fringe benefits might also be accounted for. Additional budget data might include the funds allocated to support expected and scheduled staff training and professional development costs, such as registration and travel.

Box 5.1 illustrates other inputs critical to the understanding of staff capacity at the beginning of each fiscal year.

BOX 5.2 **STAFFING EXPENDITURES**

Total library expenditures (in dollar amounts)

» For all information resources (library materials), one time and continuations
» For all staff and student assistants (including fringe benefits)
» For all other operating expenditures

Percentage of total library budget expended

» For all information resources (library materials), one time and continuations
» For all staff and student assistants (including fringe benefits)
» For all other operating expenditures

Total salaries and wages as expenditures

» All staff
  – Full-time
  – Part-time
  – Student assistants (if appropriate)

» Professional librarians (master's degree in librarianship or equivalent)
» Other professionals (required education in related fields)
» Support staff (technical and clerical)
» Student assistants (if appropriate)
» Fringe benefits (if expended through the library)

Expenditures as a percentage of total staffing by type of staff

» Professional librarian FTE as a percentage of total library FTE
» Other professionals as a percentage of total library FTE
» Support staff FTE as a percentage of total library FTE
» Student assistants (if appropriate) FTE as a percentage of total library FTE

Staffing expenditures by library department or function

» Public services
» Collection development and management
» Information processing (cataloging and other technical services)

» Information technology and digital development
» Administration

Staffing expenditures as a percentage of total staffing by library department or function

» Public services as a percentage of total library FTE
» Collection development and management as a percentage of total library FTE
» Information processing (cataloging and other technical services) as a percentage of total library FTE
» Information technology and digital development as a percentage of total library FTE
» Administration as a percentage of total library FTE

Staffing expenditures on staff development and training attendance at

» Workshops
» Conferences
» Other professional development sessions

Staffing expenditures per capita (e.g., population, student, faculty)

Staffing expenditures per 1,000 capita (e.g., population, student, faculty)

METRICS TO COLLECT CONCERNING OCCURRENCES

There are differences between the metrics collected for capacity (inputs) and those gathered for occurrences (outputs). Although inputs are important to understanding what the library can accomplish, the reality is that what is scheduled, expected, and anticipated seldom happens as planned. Measured outputs may fall short of achieving stated objectives for a number of reasons, including changes in budgets during the fiscal year (e.g., rescissions), planned/scheduled days open lost to weather-related events (e.g., storms) that close an otherwise open library, and changes in staffing levels for a variety of reasons, such as staff turnover or reassignments to projects that ultimately reduce staffing capacity in the allotted departmental or functional areas (e.g., cataloging an unexpected and large monographs gift takes allotted time away from a collection weeding project). It may be more important to measure and report about occurrences rather than capacity because stakeholders want to know as much as possible about what happened versus what was planned.

There are many metrics to collect about staffing for a fiscal year. Data collection includes how much was expended financially for staffing as well as how many activity or functional transactions were accomplished by staff as workload indicators. It is also noteworthy to learn about staffing from a variety of ratios measured at the end of the fiscal year.

Expenditures data provide numerous and important metrics (see box 5.2). The three main expenditure categories (staff, collections, and other expenditures) provide the total expended as well as the percentage of total library funds expended for all information resources (library materials), staff (which may include fringe benefits), and other operating expenditures. The total expended as salaries and wages can be calculated and summed.

BOX 5.3 **COSTS**

In general
» Total cost per identified activity, such as number of public service outlets staffed
Cost of operating the library
» Cost to acquire and make available a book in print versus electronic format
» Cost of staff to circulate a book to a user
Information resources
» Cost to acquire and make available a book in print versus electronic format
» Cost of staff to circulate a book to a user
Reference
» Cost of staff to answer a reference question
Interlibrary loan
» Cost to borrow an item
» Cost to lend an item
Library administrative cost per library employee

Related to expenditures are data about activity or transaction costs that are dependent on staff involvement to accomplish. These costs require knowing the number of transactions or level of activity undertaken during the fiscal year as well as quantifying staff involvement (see box 5.3). Some of these costs will be discussed later in this chapter as subjects of internal staffing studies. Although individual workload indicators are not discussed here, these can be interpolated from the costs data calculated.

Along with the importance of expenditure data at the end of the fiscal year is the compilation of data about staffing (see box 5.4). Expressed in terms of full-time equivalents, two sets of useful information for internal analysis would include total staff and FTE for each staff type (e.g., professional librarians and support staff) and then by library department or function. A third set would provide ratios of staffing types in FTE to all staff FTE (e.g., support staff FTE as a percentage of all library FTE); such ratios when graphed on a stacked bar chart for each fiscal year over a few years provide a useful visual of the mix of staffing types.

Although not as commonly or frequently compiled as data about staff and staffing expenditures, staff development information reflects the alignment of staff qualifications with current customer needs and is useful for improving efficiency and effectiveness in service delivery (see box 5.5). Additionally, information about library staff involvement in community engagement and professional associations may help to illustrate the library's external involvement.

Many staff-related metrics might be collected concerning the local library situation (see box 5.6). An example is library visits or gate counts, which are dependent on the library being open and staffed. Depending on the granularity of the visits / gate counts data, one could identify the busiest hour of the day, day of the week, week of the month, and month of the year. Another example is the amount of funds raised by staff through fund-raising efforts or fees and other library fees. If a library has an active staff development program, it may consider collecting information about mentoring, such as professional librarians mentoring support staff or library staff mentoring student assistants.[2]

STAFFING STUDIES FOR INTERNAL DECISION MAKING

With capacity and occurrence data collected, library decision makers can conduct internal studies involving library staff. A couple of basic studies include the following:

» Simple studies could reveal staffing trends over two or more fiscal years by reviewing changes in total staff expressed as FTE, the percentage of each type of library staff to total library staff, and total staff FTE per capita or per 1,000 capita or both. A similar study could review changes in time of the type of library staff FTE per capita or per 1,000 capita or both. Staff turnover and absentee rates could also be calculated and compared using simple trend analysis.

» With the shift of some collections to focus on electronic formats rather than traditional print, and the shift to increase customer self-service through online information delivery or the application of such technologies as user self-checkout, studies can help to determine which

BOX 5.4 **STAFFING**

Expressed in terms of FTE

- » Total library staff
- » Professional librarians (master's degree in librarianship or equivalent)
- » Other professionals (required education in related fields)
- » Support staff (technical and clerical)
- » Student assistants (if appropriate)

Library FTE

- » Ratio of FTE library staff to student FTE
- » Ratio of FTE library staff to faculty FTE
- » Professional librarians FTE as a percentage of library FTE
- » Other professionals FTE as a percentage of library FTE
- » Support staff FTE as a percentage of library FTE
- » Student assistants (if appropriate) FTE as a percentage of library FTE

Library staff FTE per organizational function

- » Public services
- » Collection development and management
- » Information processing (cataloging and other technical services)
- » Information technology and digital development
- » Administration

Total library staff FTE per capita

TYPE OF LIBRARY STAFF FTE PER CAPITA

- » Professional librarians (master's degree in librarianship or equivalent)
- » Other professionals (required education in related fields)
- » Support staff (technical and clerical)
- » Student assistants (if appropriate)

LIBRARY STAFF FTE PER ORGANIZATIONAL FUNCTION PER CAPITA

- » Public services
- » Collection development and management
- » Information processing (cataloging and other technical services)
- » Information technology and digital development
- » Administration

Total library staff FTE per 1,000 capita

TYPE OF STAFF PER 1,000 CAPITA

- » Professional librarians (master's degree in librarianship or equivalent)
- » Other professionals (required education in related fields)
- » Support staff (technical and clerical)
- » Student assistants (if appropriate)

LIBRARY STAFF FTE PER ORGANIZATIONAL FUNCTION PER 1,000 CAPITA

- » Public services
- » Collection development and management
- » Information processing (cataloging and other technical services)
- » Information technology and digital development
- » Administration

Staff turnover

- » Number that joined the staff
- » Number that left the staff
- » Turnover rate = the number of staff divided by the number of staff who left, then multiplied by 100

Staff absentee rate

- » Number of total staff hours worked (do not include sick leave reported)
- » Number of total staff hours reported as sick leave
- » Absentee rate = the number of total staff hours reported as sick leave divided by the number of total staff hours worked, expressed as a percentage

BOX 5.5 **STAFF DEVELOPMENT**

Staff training

» Total number of hours received

» Formal training hours per staff FTE

Staff attendance in hours and number of occurrences

» Workshops

» Conferences

» Other professional development sessions

Service

» Number of staff who served on internal library committees
» Number of staff who served on committees external to the library
» Number of internal and external committees on which staff participate
» Number of staff hours spent on internal and external committee work

Types of publications

» Articles (in peer reviewed and non–peer reviewed journals)
» Conference papers

» Books
» Poster sessions

Speeches or presentations delivered

» Locally
» State level
» Regionally

» Nationally
» Internationally

existing staff functions are still relevant. For example, how does the adoption of the e-journals format affect staff who process print journal issues for shelving or those who manage the binding of issues into volumes? Are the same number of staff hours needed, or can some hours be reallocated elsewhere internally? Surveys and job observations, time and motion studies, and compilation and analysis of output data are means to review staff alignment with needed tasks and activities.

» Staff efficiencies could be discovered for re-shelving items, ordering and processing new items, putting an item on reserve, and processing interlibrary loans.

» A staffing study of the reference public service desk might determine the cost-appropriate mix of professional librarians to support staff. For example, for two months beginning in October 2002, Stetson University (Florida) reference librarians recorded all reference questions asked at the reference desk along with the source(s) used to try to answer them. All questions were recorded that came to the reference desk in person, by phone, or by e-mail. The two-month study was repeated in spring 2003, spring 2006, and fall 2006 to account for changes in class

BOX 5.6 **OTHER STAFFING METRICS**

Library visitors (in-person)

LIBRARY VISITS

» Per capita

» Per capita per hour open

» Per staff FTE per fiscal year (or month, etc.)

NUMBER OF LIBRARY VISITS/
GATE COUNTS TO DETERMINE BUSIEST

» Hour of the day

» Day of week

» Week of the month

» Month of year

Amount of funds raised by source

» Fund-raising efforts involving staff (e.g., book sale)

» Fees collected for library use

» Fines as levied by library staff

Number of staff and/or student assistants formally mentored by library staff

assignments and changes over time. To calculate the cost-effectiveness of staffing the reference desk, each reference librarian's salary during the four study periods was first translated to hourly rates (based on 1,950 paid work hours per person per fiscal year) and then averaged to come up with a single hourly rate for each librarian during the four-year study period. Then the exact number of hours that each librarian worked during the study periods was determined using reference schedules and library calendars to ensure accuracy. By multiplying the hours worked by each librarian during the eight-month period by his or her average hourly rate, the estimated cost of staffing the reference desk was obtained. Dividing that amount by the sum of all desk transactions by the sum of the personnel costs resulted in an average expenditure of $7.09 per transaction. The type of transaction was also recorded, including noninformation directional, information-oriented directional, information-oriented technology, research, catalog search, citation help, database help, and personal knowledge/referral, among other question categories. Susan M. Ryan, the author of the study, found that, though the expense to answer the 784 "research" questions ($5,559) was not high, during the same time frame the library spent $7.09 on each of the 2,528 times that a printer cartridge was changed, or a paper jam was fixed, or directions were given to a building across campus—a cost totaling $17,924.[3] This staffing study could be easily replicated elsewhere. The study might determine the number of hours as well as the percentage of total desk coverage by each type of staff. The cost per transaction could be reduced by replacing some of the hours at the reference desk staffed by professional librarians with less expensive, but trained and qualified, support staff.

BOX 5.7 **STAFFING STUDIES INVOLVING SERVICE PERFORMANCE METRICS**

Number of hours open for public service (access)

Number of entrances (physical layout), which affects the number of staffed service points (services)

Staff public work hours per typical full-service week
» Number of total hours (overlapping) of staffed circulation service
» Number of nonoverlapping hours of staffed reference service
» Number of total hours (overlapping) of staffed reference service

Average customer wait time (e.g., at reference and circulation desks; wait time for a reserve before filled)
» Number of rings before phone is answered

Circulation transactions (usage)
» Total number of circulation transactions by type of item (e.g., print monographs, reserve items, audio items, and image items)
» Circulation transactions by type of item (e.g., print monographs, reserve items, audio items, and image items) per capita

Information resources
» Accuracy of book processing, such as correctly matching the applied item bar code to the item record
» Placement accuracy of items shelved
» Turnaround time for shelving/re-shelving

Reference transactions (usage)
» Number of reference questions answered per capita
» Number of reference questions answered by:
  – Face-to-face
  – Mail (physical)
  – Telephone
  – Electronic
    › chat
    › e-mail
    › text messaging
» Number of reference questions answered correctly
  – Average time to answer a reference question
  – Accuracy rate of providing the correct answer to a question

Research consultations conducted
» Number of hours

Number of library-created and -maintained subject/topic guides to resources (help guides)
» Number of subject/topic guides created by the library to support a specific course

Interlibrary loans
» Number borrowed (received from another library)
» Number loaned (provided to another library)
» Turnaround time (length of time) to fill an interlibrary loan request
» Turnaround time (length of time) to fill an intercampus loan request

Programs and presentations (excluding library instruction)
» Sponsored by the library
» Attendance

Library instruction sessions

» Number conducted

» Number of librarian-led program/discipline- or course-based instruction sessions

 – Number of program/discipline- or course-based instruction sessions in which a librarian provides a supporting role to the faculty member

» Number of participants attending library instructional sessions

 – Total number

 – Average number attending per instruction session

 – Attendance per capita

Presentations to groups (e.g., orientations, library tours)

» Total number conducted

» Number conducted per capita

» Total number attending

» Average number attending per presentation

» Attendance per capita

Other studies might involve the compilation and analysis of service performance metrics that are affected by staffing levels and types of staff (see box 5.7). These would include the number of hours open; the number of visits /gate entrances; the number of public service hours provided; workload indicators for reference, library instruction, interlibrary loan, and circulation; program attendance; and presentations to groups.

STAFFING STUDIES USING EXTERNAL DATA

In addition to conducting internal studies about staffing, library decision makers may want to learn how their libraries compare with others. Fortunately, there are two means of benchmarking library staffing: by reviewing the professional literature and by compiling data from national sources to customize studies for local review, analysis, and reporting (see also chapter 6).

The professional literature occasionally reports on national staffing metrics that can be used for local library benchmarking. In a study of academic and public library salaries and library staffing expenditures trends from 2000 to 2009, Denise M. Davis found the following:

» Public and academic library salaries/wages and benefits expenditures consume as much as 70 percent of some library operating budgets.

» Overall, academic libraries expended 49.3 percent of their operating budgets on salaries and wages in 2008, down from 50.1 percent in 2000.

» Public libraries expended 65.5 percent of their operating budgets on salaries and wages in 2007, an increase from 64.2 percent in 2000.

» When considering higher education institutional degree-granting levels in FY2008, those offering less than a four-year degree reported the largest proportion of the budget for salaries (71.6 percent), followed by bachelor's degree-granting institutions (54.4 percent), master's degree (53.9 percent), and doctoral degree (45 percent). Overall, degree-granting institutions at four-year and above reported an average of 46.5 percent of operating budget for staffing.

» Additionally in FY2008, the proportions of professional (MLS) and other professional and support staff by degree-granting level in academic libraries were 32.5 percent MLS and 65.5 percent non-MLS for less than four-year degree institutions; 31.8 percent MLS and 68.2 percent non-MLS for bachelor's degree institutions; and 28 percent MLS and 72 percent non-MLS for master's and doctorate degree institutions.[4]

In another study, when comparing academic library spending with that of public and school libraries in a ten-year span from 1998 through 2008, John J. Regazzi found the following:

» Academic and public libraries have different investment and spending priorities. Academic libraries as a group have reduced staff to invest in collection development and electronic information. Public libraries are not significantly expanding their collections but are investing proportionally more in staff expansion and development so as to provide more community programs and services.

» With regard to staffing, though academic libraries increased their allotment of master's-degree librarians by 9 percent from 1998 to 2008, they shed other types of jobs tied to nonprofessional staff and the use of student assistants. Academic libraries reduced their FTE staffing by nearly 4 percent, while public libraries increased staffing by nearly 20 percent.[5]

An academic library staffing study of professional librarians published in 2007 found that

» most professional librarians at baccalaureate degree–granting college libraries have about four colleagues;

» master's degree–granting institutions have about fourteen professional librarians;

» most professional librarians working in doctoral institutions have over fifty colleagues;

» there are usually about two nonlibrarian staff members to each librarian in larger academic libraries;

» in small private institutions the ratio is closer to one nonlibrarian staff member for each librarian;

» librarians at larger institutional libraries generally serve fewer than twenty-two faculty members for each professional librarian FTE;

» librarians at medium-sized institutional libraries serve thirty faculty members for each professional librarian FTE; and

» librarians at medium-sized and small institutional libraries serve forty faculty members for each professional librarian FTE.[6]

These studies provide decision makers with several metrics for which to benchmark staffing in their libraries. A drawback to these well-done studies is the time lag of the analyzed and reported data to their availability via publication in the professional literature. Therefore, libraries may want to update these nationally derived aggregate metrics to more current numbers or may want to benchmark only with their peers.

Benchmarking, which is discussed more fully in chapter 6, facilitates the comparisons of selected metrics in libraries based on the careful selection of peers. Many higher education institutions have undertaken a process to identify peer institutions, often based upon the Carnegie Classification for common characteristics. The selection of peers is less common in municipal or county governments. Public libraries, however, might consider selecting peers within their population range or those more closely sharing their registered borrowers' demographics.

Once the peers have been selected, libraries will then want to choose which staffing metrics to benchmark. Those metrics identified in this chapter may be useful depending on what decision makers want to know or what stakeholders request.

Box 5.8 indicates the most commonly requested and useful comparative staffing metrics. The last benchmark in the box provides three key expenditure metrics. Using PLA*metrics* for this benchmark, we can determine if a suitable report already exists in the data service, one that might be updated. For this example (see example 5.1), we can create a new report to illustrate the process, as outlined in the table. The example shows the resulting spreadsheet for library materials and all other expenses for each library. A local library could use the data from the resultant report as a benchmark concerning the ratios for the three expenditure categories.

Please note that several state library agencies also gather input and output metrics from public libraries. Often the compiled and validated data are later accessible and available for benchmarking use via the agency's website.

BOX 5.8 **COMPARATIVE STAFFING METRICS**

Staff by type (classification) in FTE
» Number of professional librarians
» Number of other professionals
» Number of support staff
» Number of student assistants (if appropriate)
Staffing types as ratios to all library staff FTE
Ratio of FTE library staff to per capita
Staff expenditures, collection expenditures, and all other expenditures, each expressed as a percentage of all expenditures

EXAMPLE 5.1 **COMPARATIVE BENCHMARKING DATA**

STEP 1   Log on to the Counting Opinions Manage Reports function to begin.

STEP 2   Because we are creating a new report for this example, click on the tab labeled PLA and then select the most current fiscal year available for detailed summary tables. In this example, it was FY2012.

STEP 3   We want to create a report concerning expenditures for materials, staffing, and collections. A summary table exists titled "Operating Expenditure Report" arranged by service population ranges. For this example, "Operating Expenditure Report 250,000–499,999" was selected for its population range of 250,000 to 499,999.

STEP 4   You may vary your approach at this point, but for this example, we will revise this report. Therefore, select Save as New Report so that we may make changes. Saving this report places a copy under the Local tab, and then under Reports. Go to this newly saved report and open it.

STEP 5   Change the report name to "Ratio of Expenditures FY2012" and click the Save button. This changes the title of the report in the Local Reports tab.

STEP 6   Review the indicators. Note that there are two staff expenditure indicators—one for salaries and wages, and another for employee benefits. There is one indicator available in the selection box for "Operating Expenditures—Staff." Using this one indicator will simplify this calculation of the ratio. Therefore, remove the two staff indicators from the existing report and replace them with this new one, and click the Save button.

STEP 7   As a result, you now have information on "Expenditures on all other items," which is what we need for "Other expenditures," "Total expenditures," and "Operating expenditures—Staff." We are missing the materials expenditures. Using the Indicators box, find the indicator labeled "Total expenditures for library materials," add it to the report, and then Save.

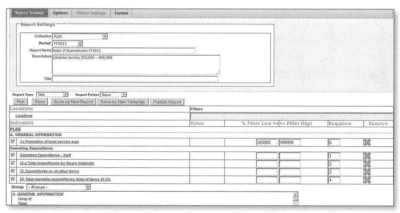

STEP 8   Run the report, and the results are displayed. In this example, information from eighty-five libraries is available.

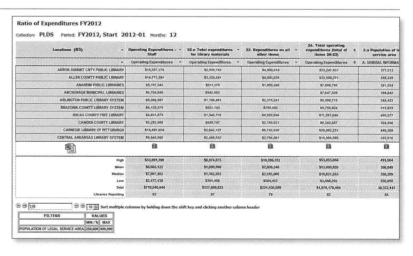

STEP 9 This custom report may be further modified by revising the filters. For example, you may further refine the existing "Population of legal service area" of "250,000–499,999" by revising the filters to narrow the population range, thereby reducing the number of results. The population range was revised in this example by reducing the high filter from 499,999 to 350,000. Again, the report was saved and then run again, reducing the number of libraries identified from eighty-five to forty-two.

Ratio of Expenditures FY2012

Collection: PLDS   Period: FY2012, Start 2012-01   Months: 12

Locations (42)	Operating Expenditures - Staff	22.c Total expenditures for library materials	23. Expenditures on all other items	24. Total operating expenditures (total of items 20-23)	2.a Population of legal service area
	Operating Expenditures	Operating Expenditures	Operating Expenditures	Operating Expenditures	A. GENERAL INFORMATION
ANAHEIM PUBLIC LIBRARIES	$5,197,342	$511,178	$1,090,240	$7,698,760	341,034
ANCHORAGE MUNICIPAL LIBRARIES	$6,764,545	$942,982		$7,647,528	298,542
BRAZORIA COUNTY LIBRARY SYSTEM	$4,150,375	$821,145	$790,303	$5,765,924	319,373
CAMDEN COUNTY LIBRARY	$6,292,909	$808,747	$2,190,031	$9,342,887	324,358
CENTRAL ARKANSAS LIBRARY SYSTEM	$9,846,980	$2,405,532	$2,754,081	$15,006,593	332,076
CENTRAL RAPPAHANNOCK REGIONAL LIBRARY	$8,838,562	$899,278	$1,294,456	$10,832,296	300,972
CHESTERFIELD COUNTY PUBLIC LIBRARY	$5,354,074	$836,937	$935,472	$7,126,483	310,000
COLLIER COUNTY PUBLIC LIBRARY	$4,912,926	$1,269,541	$1,458,658	$7,641,055	321,520
CUMBERLAND COUNTY PUBLIC LIBRARY & INFORMATION CENTER	$7,286,711	$1,092,566	$1,363,617	$9,742,894	327,643
DAVIS COUNTY LIBRARY	$4,150,435	$899,018	$812,564	$5,572,017	312,090

High	$12,974,822	$2,539,736	$6,096,220	$19,662,482	341,034
Mean	$6,498,639	$1,174,255	$1,961,227	$9,487,029	297,633
Median	$6,224,637	$1,012,335	$1,458,658	$8,893,352	297,414
Low	$2,177,138	$291,458	$618,591	$3,568,292	250,860
Total	$259,945,547	$46,970,213	$72,565,350	$379,481,157	12,500,590
Libraries Reporting	40	40	37	40	42

1/5   10   Sort multiple columns by holding down the shift key and clicking another column header

FILTERS	VALUES	
	MIN / %	MAX
POPULATION OF LEGAL SERVICE AREA	250,000	350,000

STEP 10 Once you have the report results as you want them, save the data to an Excel spreadsheet by clicking on the Excel icon on the results page.

STEP 11 Open the saved spreadsheet to review. Again, individual local approaches will vary as to processing the information. For example, one approach would be to delete from the spreadsheet those libraries that did not report all of the data. Then, the expenditure data (dollars) can be converted into ratios of total expenditures for staff, library materials, and all other expenses for each library. This option produces the following spreadsheet for the first ten libraries in the staffing study.

Location	Staff	Library materials	All other	Total expenditures	Legal service area pop.
Saint Louis Public Library	65.98%	15.13%	18.89%	$19,662,482	319,294
San Mateo County Library	68.67%	8.85%	22.47%	$18,284,150	270,925
Douglas County Libraries	66.98%	20.21%	12.81%	$17,513,320	291,083
Saint Paul Public Library	67.63%	9.77%	22.59%	$16,236,977	285,068
Henrico County Public Library	68.32%	12.44%	19.24%	$14,716,462	311,726
Central Arkansas Library System	65.62%	16.03%	18.35%	$15,006,593	332,076
Vaughan Public Libraries	70.47%	11.98%	17.56%	$13,482,842	304,639
Central Rappahannock Regional Library	81.59%	6.46%	11.95%	$10,832,296	300,972
Newark	82.56%	2.76%	14.68%	$10,567,620	277,140
Shreve Memorial Library	56.56%	8.99%	34.44%	$14,906,264	253,623

For academic libraries, example 5.2 creates a report about the ratio of staffing types as expressed in FTE using the National Center for Education Statistics (NCES) Compare Academic Libraries function. This function is located by clicking on Peer Comparison Tools found under the Data & Tools option on the NCES home page, http://nces.ed.gov/. (Note: This information is also available using ACRL*Metrics*.)

EXAMPLE 5.2 **RATIO OF STAFFING TYPES (FTE)**

STEP 1 After accessing the NCES Compare Academic Libraries tool (http://nces.ed.gov/surveys/libraries/compare/Default.aspx), click on Start Search.

STEP 2 Unlike with Counting Opinions, you must "Select Target Library" when using this NCES comparison tool. A suggestion is that you self-select your own academic library and then continue.

STEP 3 Choose a comparison group by selecting the institution's peers. Once all of the peers are added to the comparison list, continue to the next step. In this example, there are a total of eleven libraries: the target library and its ten peers.

STEP 4 Add the variables for the study. They are grouped under staff. Select "Librarians," "Other Professional Staff," "All Other Paid Staff," "Student Assistants," "Total Staff," and, because it is available, "Total Staff Per 1,000 FTE Students." Then, continue to the next step.

STEP 5 Now the report can be viewed and downloaded as an Excel worksheet.

STEP 6 The spreadsheet has been downloaded, edited to improve clarity, and sorted for review and analysis.

NCES Academic Libraries Survey Fiscal Year: 2012 sorted on "Total Staff"						
Institution	Librarians	Other Professional Staff	All Other Paid Staff	Student Assistants	Total Staff	Total Staff Per 1,000 FTE Students
Indiana State University, IN	19.00	4.00	27.00	21.00	71.00	7.10
Valdosta State University, GA	18.00	8.00	21.88	14.50	62.38	5.56
Stephen F Austin State University, TX	15.00	12.00	17.00	16.00	60.00	5.33
Western Carolina University, NC	20.00	2.00	26.50	6.40	54.90	6.89
University of Massachusetts-Lowell, MA	13.61	8.00	7.65	25.00	54.26	4.62
East Tennessee State University, TN	18.00	6.00	27.00	2.25	53.25	3.94
University of West Georgia, GA	18.00	10.00	10.00	11.50	49.50	6.16
Rowan University, NJ	12.17	7.00	22.31	5.10	46.58	4.57
The University of West Florida, FL	10.60	0.00	24.00	8.67	43.27	4.64
University of South Dakota, SD	12.00	0.00	18.48	9.36	39.84	5.35
University of Arkansas at Little Rock, AR	12.00	4.00	15.00	8.00	39.00	4.17

NCES Academic Libraries Survey Fiscal Year: 2012 sorted on "Total Staff"						
Institution	Librarians	Other Professional Staff	All Other Paid Staff	Student Assistants	Total Staff	Total Staff Per 1,000 FTE Students
Indiana State University, IN	26.76%	5.63%	38.03%	29.58%	71.00	7.10
Valdosta State University, GA	28.86%	12.82%	35.08%	23.24%	62.38	5.56
Stephen F Austin State University, TX	25.00%	20.00%	28.33%	26.67%	60.00	5.33
Western Carolina University, NC	36.43%	3.64%	48.27%	11.66%	54.90	6.89
University of Massachusetts-Lowell, MA	25.08%	14.74%	14.10%	46.07%	54.26	4.62
East Tennessee State University, TN	33.80%	11.27%	50.70%	4.23%	53.25	3.94
University of West Georgia, GA	36.36%	20.20%	20.20%	23.23%	49.50	6.16
Rowan University, NJ	26.13%	15.03%	47.90%	10.95%	46.58	4.57
The University of West Florida, FL	24.50%	0.00%	55.47%	20.04%	43.27	4.64
University of South Dakota, SD	30.12%	0.00%	46.39%	23.49%	39.84	5.35
University of Arkansas at Little Rock, AR	30.77%	10.26%	38.46%	20.51%	39.00	4.17

NOTE: The spreadsheet could be further revised to replace the FTE with percentage ratios for each staffing category to the number of total staff FTE.

LIBRARY STANDARDS AND BEST PRACTICES (STAFFING)

Many libraries of all types seek guidance on the standards and best practices concerning staff to explain the appropriate or desirable number of staff FTE per capita, the ratio of librarians per 1,000 capita (e.g., legal service population, FTE students), the most efficient mixture of circulation and reference librarians, and the most effective mixture of professionally credentialed librarians and support staff within libraries by type of library or by population ranges (again, e.g., legal service population, FTE students).

The American Library Association (ALA) and its divisions no longer establish or support prescriptive standards. The Public Library Association (PLA) rejected the idea of national standards on any aspect of library service in favor of an outcomes-based planning and assessment process recognizing the differences in user needs based upon the community. Library consultant Jeanne Goodrich found that the PLA could not provide guidance about desirable or appropriate staffing metrics, because "there are simply too many local variables to make such a pronouncement prudent, or even truly helpful. Who are the people in the community? What has the community told the library they need?"[7]

Several states apply regulatory standards concerning library staffing to ensure quality public library services at local levels in order to receive state or federal funding, or both, through state library agencies. For example, Massachusetts requires that the minimum general and professional education requirement for library directors in municipalities with populations over 10,000 is a master's degree from an ALA-accredited program of library and information science.[8] Virginia's *Planning for Library Excellence: Standards for Virginia Public Libraries* provides three progressive levels of service measure ratings: A (core) to AA to AAA (highest). Full-time equivalent staffing levels increase from .3 FTE per 1,000 persons in the library service area at level A to .5 FTE at level AA and to .6 FTE at level AAA. As to staff qualifications, for every 25,000 in population, the library shall have 2.5 FTEs in professional staff positions with ALA-accredited education/training at level A, 4.5 at level AA, and 6.5 at level AAA.[9]

In place of prescriptive standards, the Association of College and Research Libraries (ACRL) articulates expectations for library contributions to institutional effectiveness in its current *Standards for Libraries in Higher Education*, which provides a comprehensive framework using an outcomes-based approach, with evidence collected in ways most appropriate for each institution.[10]

National library associations support best practices in lieu of prescriptive standards (see also chapter 7). Briefly, a best practice is an activity or procedure that has produced outstanding results in a situation that could be replicated to improve either effectiveness or efficiency in a similar situation. Examples of best practices include low costs that yield effective results, such as discovering the staff costs to circulate a book, answer a reference question, and lend or borrow items through interlibrary loan. Best practices can also be discovered through benchmarking. For example, returning to the public library example (see example 5.1), we can review the variations in the three expenditure metrics. Based on these reported figures, Newark, with a service population of 277,140, expended less than

3 percent of its operating budget on library materials, while Douglas County expended more than 20 percent on its service population of 291,083. Why is there such a difference? Was it because Newark expended over 80 percent of its operating expenditures on staffing while Douglas County expended 67 percent? Or, is the difference in the amount of expenditures? Newark expended $10,567,620 for a per capita of $38.13; Douglas County expended $60.17 per capita, a difference of 36.6 percent. A best practices process would identify these benchmarks and seek to understand the differences.

Academic libraries often consider the triad metric: the percentages of operating expenditures on staffing, library materials, and other operating costs. What are the optimal ratios? A library's strategic objective may be to expend annually more than 50 percent of its operating expenditures on library materials, while expending less than 50 percent on staffing and thereby holding other direct costs to single digits (e.g., materials expended at 51 percent, staffing at 43 percent, and other direct costs at 6 percent). Using ACRL*Metrics*, an academic library can identify those academic libraries expending less than 50 percent of operating expenditures on library staffing and then study or otherwise contact the libraries to learn how they are successfully meeting this objective as a desired best practice.

CONCLUDING THOUGHTS

There are several studies that libraries may want to undertake to learn about staffing's contributions to their customers as they address how staff directly contribute to accessibility (may be measures of the number of hours open and when), availability (staff shelve materials in a timely manner accurately), and affordability (customers save their own time and money by depending on library staff to answer questions, or staff provide other assistance through direct or indirect mediation such as how-to guides). Public libraries may want to learn how staff contribute to customer satisfaction, which results in repeat use or a high number of library visits per capita. Academic libraries are always seeking to learn if, and how, staff contribute to student recruitment (library staff conduct or contribute to effective library tours for prospective students and parents), retention (is the library mentioned as a factor in student decisions to leave or stay at an institution), and completion (most often measured as graduation), while also supporting accreditation studies and program reviews (such as providing evidence that staff qualifications help to develop quality collections and provide exemplary services).

All libraries and their stakeholders want to know how they add value to their community or institution. Because of the proportion of allocated funds expended on staffing, it is critical for libraries to understand and report on a multiplicity of staffing characteristics informed by data and to be prepared to explain how they compare, and why, with similar libraries.

EXERCISES

Answers to the following questions are in the "Appendix" at the back of the book. We encourage different members of a library staff to work on the exercises together and to discuss the results. Managers might also participate in that discussion.

QUESTION 1 Staff types may vary by library, but they might comprise, for example, professional librarians, others with professional qualifications (not librarians), support staff, and student assistants. How could you visually report staff type classifications over a five-year period to your library's stakeholders?

QUESTION 2 A public library wants to know how its staffing levels per circulation, reference, and library visits transactions compare with those of its benchmarking partners. How may the library create this report?

QUESTION 3 An academic library wants to review information about staff and reference transactions and how they compare with those of its peers. How may the library develop this report?

QUESTION 4 A public library now wants to report staff expenditures data for circulation, reference, and library visits transactions and then compare staff costs with those of its benchmarking partners. How might it develop this report?

QUESTION 5 An academic library wants to review staff salary expenditures data and how these expenditures compare with those of its peers. How might the library find and report such data?

Notes

1. Denise M. Davis, "Academic and Public Library Salaries and Library Staffing Expenditures Trends, 2000–2009," *Library Trends* 59, nos. 1–2 (2010): 43.

2. See also the various appendixes in Robert E. Dugan, Peter Hernon, and Danuta A. Nitecki, *Viewing Library Metrics from Different Perspectives: Inputs, Outputs and Outcomes* (Santa Barbara, CA: Libraries Unlimited, 2009).

3. Susan M. Ryan, "Reference Transactions Analysis: The Cost-Effectiveness of Staffing a Traditional Academic Reference Desk," *Journal of Academic Librarianship* 34, no. 5 (September 2008): 391–93, 396.

4. Davis, "Academic and Public Library Salaries and Library Staffing Expenditures Trends, 2000–2009," 43, 45, 46, 51, 52, 53, 57.

5. John J. Regazzi, "Comparing Academic Library Spending with Public Libraries, Public K–12 Schools, Higher Education Public Institutions, and Public Hospitals between 1998–2008," *Journal of Academic Librarianship* 38, no. 4 (July 2012): 205, 210, 211, 215.

6. Rachael Applegate, "Charting Academic Library Staffing: Data from National Surveys," *College & Research Libraries* 68, no. 1 (January 2007): 65, 66.

7. Jeanne Goodrich, "Staffing Public Libraries: Are There Models or Best Practices?" *Public Libraries* 44, no. 5 (September/October 2005): 281.

8. Massachusetts Board of Library Commissioners, "Minimum Standards: Director Personnel Requirements in Populations 10,000 and Up," http://mblc.state.ma.us/grants/state_aid/policies/stanper2.php.

9. Library of Virginia, *Planning for Library Excellence: Standards for Virginia Public Libraries* (2009), 24–25, www.lva.virginia.gov/lib-edu/ldnd/standards/PFLE.pdf.

10. Association of College and Research Libraries, *Standards for Libraries in Higher Education* (October 2011), 10, www.ala.org/acrl/sites/ala.org.acrl/files/content/standards/slhe.pdf.

Benchmarking and Benchmarking Studies

BENCHMARKING IS A TOOL to measure and compare the performance of libraries. Initiating a benchmarking process is a result of the library leadership's investigation into whether another library's performance or efficiencies and related outputs are recognized as indicating best practices in specific functions and services. The goals of benchmarking as a managerial learning process are to find an external standard for measuring the quality and quantity of performance or the means and cost of internal processes and to help the library discover how it can best improve the services offered to its users. The technique of benchmarking enables librarians to learn from one another by looking at why there are differences in performance results among organizations undertaking similar functions.[1]

WHY SHOULD LIBRARIES BENCHMARK?

Libraries have a multiplicity of institutional and external stakeholders that hold library managers accountable to demonstrate continuous improvement and the value added to services and outcomes. Although measuring an increase or decrease in use of services from one year to the next in a single library can be accomplished with a variety of methods, such self-assessment or comparison, while useful for tracking internal progress, is a limited evaluative tool. A best practice uses a benchmarking process to undertake external comparisons with peer libraries.[2]

Libraries use benchmarking to improve resources and services. Benchmarking is a useful technique that provides administrators with indicators of performance. An analysis of metrics compiled from this process can reveal how an organization is performing with respect to its peers and identify those demonstrating best practices. The discovery of methods deployed by other libraries to attain successful processes, services, and outcomes can help the library improve its own performance by duplicating the beneficial methods of these successful libraries.[3]

Benchmarking, a comparative technique, should not be construed as a competitive activity among libraries.[4] One factor in the growing level of acceptance of benchmarking as a tool is libraries' tradition of sharing information about inputs, outputs, processes, practices, and policies. Information has been exchanged formally through association and government surveys as well as informally at professional meetings, visits to other institutions, study tours, and direct contact with colleagues at other libraries in the course of daily work.[5]

TYPES OF BENCHMARKING PROCESSES

Performance benchmarking, also known by such names as *comparative/metric benchmarking*, compiles and compares measures of performance, such as the library's ratio of inputs (e.g., budget) to outputs (e.g., services provided), to determine how the library's operation compares with that of similar libraries. Library managers often use the comparison to demonstrate to relevant stakeholders the level to which the local library's resources and activities are supported (e.g., above average, below average, at average). Although performance benchmarking is an important step in a library's quality improvement program, it does not provide a definitive idea or plan about what to improve to gain better quality.[6]

Process or functional benchmarking compares the methods and practices, or sequence of activities, used to perform a process. It compares local processes with similar functions in partner or peer institutions that are identified as having best practices. To compare processes, the library must identify specific benchmarking partners or determine which organization has the most effective system for handling the targeted process. Once the leader in efficiency or effectiveness is identified, the process used is documented and then implemented. An example of process benchmarking would be to compare the accuracy of re-shelving books with that of other libraries to learn how better-performing libraries (those with higher accuracy) re-shelve books. Another example would be to compare turnaround times for lending materials via interlibrary loan. Process benchmarking is the point where quality improvement comes into benchmarking activities; the result of the benchmarking may be an improved process.[7]

Competitive benchmarking specifically compares a firm's own performance in a process or service with that of a competitor in the same industry. Although librarians generally regard each other as colleagues, variation does exist among libraries; they are not uniformly excellent, and the reasons vary, including differing contexts, levels of funding, priorities, and stages of organizational development.

An example of competitive benchmarking is the comparison of when and how many hours neighboring libraries are open. Another example is alternative service providers that library customers use: where do they go if they cannot receive a desired service from the local library? Competitive benchmarking may help to explain why libraries sought to provide coffee services within their outlets. Observing, documenting, and emulating the best practices of a competitor can provide helpful insights.[8]

STEPS IN THE BENCHMARKING PROCESS

Performance benchmarking is the easiest benchmarking exercise to undertake. This type of benchmarking compiles readily available data from the divisions of the American Library Association or from federal and state government agencies, or from any combination of these. Additionally, public libraries may use the annual *LJ Index*, which groups libraries by their total operating expenditures. Comparing local metrics with those of other libraries (e.g., circulation per capita) does not require direct communications with the target libraries to undertake the performance benchmarking process successfully. Performance benchmarking is also useful for identifying potential priorities and opportunities for improvement.

Process benchmarking, which is more complicated, should be viewed as a continual process, designed to generate improvements to a service that has value for library managers as well as library customers. This type of benchmarking

- » identifies a process that is critical to the success of the library, such as re-shelving books or interlibrary loan. Although any process can be benchmarked, it is suggested to begin benchmarking exercises with processes that are easy to observe and quantify.
- » measures the service locally and selects the aspects to be benchmarked. There is little or no value to be gained from benchmarking areas that are not easily changed. Document or map the subprocesses that are carried out as part of the activity; measurements may include the cost or time it takes to deliver a service, as well as the volume and accuracy or quality of that service.
- » analyzes the results from the measurements.
- » identifies appropriate benchmarking partners in order to compare the results with other libraries using a similar process. For benchmarking to be effective, the philosophy, aims, and objectives of the libraries must be similar, at least in respect of the level of services under consideration.
- » identifies best practices (i.e., the methods used by the benchmarked libraries, which can be adopted locally in order to improve the level of service).
- » implements the process changes locally.
- » remeasures the local service at an appropriate later time to assess or evaluate the impact of the change.[9]

WHAT DO LIBRARIES BENCHMARK?

Libraries have used performance and process benchmarking methods to extract comparable data with the intention of studying and discussing possible process improvement in the areas depicted in box 6.1.

IDENTIFYING BENCHMARKING PARTNERS

Finding appropriate libraries to use as benchmarking partners may be the most difficult aspect of benchmarking. Professional associations as well as state and federal government agencies collect and provide access to library statistics that can be used for identifying libraries for benchmarking studies. Some of the characteristics you may use to identify libraries against which to benchmark include similar

» population size of the library's parent organization. This would include the students, faculty, and staff of a K–20 educational institution or the population of a geographic area the organization has the responsibility to serve (also known as a legal service area), such as a municipality, county, or a multi-jurisdictional library district.

BOX 6.1 **BENCHMARKING FOR PROCESS IMPROVEMENTS***

» Library use as measured by physical visits and registered borrowers as a percentage of the service population

» Effectiveness in reaching service populations, such as registered borrowers to total population (per capita)

» Material use, including circulation, in-library use of materials, proportion of sought material obtained at the time of visit, holds, and collection turnover rate

» Number of staff by function and total full-time equivalents

» Qualifications of library staff, including degrees held and years of library service

» Facilities in terms of square feet; physical location in the service area (e.g., proximity to the geographic center of the legal service area)

» Public and staff physical space utilization

» Material access as measured by fill rates and document delivery time (user waits for materials)

» Availability of electronic services

» Quality of electronic services

» Reference services measured by transactions and completion rate (ratio of questions answered satisfactorily)

» Innovation in reference services

» Wait times at public service desks

» Information literacy skills and measured outcomes

» Programming, including number of programs and attendance

» Interlibrary loans (net lender or borrower)

» Time to shelve and re-shelve a book

» Accuracy in shelving and re-shelving books

» Adequacy/quality of the collections

» Acquisitions, such as monograph purchase and processing

» Time to acquire and process a user-requested new book

» Original cataloging processes

» Research support and to whom

» Costing core processes (e.g., circulation and reference transactions, cost to open per hour)

» User satisfaction

» Staff satisfaction

» Website usage

» Ratio of retired and added titles/volumes to collection

*See Leeanne Pitman, Isabella Trahn, and Anne Wilson, "Working towards Best Practice in Australian University Libraries: Reflections on a National Project," *Australian Academic and Research Libraries* 32, no. 1 (March 2001): 6–9; and Claire Creaser, "Performance Measurement and Benchmarking for Schools Library Services," *Journal of Librarianship and Information Science* 33, no. 3 (September 2001): 131–32.

» Carnegie Classification for higher education institutions.
» geographic area setting, such as urban/suburban/rural.
» organizational structure. An example would be a single outlet library; another example would be a system with a central or main library and a range of branch libraries (e.g., less than five; more than fifteen) or other outlets in addition to the main library, such as bookmobiles. Another related characteristic includes outlets' gross square feet.
» size of annual operating budget or expenditures.
» collection size (typically based on the number of volumes in a library's collection).
» legal basis or governance structure. Institutional governance structures include mayor, city council, county, elected board of trustees, appointed board of trustees, and special purpose local government, such as school districts and those with the legal authority to levy taxes.
» staffing configuration. This could include the number of full-time equivalent staff and their qualifications or other credentials.
» per capita funding or expenditures.[10]

Or, a library could use some combination of the preceding characteristics to select appropriate libraries for benchmarking.

Academic Libraries

Most higher education institutions have identified peers (truly comparable institutions with a similar role, scope, and mission) when they make comparisons for institutional and program accreditations and for program reviews. Other types of comparison groups include

» **competitors** (institutions that focus on the same types of incoming students, attempts to recruit the same faculty members, and fund-raising);
» **aspirants** (what the institution wants to become as a result of successfully implementing the goals and objectives of its current strategic plan) when undertaking comparisons for institutional and program accreditations and for program reviews; or
» **predetermined** (examples include *natural*, such as athletic conference or geographical region; *traditional*, such as historical relationships or Ivy League; *jurisdictional*, such as legal or political boundaries like state lines; and *some type of recognized classification*, such as national reporting like Carnegie).[11]

Peer and aspirant institutions are selected because of institutional mission, reputation, selectivity for admission, size of budget, program mix (types of programs offered), control (public versus private), and size of endowment among other characteristics and demographics. Academic libraries are encouraged to use existing institutional peer groups for comparisons. Some academic libraries have also identified peer and aspirant organizations separate from those on their own institutions' lists either to expand the number of libraries for comparison or because they have concluded that their institutions' peers and aspirants are inadequate for their benchmarking use.

Public Libraries

Often the public library's institution (e.g., city or county) has not identified institutional peers for benchmarking. If that is the case, a public library may identify peers using one of several means, including a rating tool such as *Library Journal's LJ Index (Star Index)*, the federal Institute of Museum and Library Services (IMLS), or the PLA*metrics* portal. The *LJ Index* divides libraries into nine peer comparison groups based on total operating expenditures. Within each group the highest-scoring libraries are recognized by assigning a ranking of five (highest), four, or three stars. Each star-rating group contains ten star libraries, except for the $30 million and above group for which each star rating contains five libraries. Star ratings are based on scores. The *LJ Index* scores are based on four weighted and averaged per capita service outputs: library visits, circulation, program attendance, and public Internet computer use.

The *Index* authors state that the "four measures are closely related to one another statistically" but "don't measure quality, value, excellence, or relevance of services to the community."[12] However, it is a useful starting point for identifying benchmarking peers. A public library seeking to identify peers could first look in the same expenditures range. If there are too many, the library can limit the search; the *LJ Index* spreadsheet can be sorted by state, service population, and total operating expenditures or by using a key ratio. Searchers may also sort by the four per capita service outputs previously listed.

A second means is to identify peers through the IMLS website. Example 6.1 identifies the steps to follow. A third means is to use the PLA*metrics* subscription database maintained by Counting Opinions (see example 6.2).

METRICS FOR LIBRARY BENCHMARKING STUDIES

Once the library's partners have been identified for the benchmarking study, this question arises: What metrics will be used for the analysis? The answer depends on what the library wants to benchmark. It could be that a benchmark of all metrics can help to reveal potential opportunities to consider as priorities for improvement or to find areas where the library currently excels. Box 6.2 provides a general, not an exhaustive, list of benchmarking metrics for libraries; not all of them apply to both academic and public libraries.[13] In addition to this list, libraries may create tables to compare a multiplicity of metrics for benchmarking, such as the following:

- » Items circulated per registered borrower compared with the operating costs per registered borrower, providing a ratio of cost per use for core services
- » Total librarians, total other staff, total staff, circulation per FTE staff hour, and FTE staff per 1,000 population to compare staffing levels per circulation
- » Total collections expenditures, total collections expenditures per capita, collections expenditures as a percentage of all expenditures, circulation, and circulation per capita to compare collections expenditures and circulation

EXAMPLE 6.1 **USE OF IMLS WEBSITE FOR BENCHMARKING**

STEP 1	Go to the home page of the Institute of Museum and Library Services, www.imls.gov.
STEP 2	Click on the link titled Research.
STEP 3	Click on the link titled Data Collection.
STEP 4	Click on the link titled Public Library Survey.
STEP 5	Click on the link titled Compare Public Libraries (https://harvester.census.gov/imls/compare/index.asp).
STEP 6	Click on the link titled Begin Search.
STEP 7	On the next web page, "Select Library of Interest," enter your library's name, city, state, and zip code, and click on the link titled Continue. (However, if you want to duplicate the screen image given here, then type in West Florida Public Library.)
STEP 8	Select the radio button for the library of interest (yours).
STEP 9	Two methods to select a comparison (benchmarking) group are presented: » Choose Similar Libraries (Comparison Group) By Variable » Specific Public Libraries For Your Comparison Group Because we are seeking to identify benchmarking partners, we chose the first option.
STEP 10	Select from eight general variables presented. For this example, we chose "Organizational Characteristics." Select "Number of Outlets" (main library, branches, and bookmobiles) and then accept Method 1 with the default of 20 percent. That will return a number of libraries meeting those criteria. If the resulting number is too high (such as hundreds), select the link titled Add a Variable To Refine Your Comparison Group. Because there was a return of hundreds for a search of the West Florida Public Library, which is too many for a benchmarking study, we decided to add another variable.
STEP 11	Return to "Organizational Characteristics." Select "Population of Legal Service Area," choose Method 1, and again accept the default of 20 percent. The resulting search for the West Florida Public Library yielded fewer than one hundred libraries.
STEP 12	With two library variables selected, for the West Florida Public Library, it was decided to add one more variable. Select "Paid Full-Time Equivalent Staff (FTE)" and then select "Total Staff per 1,000 Population" rather than the option for "ALA-MLS Librarian per 1,000 Population." Choose Method 1 and accept the default of 20 percent. The yield was very high (in the hundreds), but there are now three search criteria.

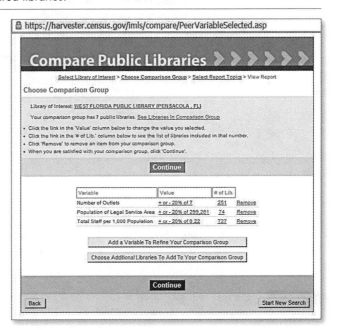

Continued on next page.

EXAMPLE 6.1 (continued)

STEP 13

When you are ready to see the list of libraries, click the link labeled Continue. Another screen appears, and you may choose up to seven topics (measures or indicators) from the eleven categories presented. For this example, the following were chosen:

» from Paid Full-Time Equivalent Staff (FTE): Total Staff

» from Operating Expenditures: Total Operating Expenditures

» from Services (Per Year):

   – Total Circulation per Capita

   – Library Visits per Capita

   – Reference Transactions per Capita

   – Average Number of Weekly Public Service Hours per Outlet

STEP 14

Once the topics are selected, click Continue. The report is presented, and you may count the number of libraries found (the selected library is also displayed and should not be counted; in other words, if the return is eight libraries, the search identified seven possible benchmarking partners). The report may be saved or exported to a spreadsheet.

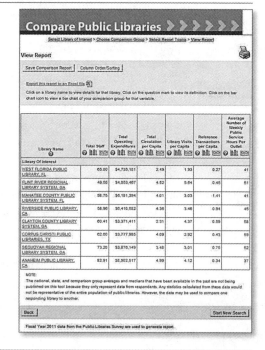

Compare Public Libraries › › › › › ›

Select Library of Interest > Choose Comparison Group > Select Report Topics > **View Report**

View Report

| Save Comparison Report | Column Order/Sorting |

Export this report to an Excel file

Click on a library name to view details for that library. Click on the question mark to view its definition. Click on the bar chart icon to view a bar chart of your comparison group for that variable.

Library Name	Total Staff	Total Operating Expenditures	Total Circulation per Capita	Library Visits per Capita	Reference Transactions per Capita	Average Number of Weekly Public Service Hours Per Outlet
Library Of Interest						
WEST FLORIDA PUBLIC LIBRARY, FL	65.00	$4,735,181	2.49	1.93	0.27	41
FLINT RIVER REGIONAL LIBRARY SYSTEM, GA	49.50	$4,053,467	4.52	5.64	0.45	51
MANATEE COUNTY PUBLIC LIBRARY SYSTEM, FL	58.75	$6,191,394	4.01	3.03	1.41	41
RIVERSIDE PUBLIC LIBRARY, CA	58.96	$6,410,582	4.36	3.46	0.94	45
CLAYTON COUNTY LIBRARY SYSTEM, GA	60.41	$3,371,411	2.31	4.37	0.59	58
CORPUS CHRISTI PUBLIC LIBRARIES, TX	62.60	$3,777,985	4.69	2.92	0.43	59
SEQUOYAH REGIONAL LIBRARY SYSTEM, GA	73.20	$3,876,149	3.48	3.01	0.75	52
ANAHEIM PUBLIC LIBRARY, CA	82.91	$8,902,517	4.99	4.12	0.34	37

NOTE:
The national, state, and comparison group averages and medians that have been available in the past are not being published on this tool because they only represent data from respondents. Any statistics calculated from these data would not be representative of the entire population of public libraries. However, the data may be used to compare one responding library to another.

| Back | | Start New Search |

Fiscal Year 2011 data from the Public Libraries Survey are used to generate report.

STEP 15

The resultant list of benchmarking partners may not be ideal, but it is a place to start. The search can be revised until a usable set of benchmarking partners is created.

EXAMPLE 6.2 **USE OF THE COUNTING OPINIONS WEBSITE FOR BENCHMARKING**

STEP 1	Log on to the Counting Opinions public libraries site, https://public.countingopinions.com/.
STEP 2	Click on the link titled Reports.
STEP 3	Click on the tab labeled Local and then the link labeled Add.
STEP 4	For Collection, select PLDS (Note: IMLS data sets are also available).
STEP 5	Select a Period (for this example, FY2011).
STEP 6	Type in a Report Name, such as "Identifying Benchmark Partners."
STEP 7	Type in a Description, such as "FY2011 PLDS data to identify benchmarking partners."
STEP 8	Type in a title if desired.
STEP 9	Select a Group or use the default All groups.
STEP 10	To start identifying benchmark partners, we chose "Population of Legal Service Area" under General Information, and then "Operating Expenditures—Staff," "Total Expenditures for Library Materials," "Expenditures on All Other Items," and "Total Operating Expenditures" to begin the search for this example.
STEP 11	The report was saved and then run. It returns many libraries (in the hundreds) and possibly too many to identify study partners.
STEP 12	Return to the report and add filters. To find libraries with similar population size, locate the line for "Population of Legal Service Area" and enter a low number in the filter as well as a high number— a population range. In this example, the population range was 10 percent below and 10 percent above the population for the local library. Run the report again. For our example, the result was a more manageable thirty-two libraries. (Note: If you are using the continuous reporting libraries that are in the public.co.com website, there will likely be fewer than thirty-two libraries.) Make sure your local library is on the resulting list.
STEP 13	Because fewer peer libraries were wanted, another filter was added. A range on the line for Total Operating Expenditures was added with 10 percent below the local library's total expenditures as the low and 10 percent above as the high, and the report was run again. The result yielded too few libraries as benchmarking partners.
STEP 14	If there are too few libraries, return to the report, remove a filter, and run the report again. That will increase the number of libraries returned. Continue this process of applying a variety of filters, or of adding additional indicators, until a manageable list of partner libraries to use for the benchmarking study is created.

BOX 6.2 **BENCHMARKING METRICS**

Demographics

- » Population of the legal service area
- » Square miles of the legal service area
- » Card holders
- » Card holders as a percentage of the legal service area

Facilities

- » Number of facilities service outlets
- » Number of bookmobiles
- » Total of facilities square feet
- » Facilities square feet per capita
- » Branch libraries per square mile
- » Number of branch libraries per 100,000 population
- » Linear feet of shelving
- » Total number of user seats
- » Number of user seats at equipment
- » Number of user seats not at equipment

Financial

- » Total revenue (budget allocation)
- » Total revenue (budget allocation) per capita
- » Operating expenditures, total
- » Operating expenditures per capita
- » Total staff expenditures, compared to average (considered an indicator of staffing efficiencies)
- » Personnel expenditures as a percentage of total operating expenditures
- » Collections expenditures as a percentage of total operating expenditures
- » Other direct expenditures (non-staff and non-collections) as a percentage of total operating expenditures
- » Total collections expenditures Total collections expenditures per capita
- » Collections expenditures on print materials
- » Collections expenditures on audio materials
- » Collections expenditures on video materials
- » Collections expenditures for electronic resources
- » Collections expenditures for other (undefined)
- » Operating cost per hour open
- » Operating cost per circulation transaction
- » Operating cost per physical visit
- » Operating cost per registered borrower

Collections

- » Total holdings
- » Holdings per capita for print books, e-books, serial volumes, audio materials, video materials, and serials subscriptions
- » Holdings per 1,000 population for print books, e-books, serial volumes, audio materials, video materials, and serials subscriptions
- » Ratio of holdings to total holdings for print books, e-books, audio, video, and e-materials
- » Total serials subscriptions
- » Turnover rate
- » Percentage of library resources less than _____ years old
- » Fill rates (title, subject, and author)—the extent of users' success in securing the materials that they were seeking
- » Percentage of the collection measured against a generally accepted bibliography or book list (e.g., *Choice: Current Reviews for Academic Libraries*)

Personnel

- » Number of staff
  - Professional librarians
  - Total of professional librarians in FTE
  - Other paid FTE library staff
  - Total paid FTE library staff
- » Percentage of FTEs that are librarians
- » Percentage of FTEs that are librarians versus nonlibrarians
- » FTE library staff per 1,000 population

Services

- » Total number of service hours open
- » Number of public service points
- » Measured time in queue at public service points
- » Time it takes to process a new acquisition by format (e.g., newspaper, print monograph, e-book, microform, print journal, audio item, video item)
- » Total circulation transactions
- » Circulation transactions per capita
- » Circulation transactions from branches
- » Circulation transactions from main library
- » Circulation transactions per physical visit
- » Circulation transactions per hour
- » Ratio (percentage) of circulation transactions of branches to main circulation
- » Circulation transactions per FTE staff
- » Circulation transactions per FTE staff hour
- » Circulation transactions of children's materials
- » Children's circulation transactions as a percentage of all circulation
- » In-library use of materials (used but did not leave the facility, such as serials)
- » In-library use of materials per capita
- » Time to shelve/re-shelve a volume
- » Accuracy in shelving/re-shelving a volume
- » Total number of borrowers
- » Number of borrowers per capita
- » Percentage of borrowers borrowing from the library in the past year
- » Circulation per borrower
- » Collection turnover rate
- » Total physical visits
- » Central library physical visits
- » Branch library physical visits
- » Ratio (percentage) of physical visits of branches to main
- » Physical visits per hour open
- » Physical visits per FTE staff

- » Total Web visits
- » Total public access computers
- » Public access computers per 1,000 population
- » Uses of computers
- » Uses of Internet computers
- » Number of child personal computers connected to the Internet
- » Number of child personal computers not connected to the Internet
- » Total reference transactions
- » Reference transactions at main
- » Reference transactions at branches
- » Reference transactions per capita
- » Reference transactions per physical visit
- » Reference transactions per 1,000 population
- » Measured time it takes to answer a reference question
- » Reference completion rate
- » Total number of library programs
- » Total program attendance
- » Adult program attendance
- » Children's program attendance
- » Program attendance per capita
- » Number of programs per capita
- » Program attendance per 1,000 population
- » Program attendance per FTE staff
- » Average attendance per program
- » Interlibrary loans—borrowed from and loaned to
- » Interlibrary loans (borrowed and loaned) per 1,000 population
- » Measured time to deliver materials to user
- » Librarian-led instruction sessions
- » Number of participants at librarian-led instruction sessions
- » Ratio of participants at librarian-led instruction sessions to population

» Total circulation, circulation per capita, circulation per visit, and circulation per hour to compare circulation transaction workloads

» Number of outlets, average public service hours per outlet, visits, visits per capita, and visits per hour to compare "busyness" by outlet

» Total library programs, total program attendance, and program attendance per capita to compare program attendance

» Number of users of public Internet computers, number of public Internet terminals, average Internet terminals per outlet, and public computer use per capita to compare public Internet computer use

» Holdings per capita, circulation per capita, and expenditures per capita to compare three of the most frequently referred-to outputs

SOURCES OF, AND COMPILING, LIBRARY BENCHMARKING DATA

Once the list of metrics and indicators is created, the next question, which this section addresses, is, "Where does the library find the benchmarking data?"

Statistical Benchmarking Data for Public Libraries

Statistical resources for public library benchmarking include the *LJ Index*, the annual report from the IMLS Statistics Program, and the Counting Opinions database of public library measures. The annual *LJ Index* is easy to use for a benchmarking study although limited to the four weighted and averaged per capita service outputs of library visits, circulation, program attendance, and public Internet computer use. To use the *LJ Index* for a benchmarking study, cut and paste the peer library data from the *LJ Index* spreadsheet, which can be downloaded from the American Star Libraries page.[14] Once the data from the *LJ Index* for the local library and its identified peers are loaded into a local spreadsheet, the data can be sorted and analyzed.

A second source of comparable measures is the IMLS Public Library Survey. Example 6.3 identifies the steps to follow. Unfortunately, this survey may experience a two-year lag for data gathering and compilation.

A third source, the Public Library Data Service (PLDS) Statistical Report, includes data from the prior calendar year and is mounted as PLA*metrics*, a subscription-based service of the Public Library Association. This is an annual compilation of data collected from more than one thousand public libraries. Example 6.4 depicts the steps to follow.

EXAMPLE 6.3 **IMLS PUBLIC LIBRARY SURVEY**

STEP 1   Go to the IMLS home page, www.imls.gov.

STEP 2   Click on the link titled Research.

STEP 3   Click on the link titled Data Collection.

STEP 4   Click on the link titled Public Library Survey.

STEP 5   Click on the link titled Compare Public Libraries (https://harvester.census.gov/imls/compare/index.asp).

STEP 6   Click on the link titled Begin Search.

STEP 7   On the next web page, "Select Library of Interest," enter the library's name, city, state, and zip code, and click on the link titled Continue.

STEP 8   Select the radio button for the library of interest (yours).

STEP 9   Two methods to select a comparison (benchmarking) group are presented:
  » Choose Similar Libraries (Comparison Group) By Variable
  » Specific Public Libraries For Your Comparison Group

Because the benchmarking partners are known, choose the second option.

STEP 10   Enter the information for the first peer library, and click on the link titled Continue.

STEP 11   Ascertain that the correct peer library was found. To add another peer, click the link titled Continue on the next page. Then, click the link titled Choose Additional Libraries To Add To Your Comparison Group.

STEP 12   Continue to add the peer libraries for the benchmarking study. Then, when the last peer library has been added and found, click the link titled Continue.

STEP 13   The next screen enables you to choose up to seven topics (measures and indicators) from the eleven categories presented. For this report, the following were chosen:
  » from Paid Full-Time Equivalent Staff (FTE): Total staff
  » from Operating Expenditures: Total Operating Expenditures
  » from Services (Per Year):
    – Total Circulation per Capita
    – Library Visits per Capita
    – Reference Transactions per Capita
    – Average Number of Weekly Public Service Hours Per Outlet
  » from Electronic Measures: Number of Public Internet Computers

STEP 14   Click on the link titled Continue. The report is presented; it may be saved or exported to a spreadsheet for additional analysis, such as ratios.

Statistical Benchmarking Data for Academic Libraries

Sources of comparative data include

» the biennial Academic Library Survey (ALS) from the National Center for Education Statistics (NCES), which provides descriptive statistics on about 3,700 academic libraries in fifty states and the District of Columbia. NCES is the primary federal entity for collecting and analyzing data related to education. The last ALS data collected were for FY2012 data. IPEDS began to collect annually the Academic Library (AL) component with the FY2014 data elements.

» the Association of Research Libraries (ARL) collection of quantitative and qualitative data for more than 120 of the largest research libraries in North America. The data describe the collections, expenditures, staffing, and service activities.

EXAMPLE 6.4 **PUBLIC LIBRARY DATA SERVICE (PLDS) STATISTICAL REPORT**

STEP 1 Log on to the Counting Opinions public libraries site, https://public.countingopinions.com.

STEP 2 Click on the link titled Reports.

STEP 3 Click on the tab labeled Local and then the link labeled Add.

STEP 4 For Collection, select "PLA PLDS."

STEP 5 Select a Period (for this example, FY2011).

STEP 6 Type in a Report Name, such as "Identifying Benchmark Partners."

STEP 7 Type in a Description, such as "FY2011 PLDS data to identify benchmarking partners."

STEP 8 Type in a title if desired.

STEP 9 Select a Group or use the default All groups.

STEP 10 Select one or more indicators from the list of metrics. For this benchmarking study, find circulation and reference transactions. Therefore, choose:
  » Circulation per Capita
  » Circulation per Hour
  » Reference Transactions per Capita
  » Reference Transactions per Hour

A welcome feature of using Counting Opinions, unlike IMLS, is that more than seven indicators can be selected for inclusion in a benchmarking study.

STEP 11 When the indicators have been chosen, the ability to add Locations is available. Click on Locations and find and choose the identified benchmarking partners.

STEP 12 Run the report, which may be saved as a spreadsheet for additional analysis.

» ACRL's annual survey of academic libraries, which offers an online subscription service through ACRL*Metrics* that covers ACRL and NCES survey data starting from 1998 and 2000, respectively. Because of the limited number of libraries in the ACRL collection, it will not be discussed in detail here.

When using the NCES data set for benchmarking studies, follow the steps shown in example 6.5.

ACRL*Metrics* enables the academic library to conduct benchmarking studies using ACRL reported data as well as the data from academic libraries reported to NCES and IPEDS. Example 6.6 provides the steps to follow.

To include NCES data with the ACRL data, select the NCES Academic Libraries Survey under Collection. If indicators containing ACRL data are already selected, NCES indicators will be added to the same report.

EXAMPLE 6.5 **USE OF NCES DATA SET FOR BENCHMARKING**

STEP 1 From the NCES home page (http://nces.ed.gov), click on the link titled Surveys & Programs.

STEP 2 Find the link for Library Statistics Program.

STEP 3 Click on the link titled Academic Libraries.

STEP 4 Click on Compare Academic Libraries (http://nces.ed.gov/surveys/libraries/compare).

STEP 5 Start the search and click on the link titled Select Target Library, which is the one you want to compare with the peers. Type in enough information to find and select the target.

STEP 6 Under the heading for "Step 2 Select Comparison Institution Libraries (In Progress)," click on the link titled Choose Comparison Group.

STEP 7 Ensure that the tab titled Choose Comparison Libraries is available for use by presenting text boxes for the library name, state, city, and zip code.

STEP 8 Search for and select the peer libraries for inclusion in the benchmarking study by using these text search boxes, and then clicking on the link titled Add to List. Once all of the peer libraries have been added, click on the link titled Continue to Next Step.

STEP 9 Select the report variables. Selected for this example were:
   » Total Staff per 1,000 FTE Students
   » Total Salaries (Expenditures)
   » Total Library Expenditures per FTE Student
   » Circulation Transactions (including reserves) per FTE Student
   » Hours Open in a Typical Week

Once the variables have been added, click on the link titled Continue to Next Step and then View the Report.

STEP 10 The report generated includes the selected variables for the peer libraries, as well as the averages and medians for the comparison group, the state, and the nation. The report can be printed, saved, or exported to a spreadsheet.

EXAMPLE 6.6 **USE OF ACRL*METRICS* FOR BENCHMARKING**

STEP 1	Log on to the ACRL*Metrics* site, www.acrlmetrics.com.
STEP 2	Click on the link titled Reports.
STEP 3	Click on the tab labeled Local and then the link labeled Add.
STEP 4	For Collection, select "ACRL" for this example. (Note: NCES and select IPEDS data sets are also available.)
STEP 5	Select a Period; for this example, 2012 was selected.
STEP 6	Type a Report Name, such as "Expenditures of Benchmarking Peers."
STEP 7	Type a Description, such as "2012 ACRL expenditures data."
STEP 8	Type a title if desired.
STEP 9	Select a Group or use the default All groups.
STEP 10	Select one or more indicators from the list of measures. For this benchmarking study, find expenditures information per enrolled full-time students. Therefore, choose:

- » Total Expenditures per Enrolled FT Students
- » Total Library Materials Expenditures per Enrolled FT Students
- » Total Staff Expenditures per Enrolled FT Students
- » Operating Expenditures on Other Per Enrolled FT Students

Choose as many indicators as needed/wanted. Then, click Add.

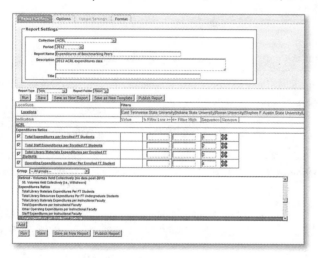

| STEP 11 | When the indicators have been chosen, the ability to add Locations is available. Click on Locations and find and choose the identified benchmarking partners. |
| STEP 12 | Run the report, which may be saved as a spreadsheet for additional analysis. |

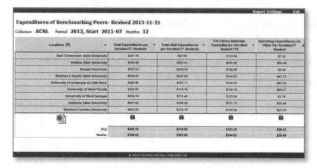

BENCHMARKING ASSOCIATION
AND STATE LIBRARY STANDARDS AND GUIDELINES

Benchmarking is often connected to generally accepted or approved standards. A library benchmarking study would compare itself to these standards to help gauge performance and adequacy. Prior to 1965, public libraries often depended upon prescriptive standards to assess their performance.[15] The American Library Association developed recommended minimum standards for public libraries, including per capita financial support, maintaining a collection adequate to the needs of the community, and maintaining a professional staff of high quality and adequate number. These qualitative standards were later replaced by quantitative recommended standards, including acceptable travel time for library patrons, library operating hours, collection size and quality, collection maintenance practices, library staffing levels, and physical characteristics of the library facility. It was easy for public libraries to conduct a performance or comparative/metric benchmarking process. However, qualitative and quantitative national standards were criticized for failing to recognize the variations in services offered as a result of the differences in service populations from one community to another. Furthermore, while those performing below these minimum standards were able to use the benchmarks to show inadequacy to budget officials and governing bodies, those performing above the standards found that their success could be penalized by these stakeholders seeking to divert resources to other needs. The Public Library Association abandoned prescriptive quantitative standards in the late 1980s and instead advocated an outcomes-based assessment process, recognizing that each library must provide services that meet the differing needs of differing communities.[16]

Several states have legislated or otherwise regulated public library standards as a condition for qualifying to receive state or federal financial assistance. For example, Vermont sets a standard for hours open of "at least 14 hours a week, including at least 4 hours after 5 pm or on weekends (Saturdays and/or Sundays)." Additionally, "The library . . . [r]eceives and expends total support (including tax support, interest on endowments, local fundraising, carefully documented in-kind support, etc.) of at least $5.00 per capita." These minimum standards become simple benchmarks; complying "with the standards makes a library eligible for selected services from the Department of Libraries."[17]

Other states identify levels of service that can be used by public libraries in benchmarking studies. The purpose of public library standards in Texas is "to promote quality library service to all Texans, to raise the expectations of library clientele, and to provide an authoritative document to which library administrators and supporters may refer when justifying requests for funds." Three Levels of Services are identified, and the "enhanced level builds upon the basic and the comprehensive upon the enhanced. Libraries that achieve the enhanced or comprehensive level will be those where improvement is a proactive rather than reactive process."[18]

Wisconsin's standards "provide a way to measure a basic level of quality for public library service and also provide a pathway to *excellence* in library service."

BOX 6.3 **POINTS OF SERVICE COMPARISON***

Input Metrics

» Budget and staffing devoted explicitly to undergraduate services

» Physical facilities that support undergraduate services and research and study needs and that provide an effective learning environment

» Ratio of number of students attending library instructional sessions to total number of students in specified target groups (e.g., first-year students or students in introductory-level courses)

» Collection resources supporting the undergraduate curriculum, research needs, and undergraduate information-seeking modes

» Measure of resources spent on outreach (e.g., instruction sessions, services outside the library walls, collaborations with units outside the library)

Output Metrics

» Ratio of reference transactions to student/patron FTE, including transactions that occur in any venue, whether face-to-face or virtual

» Ratio of borrowing, excluding reserve, by undergraduates to undergraduate student FTEs

» Ratio of reserves borrowing and e-reserves use for undergraduate courses to total of students in target classes

» Number and variety of outreach programs per semester and number of attendees or students reached

» Ratio of successful searches for library resources to total searches

» Average number of people in the library at a given time

» In-library materials use as separate from circulation counts

» Ratio of user FTE to service point use

» Number of links from online sites outside the library (e.g., from online course syllabi, online course directories) to undergraduate class-specific online sites or more general introductory how-to sites created by undergraduate librarians

» Ratio of orientation attendees to incoming student FTEs

» Number and kinds of partnerships with other entities on campus

*Association of College and Research Libraries, *Guidelines for University Library Services to Undergraduate Students* (October 2013), www.ala.org/acrl/standards/ulsundergraduate.

"Specific standards are recommended in the areas of governance and administration (including planning, funding, and public relations); staffing; collections and resources; services; and access and facilities. By meeting these standards, a library establishes a baseline from which it can strive for excellence." Quantitative standards for municipal populations include these: "minimum total staff is 1.0 FTE," "minimum total volumes held is 8,000 volumes," "minimum periodical titles received is 30 titles," "minimum hours open is 25 hours per week," and "minimum materials expenditures is $10,000." The state identifies four tiers of service—"basic, moderate, enhanced and excellent"—that can be used for benchmarking local library performance.[19]

ACRL does not provide prescriptive standards, but instead recommends in a set of guidelines that undergraduate libraries consider the input and output metrics depicted in box 6.3 for points of service comparison; these comparisons could be used in benchmarking studies.

ACRL's *"Standards for Libraries in Higher Education* are designed to guide academic libraries in advancing and sustaining their role as partners in educating students, achieving their institutions' missions, and positioning libraries as leaders in assessment and continuous improvement on their campuses." Appendix 2 of the standards describes the benchmarking process and emphasizes peer comparisons. Once peers have been identified, "points of comparison can be made to compare the strength of the library with its peers."[20]

CONCLUDING THOUGHTS

Librarians will encounter challenges when designing and undertaking a benchmarking study. One is data definition. Although all surveys carefully define their data points for survey reporting (e.g., a title versus a volume), some data measures are much harder to define consistently, such as online *searches*. Do, or can, we measure the number of actual searches conducted? Is a search the same as a session? Or, can we measure multiple searches during a session? And, even though the data definitions are available and their use stressed *for the good of the survey*, data collectors may stray from a strict application of the definition when compiling and reporting the data, often as a result of the diversity of ways that various systems count various activities. As a result, the reporting of reference transactions may include directional responses although the survey instrument explicitly instructs their exclusion from the reported count.

A second challenge is applicability of a data point. For example, some libraries expend funds on overhead (e.g., utilities, liability and casualty insurance, facility cleaning, facility landscaping, fringe benefits, unemployment compensation), while other libraries do not. Overhead is often defined locally and varies from institution to institution, which increases its variability. Including overhead as an expense may increase the library's expenditures so that it would not be a peer with another library that does not report similar overhead expenses.

A third challenge is the imperfect relationship between measures and quality. Quantitative measures have limited usefulness for evaluating a library's quality or performance. This is reinforced by the abandonment of most prescriptive standards by which the quality of library performance was previously assessed.

A fourth challenge is the use and subsequent reporting of results following the data collection activity. Many librarians undertake a benchmarking activity to gather data for internal use only, shared solely with specific stakeholders who requested it and hopefully others who may benefit from its compilation and analysis. Many librarians are modest about reporting benchmarking data to their external peers because they do not expect their colleagues to be particular impressed with the findings, or they do not want to single themselves out from the crowd. Similarly, librarians may conclude that their busy schedules thwart them from creating an interesting "points of pride" document for external local stakeholders who may appreciate the findings and gain an insightful picture of how the library is doing, especially when compared to its peers.

A fifth challenge is the lack of prescriptive library standards to use for benchmarking. In order to standardize a set of services against which comparisons can be made, some degree of compromise is necessary, and the difference between services and their levels based upon the clientele's needs becomes a local perspective as held by the various stakeholders. However, in practice, it is difficult to apply prescriptive standards in a performance benchmarking process involving more than the local library.[21]

EXERCISES

Answers to the following questions are in the "Appendix" at the back of the book. We encourage different members of a library staff to work on the exercises together and to discuss the results. Managers might also participate in that discussion.

QUESTION 1 Why should libraries be interested in comparisons with other libraries?

QUESTION 2 A public library wants to compare its operating expenditures with those of its benchmarking partners. How can the library develop this benchmarking report?

QUESTION 3 An academic library wants to compare its print titles and volumes, and its e-book holdings, with those of its peers. How can the library develop this benchmarking report?

QUESTION 4 A public library wants to compare its interlibrary loan transactions with those of its benchmarking partners. How can the library develop this benchmarking report?

QUESTION 5 An academic library wants to compare its number of instruction programs and attendance with those of its peers. How can the library develop this benchmarking report?

Notes

1. Lynda S. White, "The University of Virginia Library's Experiment with Benchmarking," *Virginia Libraries* 48, no. 4 (October–December 2002): 17; Rosalind Farnam Dudden, "The Medical Library Association Benchmarking Network: Development and Implementation," *Journal of the Medical Library Association* 94, no. 2 (April 2006): 109; Liz Hart, "Comparing Ourselves: Using Benchmarking Techniques to Measure Performance between Academic Libraries," *Library and Information Research News* 25, no. 80 (Autumn 2001): 23; and David N. Ammons, *Municipal Benchmarks: Assessing Local Performance and Establishing Community Standards*, 2nd ed. (Thousand Oaks, CA: Sage Publications, 2001).

2. Kathryn Robbins and Kathleen Daniels, "Benchmarking Reference Desk Service in Academic Health Science Libraries: A Preliminary Survey," *College & Research Libraries* 62, no. 4 (July 2001): 348–49.

3. L. Gehrke and J. J. Britz, "The Application of Benchmarking as a Tool to Improve the Management of Quality in Information Services," *Mousaion* 22, no. 1 (2004): 20–22.

4. Gehrke and Britz, "The Application of Benchmarking as a Tool," 22.

5. Leeanne Pitman, Isabella Trahn, and Anne Wilson, "Working Towards Best Practice in Australian University Libraries: Reflections on a National Project," *Australian Academic and Research Libraries* 32, no. 1 (March 2001): 5; and Margaret M. Robertson and Isabella Trahn, "Benchmarking Academic Libraries: An Australian Case Study," *Australian Academic and Research Libraries* 28, no. 2 (1997): 128.

6. Rosalind Farnam Dudden, *Using Benchmarking, Needs Assessment, Quality Improvement, Outcome Measurement, and Library Standards: A Medical Library Association Guide* (New York: Neal-Schuman Publishers, 2007), 116, 132, 139.

7. Dudden, *Using Benchmarking, Needs Assessment, Quality Improvement, Outcome Measurement, and Library Standards*, 116, 132.

8. Gehrke and Britz, "The Application of Benchmarking as a Tool," 24.

9. See Gehrke and Britz, "The Application of Benchmarking as a Tool," 23; and Claire Creaser, "Performance Measurement and Benchmarking for Schools Library Services," *Journal of Librarianship and Information Science* 33, no. 3 (September 2001): 127.

10. See Creaser, "Performance Measurement and Benchmarking for Schools Library Services," 130–31.

11. Deborah Teeter and Paul Brinkman, "Peer Institution," in *The Primer for Institutional Research*, ed. William Knight (Tallahassee, FL: Association for Institutional Research, 2003), 103–113.

12. "The LJ Index: Frequently Asked Questions (FAQ)," (November 8, 2013), http://lj.libraryjournal.com/stars-faq/.

13. See also the appendixes in Robert E. Dugan, Peter Hernon, and Danuta A. Nitecki, *Viewing Library Metrics from Different Perspectives: Inputs, Outputs, and Outcomes* (Santa Barbara, CA: Libraries Unlimited, 2009).

14. Keith Curry Lance and Ray Lyons, "America's Star Libraries, 2013: Top-Rated Libraries" (November 1, 2013), http://lj.libraryjournal.com/2013/11/managing-libraries/lj-index/class-of-2013/americas-star-libraries-2013-top-rated-libraries.

15. Gehrke and Britz, "The Application of Benchmarking as a Tool," 15.

16. Ammons, *Municipal Benchmarks*, 212–13.

17. Vermont Department of Libraries, *State Standards for Public Libraries* (1998, 2013), http://libraries.vermont.gov/libraries/standards.

18. Texas State Library and Archives Commission, *Texas Public Library Standards* (2004), 1, www.tsl.state.tx.us/sites/default/files/public/tslac/plstandards/tplstandards04.pdf.

19. Wisconsin Department of Public Instruction, Division for Libraries, Technology, and Community Learning, *Wisconsin Public Library Standards*, 5th ed. (August 2010), 1, 8, 37–38, http://pld.dpi.wi.gov/files/pld/pdf/standards.pdf.

20. Association of College and Research Libraries, *Standards for Libraries in Higher Education* (October 2011), 5, 22–23, www.ala.org/acrl/sites/ala.org.acrl/files/content/standards/slhe.pdf.

21. Creaser, "Performance Measurement and Benchmarking for Schools Library Services," 130–31.

Best Practices

A BEST PRACTICE IS an activity or procedure that has produced outstanding results in a situation that could be adopted through replication to improve effectiveness or efficiency, or both, in a similar situation. Best practices may be described as activities or actions that, when implemented, yield a superior outcome. Library best practices develop and change over time; they represent a consensus of ever-evolving professional judgment. Planning best practices include alignment of the library's services with its strategic plan so that both reflect the institution's mission. In that way the library can demonstrate value and relevance to stakeholders by supporting the institution's goals and objectives. Benchmarking, on the other hand, is a tool to measure and compare the performance of one library with that of other libraries (see chapter 6). As a process it compares inputs, outputs, and outcomes with identified peer or aspirant libraries. Benchmarking can help identify libraries that have one or more best practices that contribute positively to their high performance.

WHY LIBRARIES USE BEST PRACTICES

Basically, libraries seek best practices in order to improve services to their customers—to make critical service improvements—and to improve the efficient delivery of those services. The implementation of best practices helps libraries to demonstrate accountability, quality performance, and effective resource use. For example, learning how others have made staffing allocation decisions and finding ways to incorporate workload and performance metrics into the local decision-making process will likely improve service efficiencies.[1]

Best practices are helpful to library administrators trying to link organizational behavior to outcomes; they help identify the characteristics of organizational behavior that need to change to improve outcomes.[2] Improving throughput processes to increase efficiencies is often the outcome of a best practice; the improved process may increase the quality of an output but has little effect on the related input. For example, the library may be open the same number of hours with the same staffing levels, but the best practice as implemented improves the turnaround time and accuracy when re-shelving books, resulting in the library realizing its objective to increase circulation transactions per capita.

DISCOVERING BEST PRACTICES

When a library does something better than most, such as achieving cost savings, answering reference questions, or cataloging materials, the profession's modesty often stops it from widely reporting the outcomes via conferences, workshops, and the professional literature. As a result we recommend the following steps to find library best practices:

» Identify a problem that needs to be solved locally.
» Find the library(ies) that have resolved the problem.
» Learn how the library did it.
» Apply that knowledge to improve service or service efficiency.

To begin, identify a specific problem that is occurring in the library. One means is for managers to list the objectives from the strategic plan that they are not meeting and then ask why achievement of one or more of these objectives has been unobtainable. Finding the root problem—the cause of the problem and not a symptom of it—will help to focus the search for best practices. For example, a library is experiencing a declining, rather than a steady or increasing, number of circulation transactions. Managers may identify the cause of this problem as a cut in service hours or the lack of parking spaces at or near the library. However, parking may be a symptom; the cause may actually be the number of hours open or the days and times when the library is open. Undertaking an evaluation study will help to identify the problem.[3]

Once the problem has been identified, managers should search for those libraries that have resolved the problem; in other words, find those libraries that are meeting the subject library's stated objective. Unlike the business world, there is no place to go to determine which library has the best practices; there is no equal to the Malcolm Baldrige Award for libraries.[4] Finding a best practice can be difficult; considerable time and effort can be expended and little, if any, information might be found. A library cannot benefit from implementing best practices if the best practices cannot be uncovered. Still, there are several means for identifying the libraries that are achieving the subject library's objective:

» Conduct a library literature search of articles and other information resources to discover if any library has written about the problem.

- » Conduct a survey seeking libraries that are meeting the performance objective. Libraries are familiar with responding to surveys and, because of the information-sharing ethos of the profession, will complete a survey instrument if it is short, asks understandable questions, and appears relevant to a library's operation.
- » Monitor relevant electronic discussion lists, including the archives, to learn if there has been discussion about the problem and to discover which libraries responded as having addressed the problem.
- » Scan conference programs and attend meetings that may present information related to the problem.
- » Attend regional information sharing meetings or talk with colleagues to help identify libraries that have developed relevant best practices.
- » Review the reported outcomes of competitive grant projects. Among a project's evaluation criteria is, "What can be learned from the results of this project that may point to the development of best practices?"[5]
- » Search library web pages to identify best practices. Although this type of review may appear to be overwhelming, start with the library's peers.
- » Use national data compilation and reporting tools to help identify the libraries that may have a best practice in the problem area. This will be discussed later in this chapter.

On the basis of literature reviews, survey findings, or otherwise identifying libraries that may have a best practice, site visits to the libraries will reveal how and why these libraries are better performers. Being on-site facilitates a closer understanding of how the best practice really worked while enabling the site visitor to document the best practice as observed. There is no substitute for walking through a process and having an opportunity to ask questions along the way.[6]

FUNCTIONS AND SERVICES FOR BEST PRACTICES

There are general areas of library services and functions for which best practices are sought and implemented:

- » Efficiencies (e.g., the time it takes to re-shelve a book accurately)
- » Internal resource allocation models (e.g., funds are allocated by population, such as children, young adults, adults, students, faculty; or by use, in which the most used services or functions receive the highest allocation)
- » Collaboration between institutional departments (e.g., collaboration is facilitated by high activity of interdepartmental communications or by sharing a vision/mission)
- » Library instruction and information literacy (e.g., instruction is provided when needed or where needed or through course-embedded librarians)
- » Personnel development, including staff training, staff development, and staff evaluations

» Materials availability (e.g., proportion of sought material obtained at the time of visit)
» Reference services (e.g., providing users with a multiplicity of access venues, such as chat and e-mail)
» Collection use (e.g., high annual collection turnover)
» Community outreach (e.g., encouraging library staff to be engaged in the community by going to community gatherings and clubs)
» Management and leadership (e.g., having a clear organizational structure, employing data-driven decision making, and displaying high ethical standards)
» Materials selection: collection development and maintenance (e.g., creating an opportunity to involve stakeholders in selecting materials)
» Being in a position of professional librarian (e.g., keeping up with the literature and attending webinars when travel funds and time are limited)
» Space utilization (e.g., well-attended programs and high circulation in less than average square feet)
» Customer satisfaction

Box 7.1 identifies several select examples of current best practices in library services, staffing, management, and collection development. In addition, drawing on the Project for Public Spaces (PPS; www.pps.org/reference/libraryattributes), Mary Rzepczynski, assistant library director with the Delta Township District Library in Lansing, Michigan, offers fourteen strategies to help public libraries become great. These strategies, some of which are listed here, might become best practices for libraries:

» Offer a broad mix of community services.
» Build capacity for local businesses.
» Become a public gathering place.
» Boost local retail and public markets.
» Feature multiple attractions and destinations.
» Be a catalyst for community revitalization.[7]

As an example, to become a public gathering place, the library might do the following:

> The spaces inside and outside libraries are perfect for public proclamations, celebrations, fairs, and festivals—as well as smaller but no less important events that occur on a regular basis, like brown bag lectures or midday concerts. These activities reinforce the library's role as a community anchor, and leading libraries are jumping at the chance to attract people by expanding their programs. To succeed as lively gathering places, a library can offer an eclectic mix that may include outdoor exhibits on science or history, temporary public art installations, games and chess tables, or outdoor play areas linked to the children's reading room.[8]

The Association of College and Research Libraries has published a guideline of best practices of information literacy programs for academic libraries. The best practices are arranged in ten categories:

BOX 7.1 **EXAMPLES OF BEST PRACTICES**

» Test using a pilot before implementing a new service or process.

» Ensure there is adequate staffing scheduled for public service desks during the busiest use times.

» Provide users with a multiplicity of access venues for reference services, such as chat and e-mail.

» Create and maintain a Frequently Asked Questions (FAQ) web page; the FAQ becomes a user self-service that is often thought to be another best practice.

» Assess user needs, on a continuous basis, rather than concluding that the needs are obvious and known and that everyone loves the library.

» Identify costs. Common costs to identify include cost per interlibrary loan, cost per reference question answered, and cost per hour open.

» Conduct community outreach. Outreach is successful when it is specifically planned and when partnerships have been developed with local businesses, media outlets, and influential community members.

» Stabilize management and leadership. Ensure that a staff position reports to only one supervisor, not a multiplicity of supervisors.

» Use effective communications. There is no richer a communications mode than face-to-face. Technologies, such as Skype and Apple's FaceTime, may be applied as proxies in lieu of physical, face-to-face communications.

» Perform collection development and maintenance. Weeding is an effective collection maintenance tool.

» Track actions taken versus activity levels and customer feedback to demonstrate effective use of staff time and alignment with goals and objectives.

Category 1: Mission
Category 2: Goals and Objectives
Category 3: Planning
Category 4: Administrative and Institutional Support
Category 5: Articulation (program sequence) within the Curriculum
Category 6: Collaboration
Category 7: Pedagogy
Category 8: Staffing
Category 9: Outreach
Category 10: Assessment/Evaluation.[9]

As an example of an information literacy program best practice in Category 1, Mission, the program

» includes a definition of information literacy;

» is consistent with the *ACRL Information Literacy Competency Standards for Higher Education*;

» aligns with the library's mission statement to correspond with the larger mission statement of the institution;

» adheres to the format of campus strategic documents;

» incorporates the institutional stakeholders, clearly reflecting their contributions and the expected benefits;

» appears in appropriate institutional documents; and

» promotes relevant lifelong learning and professional development.[10]

NATIONAL REPORTING SOURCES

Although many best practices are qualitative, libraries can still search for one that is quantifiable by consulting some national-level reporting sources. Yet, quantitative data may serve as a proxy for qualitative characteristics when searching for libraries with best practices processes. For example, it may be that public libraries with high per capita library visits, circulation, and program attendance have become a community's gathering place, which may be the unrealized objective of your library. Because of the scarcity of literature in library and information

EXAMPLE 7.1 **USE OF THE NCES WEBSITE FOR IDENTIFYING BEST PRACTICES**

STEP 1 On the NCES home page (http://nces.ed.gov/), click on the link titled Surveys & Programs.

STEP 2 Click on the link for Library Statistics Program.

STEP 3 Click on the link titled Academic Libraries.

STEP 4 Click on Compare Academic Libraries (http://nces.ed.gov/surveys/libraries/compare/).

STEP 5 Start the search, and click on the link titled Select Target Library, which is the one you want to compare with the peers. Type in enough information to find and select the target.

STEP 6 Under the heading for "Step 2—Select Comparison Institution Libraries (In Progress)," click on the link titled Choose Comparison Group.

STEP 7 Select the tab titled Select Libraries (Comparison Group) By Variable.

STEP 8 For this example, we are seeking best practices for hours open and staffing levels. The target library has a staff of 43.27 and is open 106 hours per week. The library would like to be open longer. Therefore, the library seeks other libraries that are open longer hours with a similarly sized staff. Selected for this example are the following:

» Under the heading "Paid Full-Time Equivalent (FTE) Staff," choose Total Staff. A window opens; use the second slider, which is a Range Scale. Use a selected range of 43 to 49, and then click on Continue. You are returned to the Select Variable page, and the results of the search are displayed: forty-two libraries were found.

» Add a second variable. Under Services, select Hours Open in a Typical Week. Again, use the second slider and a selected range from 111 to 168 (24/7), and then click on Continue. The results show that 259 libraries were found.

science on best practices, this means that identifying libraries with best practices might require a considerable amount of time.

Academic Libraries

The National Center for Education Statistics (NCES; http://nces.ed.gov/) is the primary federal entity for collecting and analyzing data related to education. To compare academic libraries in the search for best practices, consult the steps outlined in example 7.1.

STEP 9   As the variables are added, the number of libraries in the comparison group is updated and displayed just above the Results screen. In this example, the combination of the search yielded seven libraries. Clicking on the link titled (Number of Libraries in Comparison Group: 7) displays the names of the seven libraries.

This example is a good starting point to learn more about how these libraries are open more hours with nearly identical staffing levels.

Library Compare Tool

Comparison Group Libraries

Library Name	Total Staff	Hours Open in a Typical Week
The University Of West Florida, Fl	43.27	106
Amherst College, Ma	43.90	111
College Of The Holy Cross, Ma	46.75	149
Lewis & Clark College, Or	47.74	141
Middlebury College, Vt	46.08	113
Pepperdine University, Ca	44.11	111
Saint Cloud State University, Mn	45.12	111
Troy University, Al	46.69	168

10 per page

ACRL*Metrics* enables the managers of an academic library to conduct studies using ACRL reported data as well as the data from the academic libraries reported to NCES and IPEDS. Example 7.2 lays out the steps to follow here.

Public Libraries

Public libraries have at least two sources of free national quantitative data and one subscription-based source. One free tool is *Library Journal's* annual *LJ Index* (*Star Index*), which divides public libraries into nine peer comparison groups that are based on total operating expenditures. Within each group the highest-scoring libraries are recognized by assigning a ranking of five (highest), four, or three stars. Each star-rating group contains ten star libraries, except for the $30 million and above group for which each star-rating group contains five libraries. Star ratings

EXAMPLE 7.2 **USE OF ACRL*METRICS* FOR ENGAGING IN BEST PRACTICES**

STEP 1	Log on to ACRL*Metrics*, www.acrlmetrics.com/.
STEP 2	Click on the link titled Reports.
STEP 3	Click on the tab labeled Local and then the link labeled Add.
STEP 4	For Collection, select "ACRL" for this example.
STEP 5	Select a Period; for this example, 2012 was selected.
STEP 6	Type in a Report Name, such as "Best Practices: Staffing and Hours Open."
STEP 7	Type in a Description, such as "2012 ACRL data—find libraries open longer with similar staff."
STEP 8	Type in a title if desired.
STEP 9	Select a Group or use the default All groups.
STEP 10	Select one or more indicators from the list of measures. For this example, we are seeking best practices for hours open and staffing levels. The target library has a staff of 43.27 and is open 106 hours per week. The library would like to be open longer. Therefore, we will seek libraries open longer hours with a similarly sized staff. Selected for this example was » Total Staff (FTE) Unfortunately, *hours open in a typical week* is no longer collected by ACRL.
STEP 11	To include hours open per week in this study, it is necessary to include NCES data. Counting Opinions includes the NCES data sets. To include the NCES data, return to Collection and highlight "NCES Academic Libraries Survey." If indicators containing ACRL data are already selected, NCES indicators will be added to the same report. Because of the years for which NCES collects academic library data, the most recent data set in Counting Opinions is FY2010.
STEP 12	Run the report. Thousands of libraries are included in the results.

are based on scores. The *LJ Index* scores are presented and reported on only four weighted and averaged per capita service outputs:

1. Library visits
2. Circulation
3. Program attendance
4. Public Internet computer use

If the best practices search is not directly or indirectly related to one of these four measures, then the *LJ Index* may not be helpful. However, if one or more of these metrics are relevant, the *LJ Index* is a useful starting point. You may download the spreadsheet data and sort by state, service population, and total operating expenditures or by the four weighted and averaged per capita service outputs just listed.[11] After identifying the top-performing libraries as a result of the analysis, managers might visit one or more of them, if possible, or have a conversation with managers there. The purpose is to reveal a best practice that can be adapted locally.

STEP 13   To limit the number of libraries in the report, use the Counting Opinions capability to filter. Based upon the local library's numbers, a fairly narrow filter can be created. The local library has a staff of 43.27 and is open 106 hours per week. Set the respective filters for Public Service Hours with a low filter of 111 and a high filter of 168 (24/7); for Total Staff set a low filter of 43 and a high filter of 45.

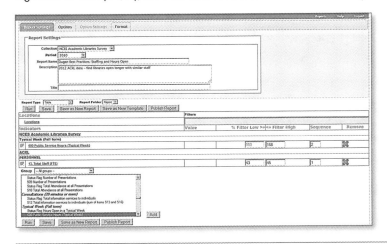

STEP 14   Run the report. The search yields two libraries. The report can be downloaded as a spreadsheet for further analysis and review.

Although only two libraries are revealed, it is a good starting point to learn more about how they are open more hours with similar staffing levels.

Dugan Best Practices: Staffing and Hours Open

Collection: **ACRL, NCES Academic Libraries Survey**   Period: **2010, Start 2010-01** Months: 12

Locations (2)	13. Total Staff (FTE)	600 Public Service Hours (Typical Week)
College of the Holy Cross	45.00	114
Swarthmore College	43.00	113

Filters	Values	
	Min / %	Max
Public Service Hours (Typical Week)	111	168
Total Staff (FTE)	43	45

For the second free tool, visit the IMLS public library data website and follow the steps outlined in example 7.3. The search process outlined in this example will help you learn more about the highest-performing libraries in three metrics: total circulation, library visits, and reference transactions per capita. Once these libraries have been identified, managers can contact them about how successful they might be in the application of one or more best practices.

EXAMPLE 7.3 **USE OF IMLS WEBSITE FOR IDENTIFYING BEST PRACTICES**

STEP 1   Go to the home page of the Institute of Museum and Library Services, www.imls.gov/.

STEP 2   Click on the link titled Research.

STEP 3   Click on the link titled Data Collection.

STEP 4   Click on the link titled Public Library Survey.

STEP 5   Click on the link titled Compare Public Libraries (https://harvester.census.gov/imls/compare/index.asp).

STEP 6   Click on the link titled Begin Search.

STEP 7   On the next web page, "Select Library of Interest," enter your library's name, city, state, and zip code, and click on the link titled Continue.

STEP 8   Select the radio button for the library of interest (yours).

STEP 9   Two methods to select a comparison group are presented:
>> Choose Similar Libraries (Comparison Group) By Variable
>> Choose Specific Public Libraries For Your Comparison Group

Because we are seeking to identify libraries based upon selected variables, choose the first option.

STEP 10   Select from eight general variables presented. For this example we will seek libraries that may be community gathering places. The thinking is that these libraries will have a high volume of circulation and reference transactions, and library visits. Therefore, select the following from the IMLS variables presented in Services:
>> Total Circulation per Capita, and then accept Method 1 with the default of 20 percent; to add additional variables, click the link titled Add a Variable To Refine Your Comparison Group.
>> Library Visits per Capita, and accept Method 1 and the default of 20 percent.
>> Reference Transactions per Capita, and accept Method 1 and the default of 20 percent.

STEP 11   Note that the IMLS box reproduced here shows that our search has yielded twenty-seven libraries. Click on the link titled See Libraries In Comparison Group.

STEP 12   The report displays the libraries that meet the search criteria from the previous steps. This chart may be downloaded as a spreadsheet to be further sorted for review.

Libraries In Your Comparison Group

Export this report to an Excel file

Click on a library name to view details for that library. Click on the question mark to view its definition.

Library Name	Total Circulation per Capita	Library Visits per Capita	Reference Transactions per Capita
F.D CAMPBELL MEMORIAL LIBRARY, PA	2.01	1.69	0.23
CITY OF GARDEN RIDGE LIBRARY, TX	2.02	2.18	0.21
WINOOSKI MEMORIAL, VT	2.09	1.85	0.25
WHITE PINE PUBLIC LIBRARY, TN	2.11	1.70	0.27
ISAAC F. UMBERHINE PUBLIC LIBRARY, ME*	2.16	2.05	0.29
RODMAN PUBLIC LIBRARY, NY	2.25	1.91	0.27
CALHOUN COUNTY PUBLIC LIBRARY, WV	2.25	1.67	0.31
LONGVIEW PUBLIC LIBRARY, TX	2.25	2.09	0.26
CUMBERLAND COUNTY PUBLIC LIBRARY, VA	2.26	2.28	0.25
BRICEVILLE PUBLIC LIBRARY, TN	2.30	1.85	0.22
ONSLOW COUNTY PUBLIC LIBRARY, NC	2.34	1.95	0.30

A third source, the Public Library Data Service (PLDS) Statistical Report, which also includes access to IMLS data, is available using the subscription-based PLA*metrics* service provided by Counting Opinions. For the steps to follow in the use of PLA*metrics*, see example 7.4.

EXAMPLE 7.4 **USE OF PLDS FOR IDENTIFYING BEST PRACTICES**

STEP 1	Log on to PLA*metrics*, https://public.countingopinions.com/.
STEP 2	Click on the link titled Reports.
STEP 3	Click on the tab labeled Local and then the link labeled Add.
STEP 4	For Collection, select "PLDS."
STEP 5	Select a Period; for this example, FY2011 was selected.
STEP 6	Type in a Report Name, such as "Libraries that may be Community Gathering Place."
STEP 7	Type in a Description, such as "looking for best practices libraries as community gathering places."
STEP 8	Type in a title if desired.
STEP 9	Select a Group or use the default All groups.
STEP 10	Select one or more indicators from the list of measures. For our sample benchmarking study, we wanted to find circulation and reference transactions. Therefore, we chose:

- » Circulation per Capita
- » Circulation per Hour
- » Visits per Capita
- » Reference Transactions per Capita
- » Reference Transactions per Hour

(Note: Counting Opinions has many more measures from which to select than are provided through the IMLS tool.)

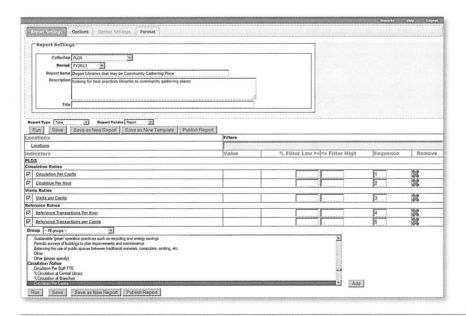

| STEP 11 | Run the report to see the results. The result of our sample search was more than 1,800 libraries, which is too large a group to review. |

EXAMPLE 7.4 (continued)

STEP 12 Knowing your library's measures, use Filters to limit the search. Unlike IMLS, Counting Opinions allows the user to establish numeric ranges through filters. Set the local library's figure as the figure for the low filter, and then set the high filter to meet the local library's stated objective. Set a low and high filter for one or more of the five measures. Four measures were chosen for our sample search:

» Circulation per Capita, low 4.00 and high 8.00

» Visits per Capita, low 2.00 and high 8.00

» Reference Transactions per Hour, low 300 and high 600

» Reference Transactions per Capita, low 1.00 and high 2.00

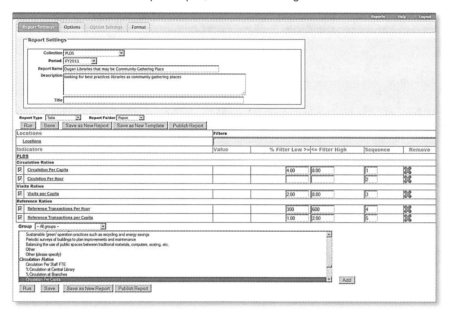

STEP 13 Run the report. The report may be saved as a spreadsheet for additional analysis.

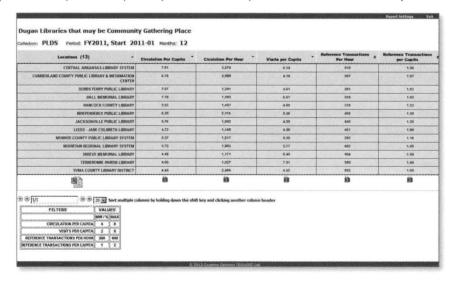

LIBRARY STANDARDS AND BEST PRACTICES

Many librarians seek standards as guidance to create best practices. However, prescriptive standards may not work for all libraries and may hinder rather than facilitate the development of best practices. Consider the example of staffing a library. What is best practice for the number of librarians to staff public service desks adequately? The answer depends on which variables are included—ones for the mission of the library, the population served, the stated needs of the population, and the resources available to the library to undertake its mission? Complicating matters, no one approach will work for all libraries. A "one size fits all" prescriptive standard is not feasible in modern libraries because, while difficult for some external stakeholders to grasp, the services provided by libraries can vastly vary from each other because of even subtle differences in characteristics such as demographics, economic environments, and user needs.[12]

Guidelines and recommended strategies from library associations and documented successes of exemplary programs suggest that a more flexible framework within which to provide services and programs is preferred instead of prescriptive standards. Two examples given in this chapter were the Project for Public Spaces' strategies for public libraries to become great and ACRL's *Characteristics of Programs of Information Literacy that Illustrate Best Practices*. Neither offers prescriptive standards, but each suggests ideas for best practices that can be used to establish, develop, and maintain services and programs that contribute to the library's attaining excellence.

CONCLUDING THOUGHTS

Library best practices represent consensus of professional judgment evolving over time as the environment in which libraries operate changes. Therefore, best practices are not suitable for standards. When confronted with a problem, librarians instinctively ask, "What are other libraries doing?" If a best practice is found, the library may not be able to duplicate the process because of the differences in the internal situations and environments between libraries. In other words, libraries may have to adapt, rather than adopt, the best practice.

John Lubans, a long-time library manager, writer, and leadership workshop facilitator, warns that the adoption/adaption of best practices promotes low-risk solutions. If everyone imitates, then innovation has no chance. This could negatively impact the creativity of the profession, the very impetus that is needed by librarians to persist in seeking, testing, implementing, and assessing best practices to resolve future problems.[13]

EXERCISES

Answers to the following questions are in the "Appendix" at the back of the book. We encourage different members of a library staff to work on the exercises together and to discuss the results. Managers might also participate in that discussion.

QUESTION 1   What best practices, if any, would you add to table 7.1? Why would you do so?

QUESTION 2   Should a library seeking to learn about a best practice limit itself to its benchmarking partners or peers? Why?

QUESTION 3   A public library has increasing user demand to circulate e-books and downloadable audio and video media. Although the library circulates some e-books, these are apparently not meeting demand. The library is not managing any downloadable media. What can its managers do?

QUESTION 4   The managers of an academic library have calculated a staff operating cost per reference transaction, which they think is high. They want to know how other libraries provide reference services at less cost per transaction. What can they do?

QUESTION 5   The managers of a public library have noticed that few people attend the programs they offer. What might they do to improve attendance?

QUESTION 6   An academic library's strategic plan directs it to increase what it spends on collections to more than 50 percent of its total operating expenditures. The library's managers want to know which other libraries have met the same objective; this collections expenditure ratio necessarily results in staffing expenditures below 50 percent of total operating expenditures. What can they do to identify libraries meeting this strategic direction?

Notes

1. Jeanne Goodrich, "Staffing Public Libraries: Are There Models or Best Practices?" *Public Libraries* 44, no. 5 (September/October 2005): 281.

2. Kathryn H. Carpenter, "Best Practices in Libraries—Not Just Another Edition of 'How I Done It Good': An Interview with Tom Kirk," *Library Administration & Management* 16, no. 2 (Spring 2002): 67.

3. See Peter Hernon, Robert E. Dugan, and Joseph R. Matthews, *Getting Started with Evaluation* (Chicago: American Library Association, 2014).

4. Lynda S. White, "The University of Virginia Library's Experiment with Benchmarking," *Virginia Libraries* 48, no. 4 (October–December 2002): 18.

5. Ann Reed and Jane Scheppke, "Oregon's LSTA State Grant Program: Excavating Best Practice, Reaching towards Transparency," *OLA Quarterly* 16, no. 3 (Fall 2010): 40.

6. See John Lubans Jr., "'From the Gutter to You Is Not Up': Worst and Best Practice," *Library Administration & Management* 16, no. 2 (Spring 2002): 92–93; White, "The University of Virginia Library's Experiment with Benchmarking," 19; and Leeanne Pitman, Isabella Trahn, and Anne Wilson, "Working towards Best Practice in Australian University Libraries: Reflections on a National Project," *Australian Academic and Research Libraries* 32, no. 1 (March 2001): 4.

7. Mary Rzepczynski, "Great Libraries," *Public Libraries* 51, no. 5 (September/October 2012): 13; and Project for Public Spaces, "How to Make Your Library Great" (n.d.), www.pps.org/reference/libraryattributes/.

8. Project for Public Spaces, "How to Make Your Library Great."

9. Association of College and Research Libraries, *Characteristics of Programs of Information Literacy that Illustrate Best Practices: A Guideline* (January 2012), www.ala.org/acrl/standards/characteristics.

10. Association of College and Research Libraries, *Characteristics of Programs of Information Literacy that Illustrate Best Practices.*

11. Keith Curry Lance and Ray Lyons, "America's Star Libraries, 2013: Top-Rated Libraries" (November 1, 2013), http://lj.libraryjournal.com/2013/11/managing-libraries/lj-index/class-of-2013/americas-star-libraries-2013-top-rated-libraries.

12. Goodrich, "Staffing Public Libraries," 280–81.

13. Lubans, "'From the Gutter to You Is Not Up,'" 92.

Moving toward Outcomes Assessment While Embracing Value

IN HIGHER EDUCATION THERE are two types of outcomes—student outcomes and student learning outcomes. The former are aggregate statistics on groups of students compiled at the program or institution level, and they paint an overall portrait of that program or institution. Examples include graduation rate, placement rate of graduates (number and length of time to gain employment in college major), student retention rate, time-to-degree rate, accessibility (ability to get into a desired program of study), rate of tuition increases, earning capacity of graduates, graduates' salaries, and amount of student debt incurred. The other type of outcomes, student learning outcomes, refers to the knowledge, skills, abilities, and competencies that students gain from their educational experiences accumulated during the time-to-completion of an undergraduate or graduate degree or the first year as an undergraduate. Faculty within a program of study, perhaps with the assistance of others (e.g., librarians), might set relevant learning goals and associated competencies that students must master—on which they demonstrate proficiency (e.g., with information literacy).

Although less frequently discussed in the literature, there are other types of outcomes in higher education. These might include research outcomes and faculty outcomes. The former are student oriented and focus on mastery of each component of research as an inquiry process or of the entire process. They, therefore, might resemble student outcomes and convey the completion rates for dissertations and the extent to which student work appears in prestigious journals of a particular discipline or field of study. They might also be similar to student learning outcomes and focus on learning experiences, such as those associated with the knowledge and abilities gained by completing a doctoral dissertation, the communication skills displayed during the defense of the doctoral dissertation, or the quality of the thesis or dissertation produced.

For faculty, an equivalent to student outcomes might be the number of dissertation committees chaired or served on in relation to the number of students engaged in dissertation work. Other traditional faculty metrics might deal with the national or international reputation of individual faculty members and the impact of their research and scholarship (e.g., the extent to which these directly lead to book contracts; book and other types of awards; opportunities for international speaking and consulting; and funding to conduct future research).

Naturally, the types of outcomes just outlined do not apply to public libraries, which serve a broader constituency. Outcomes for these libraries focus on the "benefits to people: specifically, achievements or changes in skill, knowledge, attitudes, behavior, condition, or life status for program participants."[1] Outcomes assessment for public libraries, in summary, is the process of collecting information that will indicate whether the services and programming have the desired impact on those who use them; that is, do they make a difference in their lives?

The Charlotte Mecklenburg Library in North Carolina, for instance, maintains a summer reading program to help children and adults "to learn new things, escape with a great story, or simply to relax and unwind. . . . Teachers and literacy experts agree that reading throughout the summer helps students retain skills learned during the school year. Most importantly, when parents and children enjoy summer reading together, children develop a love of books and reading that lasts a lifetime" (www.cmlibrary.org/programs/summer_reading/2014/). As noted on a previous version of the library's Summer Reading web page (www .cmlibrary.org/about_us/info.asp?id=45), "the library is making an impact on the youngest children and their parents, building critical preliteracy skills to prepare young children for school." It is noted that

> students who are struggling with reading in the third grade are likely to have trouble in all subjects, because reading is so essential to learning in grades four through 12 . . . . [R]eading is becoming an even more essential skill for all students, as North Carolina and other states move toward Common Core Standards in which literacy (reading) is embedded in all parts of the curriculum. The more children read, the better their fluency, vocabulary and comprehension.

That previous web page also pointed out that research suggests "reading four to six books over the summer helps readers maintain their skills, and reading ten to twenty books helps improve their skills." Or, as one of the researchers cited puts it, "Free voluntary reading is the best way to better reading and language development." Such a statement provides a foundation for outcomes assessment. First, how many books do students in fact read? Second, based on the use of pre- and post-tests, is there a significant improvement in their vocabulary? Third, is there similarly an increase in their reading comprehension (see note 3)? And, finally, what insights into language development emerge? For example, by the end of the program, can students read with greater ease and write better compositions?

Outcomes that matter to local government and community organizations include, among others, workforce development, reading readiness and improvement, improved literacy rates, and small business development. The data collected for demonstrating success in meeting library-based outcomes has mostly taken the form of self-reports from participants; alternatively, the data might come from research studies involving the use of experimental designs and showing what participants actually did and how their lives changed.[2]

Outcomes represent the logical evolution of performance measurement in the nonprofit sector; however, not all of them can be reduced to quantitative analysis. Some public libraries might develop outcomes for immigrants participating in a literacy program and state that participants will raise their level of reading comprehension from *literal* (what is actually stated) to *applied* (applying the concepts or ideas expressed beyond the immediate situation).[3] In other instances, some public libraries have framed an outcome as asserting that adults (participating parents and caregivers) will read to children more often. Based on participant interviews, a certain number and percentage of parents or other caretakers might do so at least five times per week. The first example is an outcome in which participating immigrants might complete a pre- and post-test of reading comprehension, with the results compared statistically. The second example is really an output! An outcome would actually focus on the results of that reading—namely, improved reading comprehension of children or their ability to read at higher grade levels. Might there be an outcome related to the parents or caregivers? The answer is yes, and it might be framed around improved or increased communication (or both), closer personal relationships with the children, increased vocabulary, or other factors. However, some public libraries may be satisfied with the simple metric (output) of increased reading to children, especially if the parents or caregivers rely on library materials.

Outcomes, especially those associated with learning, often cannot be reduced to numbers and percentages. Various programs within an academic institution, for instance, might have similar learning goals but ones that are not quantifiable. If academic programs base their information literacy programs on the standards set by the Association of College and Research Libraries, the faculty might not select all of the learning goals and stated competencies in the library standards.[4] They might even substitute competencies.

Against this general discussion, this chapter concentrates on ACRL*Metrics* and PLA*metrics* and on any questions or metrics that have implications for outcomes assessment. This chapter neither advances data collection beyond the offerings of the data services nor advocates supplementing the data services with additional metrics; such is beyond the scope of this book. The purpose here is to tweak the data services to see if any questions are relevant as outcomes—this means, most likely, student outcomes or their equivalent for public libraries. Libraries may want to extract any relevant data and recast them as stories as they try to appeal to a wider audience.

RELEVANT QUESTIONS FROM THE DATA SERVICES

From the IPEDS (Integrated Postsecondary Education Data System) survey, the relevant components for measuring student outcomes can be found in the sections on "completions,"[5] "student financial aid (undergraduates),"[6] "graduation rates,"[7] and "200 percent graduation rates."[8] None of these sections, however, mentions libraries and their contribution. Next, the Academic Libraries Survey contains questions about inputs (e.g., current serial subscriptions) and outputs (the amount of services provided). Two questions, items 800 and 801, ask about whether the "institution articulated student learning outcomes and, if so, whether information literacy was incorporated into those outcomes." Respondents merely answer both questions with a yes or no. In fact, the answers to these questions are complex and should be followed with a series of questions, not all of which could be answered quantitatively. Complicating matters, libraries might contribute to other learning outcomes. At any rate, institutional researchers can probe institutional student outcomes (e.g., graduation rate) but cannot isolate the contributions of the library or other units. In conclusion, IPEDS data, alone, do not contribute to an in-depth portrayal of program and institutional outcomes.

OTHER DATA SETS

Librarians might benefit from importing variables from other data sets, such as the National Survey of Student Engagement (NSSE; http://nsse.iub.edu/), launched in 2000 and updated in 2013, which collects data in five areas: (1) participation in different types of learning activities outside the classroom, (2) institutional requirements and coursework, (3) perceptions of the college environment, (4) estimates of educational and personal growth since starting college, and (5) background and demographic information.[9] None of the questions on the 2013 instrument addresses libraries or outcomes, although students are asked if their courses emphasized application, analysis, and evaluation, three essential components of outcomes assessment. However, these components are not linked to specific learning goals and do not show what students learned over time. Still, one question asks about use of "learning support services," but the choices do not mention libraries. Another question asks respondents about the number of papers, reports, and other writing tasks assigned during the academic year, and another asks if they prepared at least two drafts of papers before submitting them to their instructors. Such questions have major limitations but nonetheless might be added to library outputs describing the amount of use of electronic and other resources. In our opinion, the two most important questions for librarians to consider relate to whether students would go to this institution if they started college "over again" and whether they began college at this institution. Both questions provide a context for studies of library value and types of library use.

The Community College Survey of Student Engagement (CCSSE; www.ccsse .org/aboutsurvey/aboutsurvey.cfm), similar to the NSSE, focuses on respondents' college experiences. The survey asks about the amount of reading and writing students did, but there is no mention of libraries. To make such a survey relevant to libraries, there needs to be a portrayal of students beginning their freshman year and a linkage of that evidence to their use of the library and the contribution that the library makes to outcomes assessment. However, such a study is complex and unlikely to be undertaken.[10]

Although it does not focus on the library, the Beginning College Survey of Student Engagement (BCSSE; http://bcsse.iub.edu/) provides self-reports of high school experiences (e.g., writing and reading), expectations for the first year of college (e.g., hours studying), collaborative learning, perceived academic preparedness, academic perseverance, expected academic difficulty, learning strategies, and more. The survey asks respondents about their last year of high school and the number of papers, reports, and other writing tasks completed, the length of those works, and the number of hours spent doing assigned readings. Turning to the upcoming year in college, respondents are asked to reflect on the number of writing tasks and the number of pages they expect to complete, whether they expect to produce two or more drafts of papers and assignments before turning them in, and the importance of "learning support services"; the library is not specifically mentioned.

The College Senior Survey (CSS; www.heri.ucla.edu/cssoverview.php) mentions the library and its use for research and homework as well as for its electronic resources. Other questions query seniors about their perceptions of their college experiences and expectations moving forward. They also rate their satisfaction with those experiences; however, the scale likely differs from ones most commonly used to measure satisfaction. Further, there is no portrayal of the customer in terms of the gaps model (see chapter 4).

In summary, except for the CSS, none of these instruments, as currently constructed, specifically mentions libraries and their services. As a result, the surveys only provide general self-reports, some of which are highly speculative, and they do not document actual changes in student knowledge, abilities, skills, and habits of mind. Perhaps in combination with the BCSSE, institutional researchers can gain snapshots of student perceptions as they enter college and as they graduate.

VALUE OF THE LIBRARY TO ITS COMMUNITY

Value, in part, might be defined as the worth of a service or product in terms of the organizational, operational, and financial benefits to customers.[11] To them, all library services, whether delivered electronically or in the physical library, have value and a cost. That cost might refer to the time and effort to use the library or any out-of-pocket expenses incurred in getting there. Anyone would expect the benefits to exceed the costs and for the visit to be worth the time. As discussed in chapter 2 and in *Getting Started with Evaluation*,[12] return on investment (ROI), or value for money, is part of the overall picture concerning the value of a library. Value can be estimated using a combination of quantitative measures (including return on investment) as well as the intangible values (which are often discussed using qualitative measures). ROI complements other quantitative and qualitative measures concerning value so that the public library that can make the case to stakeholders and help sustain support and funding in the future. Further, it results in a statement such as "the library returns $3.34 for every $1.00 spent."

These quantifiable benefits are related to the library's direct services, for which the library tracks usage data and for which a defensible methodology can be employed to determine their value. Quantifiable benefits include the circulation of library collections and the use of a wide range of library services, including computers, trainings, programming, and other specialized services. The San Francisco Public Library (SFPL) estimated the value of most of these services by determining the market cost of a comparable service or other means of acquiring the same benefit. This market value was then multiplied by the number of uses by SFPL patrons in the 2005–2006 fiscal year. The total value of these benefits for the 2005–2006 fiscal year ranged from $87 million to $207 million.[13]

To make the findings more meaningful, they might be combined with an illustration such as figure 8.1, which identifies an array of qualitative and quantitative benefits associated with community use of the library. These benefits might shape future discussions of outcomes or impacts. The critical feature is to move the discussion of value from a focus on collections to one centered on "services supported by staff expertise that results in value for users."[14]

Social return on investment builds upon cost-benefit analysis, but it is designed to inform the practical decision making on value for users. By contrast, cost-benefit analysis, a technique rooted in social science, enables funders to determine whether their investment or grant is economically efficient. Table 8.1 is an example of social return on investment for an academic library. Using it, students can compare the value listed to the amount of their tuition and see the overall value of the library. They may want to calculate the value based on their own use patterns.

FIGURE 8.1 **QUALITATIVE AND QUANTITATIVE BENEFITS**

Quantifiable Benefits	**Qualitative Benefits**
» Materials (books, magazines, DVDs, CDs & other) » Research tools, databases » Research assistance » Public access computers, WiFi network, DVD & CD stations » Events, programs, exhibits » Senior bookmobile » Assistive technology	» Indirect benefits created by access to information
BUSINESS & JOB SEEKING » Reference & circulating materials » Assistance & reference support » Advanced training, business planning, resume support » Electronic databases & other technology	» Job creation » Career enhancement » Business development & long-term success » Enhancements to San Francisco tax base
» Children & teen materials » Children's book mobile » Electronic databases » Public access computers » Children's programming » Educational assistance: homework help, SAT	» Contributions to early literacy and school readiness » Broader access to materials for students » Safe study & social space for youth » Supplements to SFUSD library service
» Meeting space » Affinity centers » Events, programs, exhibits » Reference services & training » Public computing & training » Foreign language materials & training » Book donations	» Community building & function as a gathering place/"Third Place" » Contributions to social support network for San Francisco's most vulnerable » Immigrant support
» Branch celebrations & community events » Exhibits	» Contributions to San Francisco as a knowledge-oriented city » Contributions to city-side identity » Neighborhood vitality & redevelopment » Role in defining neighborhoods » Preservation of local history

Based on: Friends of the San Francisco Public Library, "Providing for Knowledge, Growth, and Prosperity: A Benefit Study of the San Francisco Public Library," http://sfpl.org/pdf/about/commission/berkstudysummary.pdf. Reprinted with permission.

Public library managers might substitute the categories in the table with, for instance, the number of

- » Books borrowed
- » Magazines borrowed
- » DVDs borrowed
- » Books on CD borrowed
- » Music CDs borrowed
- » Digital media downloaded
- » Magazines/newspapers used in library
- » Hours of library computer use
- » Hours of Wi-Fi use in library
- » Hours of meeting room use

- » Hours of online database use from home
- » Hours of live homework help use
- » Children's storytimes and programs attended
- » Technology programs attended
- » Teen programs attended
- » Adult lectures and programs attended
- » Reference questions asked[15]

TABLE 8.1 STUDENT RETURN ON INVESTMENT*

Service	What You Can Do During the Academic Year	Value of the Service for the Academic Year 2012–2013 (August 2012 to May 2013)
Study in the library	Study in the library for 60 minutes during the academic year	$111.02
Ask a question of reference staff	Ask one reference question as well as use two research guides	$21.09
Use the reference collection	Consult one print reference book	$93.47
Access and download full- text scholarly articles	Download 12 articles averaging five pages per article	$120.00
Use the library's proxy server to access and download full-text articles while at home or while at work	Save two trips to the library and two gallons of gas	$6.60
Borrow books from the circulating collection	Borrow two books	$35.08
Borrow books from another library	Borrow one book rather than buying it	$38.83
Borrow a DVD for a course or entertainment	Borrow one video	$3.00
Borrow a laptop computer	Borrow a library laptop once	$10.00
Use a library desktop computer to search for information	Use a library desktop computer once	$10.00

TOTAL VALUE DURING THE ACADEMIC YEAR $449.09**

*Source: University of West Florida Libraries, "Student Return on Investment," http://libguides.uwf.edu/content.php?pid=188487&sid=2183215.
**In this academic year, a full-time student paid about $336 of his or her tuition to support the libraries.

Both of the data services, ACRL*Metrics* and PLA*metrics*, contain data elements that might be selected to demonstrate value. However, the list is probably too long, and it should be reviewed against the story managers want to tell. Which data elements are most important to them and the emerging story? As cautioned in chapter 4, managers should not select the data elements without having a rationale for each one and for how, collectively, they tell an important story about the library's contribution. As well, libraries likely differ in the data elements they want to use to characterize value, and some libraries may not have provided data for certain data elements. At the same time, the data elements that have broader institutional or broader organizational relevance merit consideration.[16] Still, as academic library managers engage in a study of ROI, they might want to use multiple methods of data collection as well as to study the institutional value of library resources from a faculty perspective, such as Denise Pana, Gabrielle Wiersma, Leslie Williams, and Yem S. Fong did at the University of Colorado, Boulder. They combined ROI with a cost-benefit analysis, a citation study of journal articles written by faculty, and qualitative methods such as in-person interviews.[17]

CONCLUDING THOUGHTS

Traditionally libraries have collected and reported metrics based on inputs and outputs, as well as throughputs that characterize cost-benefit and cost-effectiveness and efficiency. Clearly, such metrics are the focus of ACRL*Metrics* and PLA*metrics*. Now institutions and others are asking libraries to refocus some of their efforts on outcomes. Outcomes can

>> be a powerful tool for communicating program and service benefits to the community;
>> be a powerful tool for demonstrating accountability and justifying funding needs to funders and resource allocators;
>> be a tool for building partnerships and promoting community collaborations;
>> help determine which programs and services should be expanded or replicated; and
>> be a tool for singling out exemplary programs and services for recognition.[18]

The IPEDS data set, which focuses on institutions, offers selected insights into outcomes such as graduation rate. As more data sets report such outcomes and as efforts to compare student learning outcomes across programs and institutions emerge, additional data sets will likely come into existence, and academic library managers might add them to the collection of metrics from ACRL*Metrics*. Public library managers can do the same for summer reading programs and measure the library's impact on the lives of those it serves. Still, such studies of impact are in their infancy.

EXERCISES

Answers to the following questions are in the "Appendix" at the back of the book. We encourage different members of a library staff to work on the exercises together and to discuss the results. Managers might also participate in that discussion. As customer satisfaction is often viewed as a key output comparable across organizations and over time, we also encourage readers to review chapter 6 of our *Getting Started with Evaluation* (ALA, 2014) and to do the exercises concluding that chapter.

QUESTION 1 From the IPEDS survey data, construct a story showing the contribution of the library to institution- or program-level learning. What evidence do you include, and how *good* is that evidence? (Note: It is easy to focus on the institution, rather than the program, level given the focus of the IPEDS data.) The University of West Florida Libraries, for instance, uses the following list of outputs: students studying in the library; borrowing books, e-books, DVDs, and laptops; students or faculty members asking reference questions or meeting with reference librarians for individual research consultations; conducting library instruction sessions; and students or faculty members using subscription databases when off campus (see http://libguides.uwf.edu/content .php?pid=188487&sid=2184200).

QUESTION 2 Looking at the research studies highlighted in chapter 1 in the section "Relevant Studies," what inputs and outputs would you use to make a case for the library's contribution to learning effectiveness? As you answer the question, we ask, "Can you make a compelling case without the inclusion of outcomes?" If not, what outcomes are most important? Further, how might you include them in your analysis?

QUESTION 3 Taking table 8.1 and either ACRL*Metrics* or PLA*metrics*, would you add or substitute any variables to characterize value on a recurring basis for a particular academic or public library? Which ones and why?

QUESTION 4 Using either of the two data services, construct a list of the variables applicable to gauging the return on investment for remote use of the library.

QUESTION 5 If you were to view a particular library from the perspective of the institution, city, or town, which variables would you select for that representation? As a guide you may want to consider the following: "students studying in the library; borrowing books, e-books, DVDs, and laptops; students or faculty members asking reference questions or meeting with reference librarians for individual research consultations; conducting library instruction sessions; and students or faculty members using subscription databases when off-campus" (see University of West Florida Libraries, "Institutional Return on Investment," http://libguides.uwf.edu/content .php?pid=188487&sid=2184200).

QUESTION 6 Turning to figure 8.1, would you add or substitute benefits for a public library? Does PLA*metrics* provide variables meaningful to documenting benefit?

QUESTION 7 Using the same figure, construct a figure applicable to an academic library. Does ACRL*Metrics* provide variables meaningful to documenting benefit?

Notes

1. Institute of Museum and Library Services, "Outcomes Based Evaluation," www.imls.gov/applicants/basics.aspx.

2. See Keith Curry Lance, Nicolle O. Steffen, Rochelle Logan, Marcia J. Rodney, Suzanne Kaller, Christie M. Koontz, and Dean K. Jue, *Counting on Results: New Tools for Outcome-Based Evaluation of Public Libraries* (Aurora, CO: Bibliographical Center for Research, 2001), www.lrs.org/documents/cor/CoR_FullFinalReport.pdf; see also Peter Hernon, Robert E. Dugan, and Danuta A. Nitecki, *Engaging in Evaluation and Assessment Research* (Santa Barbara, CA: Libraries Unlimited, 2011), 85–92.

3. See, for instance, "Levels of Comprehension," http://academic.cuesta.edu/acasupp/as/303.htm.

4. See, for example, Association of College and Research Libraries, *Information Literacy Competency Standards for Higher Education* (Chicago: American Library Association, 2000), www.ala.org/acrl/sites/ala.org.acrl/files/content/standards/standards.pdf.

5. Data collected "for award levels ranging from postsecondary certificates of less than one year to doctoral degrees include degree completions by level and other formal awards by length of program, by race/ethnicity and gender of recipient, and by program (6-digit CIP code). Note that, in 2001, IPEDS began collecting information on the number of students receiving degrees with double majors by 6-digit CIP code (for the second major) and by race/ethnicity and gender of recipient." Source: U.S. Department of Education, Institute of Education Sciences, National Center for Education Statistics, "IPEDS Survey Components and Data Collection Cycle," http://nces.ed.gov/ipeds/resource/survey_components.asp#surveycomponents.

6. Data collected regarding "federal grants, state and local government grants, institutional grants, and loans include the number of students receiving each type of financial assistance and the average amount received by type of aid. Note that these data are displayed on the College Navigator website. In addition, data are collected for the calculation of average net price, in accordance with the Higher Education Opportunity Act of 2008." Source: U.S. Department of Education, Institute of Education Sciences, National Center for Education Statistics, "IPEDS Survey Components and Data Collection Cycle," http://nces.ed.gov/ipeds/resource/survey_components.asp#surveycomponents.

7. Data collected "for full-time, first-time degree and certificate-seeking undergraduate students include the number of students entering the institution as full-time, first-time degree or certificate-seeking students in a particular year (cohort), by race/ethnicity and gender; the number of students completing their program within a time period equal to one and a half times (150%) the normal period of time, and the number of students who transferred to other institutions." Source: U.S. Department of Education, Institute of Education Sciences, National Center for Education Statistics, "IPEDS Survey Components and Data Collection Cycle," http://nces.ed.gov/ipeds/resource/survey_components.asp#surveycomponents.

8. Data are collected for "full-time, first-time, degree- and certificate-seeking undergraduate students. Numbers of students who completed within their program's normal time to completion, 150% of normal time, and 200% of normal time are used to calculate the graduation rates." Source: U.S. Department of Education, Institute of Education Sciences, National Center for Education Statistics, "IPEDS Survey Components and Data Collection Cycle," http://nces.ed.gov/ipeds/resource/survey_components.asp#surveycomponents.

9. National Survey of Student Engagement, "Survey Instrument," http://nsse.iub.edu/html/survey_instruments.cfm. It merits mention that "new in 2013, NSSE participating institutions may append up to two topical modules—short sets of questions on designated topics such as academic advising, civic engagement, experiences with diversity, technology, and writing."

10. A better approach is to replicate some of the research discussed in Nancy Fried Foster and Susan Gibbons, eds., *Studying Students: The Undergraduate Research Project at the University of Rochester* (Chicago: Association of College and Research Libraries, 2007). Such research, however, does not apply to outcomes assessment.

11. Peter Hernon, Robert E. Dugan, and Joseph R. Matthews, *Getting Started with Evaluation* (Chicago: American Library Association, 2014).

12. Hernon, Dugan, and Matthews, *Getting Started with Evaluation*, chapters 8 and 9. These chapters provide a detailed context for this section.

13. Friends of the San Francisco Public Library, "Providing for Knowledge, Growth, and Prosperity: A Benefit Study of the San Francisco Public Library," http://sfpl.org/pdf/about/commission/berkstudysummary.pdf.

14. James G. Neal, "Stop the Madness: The Insanity of ROI and the Need for New Qualitative Measures of Academic Library Success," ACRL Conference, Philadelphia, PA, March 30–April 2, 2011, 429, http://s4.goeshow.com/acrl/national/2011/client_uploads/handouts/stop_the_madness1.pdf. Neal also maintains that academic libraries should engage in entrepreneurial activities as they expand the "interest in business operations to create new income streams for the organization, to learn through these activities, and to apply these lessons to library programs. The objectives also aim to secure expanded visibility in the national library and information technology communities, and to increase credibility in the university, where the tradition for such activities in the academic divisions is established" (428).

15. Pasadena Public Library, "What Is Your Library Worth? Value of Library Services," http://cityofpasadena.net/library/about_the_library/value_calculator/. Note that this calculator focuses on monthly use. See also Library Research Service, "Return on Investment for Public Libraries," www.lrs.org/data-tools/public-libraries/return-on-investment/.

16. See, for instance, Krista M. Soria, "Factors Predicting the Importance of Libraries and Research Activities for Undergraduates," *Journal of Academic Librarianship* 39, no. 6 (November 2013): 464–70. Soria used the results from the Student Experience in the Research University (SERU) survey, developed at the Center for Studies in Higher Education, University of California, Berkeley. SERU asks undergraduates to reflect on their educational experience, including how the library contributes to that experience. Through the application of factor analysis, Soria developed additional variables for the academic engagement of students, library and research skills, satisfaction with libraries and research opportunities, and interaction with faculty. Although key terms were not defined in SERU and the response rate was only 38.1 percent, the study underscores the importance of looking at libraries from an institutional perspective and the perceived prestige of "a world-class university library" and of "a university with world-class researchers" (468).

17. Denise Pana, Gabrielle Wiersma, Leslie Williams, and Yem S. Fong, "More Than a Number: Unexpected Benefits of Return on Investment Analysis," *Journal of Academic Librarianship* 39, no. 6 (November 2013): 566–72. Other library managers might want to expand the citation analysis beyond just journal articles.

18. Peggy D. Rudd, "Documenting the Difference: Demonstrating the Value of Libraries through Outcome Measurement," in *Perspectives on Outcome Based Evaluation for Libraries and Museums* (Washington, DC: Institute of Museum and Library Services, n.d.), 20.

9

Use

LIBRARIES, AS ACCOUNTABLE ORGANIZATIONS, report information to their multiplicity of stakeholders about their ongoing efforts to meet community needs by providing high-quality services and adding value to the lives of their users. As discussed in the previous chapter, librarians want to measure impacts and outcomes and to learn how services and programs produce beneficial changes in the skills, knowledge, behavior, attitudes, and status or life conditions of library users. Identifying and measuring impacts and outcomes are critical for the library; so, too, are use metrics based on data libraries apply during their efforts to inform planning and decision making as part of a culture of assessment, evaluation, and continuous improvement.

Library use, as characterized by transaction and other output metrics, depends on users undertaking an activity that the library creates or supports. To do so, they must first have, minimally, physical or virtual access to library services and programs. Physical access is directly related to the hours when the library is open, whereas virtual access requires that resources be available even when the physical library is closed. Whether library services are available physically or virtually, accessibility is based on inputs as used by the library through its infrastructure (facilities, staff, collections, and technology) to provide services and programs. For facilities, inputs focus on the number of square feet available, user spaces (e.g., reading areas), and seating. Library staff, as measured in full-time equivalents (FTE), classified by type (professional and support staff), and often organized by function (public, technical, or administrative services), work within the facility to conduct library functions and supportive activities, such as ordering and processing books to meet user needs and managing virtual library services. Collections exist in a multiplicity of formats and are housed in or licensed by the library. They are usually described by the number of volumes, by subject, by types (e.g., reference and

129

government documents), and by formats (e.g., print and DVD), and collections include such characteristics as strengths (e.g., a strong fiction collection; a weak science collection) and age (e.g., current or dated). And, finally, technology includes the devices and applications available for users within the library facility and the means of providing access to virtual resources, such as websites and online catalogs. Data can be generated, compiled, and studied as the components of the infrastructure are used. The discussion of usage data is the focus of this chapter.

FACILITIES USE

Many of the functions undertaken to provide and maintain library services to users, including virtual services, occur in the library's facilities. Characteristics that describe the physical facility include total square feet. If possible, the library should know both the gross square feet as well as the net assignable square feet. A useful input metric is the square feet assigned to public use. Then, a public square foot per capita of service population can be calculated; when placed on a ten- or twenty-year trend line, this output may help illustrate the need for an addition or a new library facility as population grows. Another useful input metric concerns user seating. Information about user seating should be as granular as possible. For example, managers should determine the number of seats at fixed equipment (e.g., computers or microfilm machines) and the number not situated at equipment. Knowing how many seats are at tables, at carrels, in individual or group rooms, and in reading areas is also useful, as is differentiating between soft seating (lounge) and hard seats (at tables). Seats assigned to user areas, such as the reference or children's area, should also be recorded. Another useful trend metric is to calculate the ratio of seats to the service population (e.g., there are ten seats for every one thousand in the service population) or the percentage of the service population that can sit in the library concurrently (e.g., the library can seat 5 percent of the service population). Because of technology, two facility characteristics are (1) the number of user-available electrical receptacles for users to recharge their devices, and (2) the number of user-available wired network jacks so users can plug their laptops into a faster-than-wireless wired network.

Usage information about the facility also includes area spaces and seats. If there are seats in a functional area, you may calculate utilization. For example, "of the twenty soft seats in the new books area, half are used more than 50 percent of the time each weekday. This area occasionally reaches 100 percent of seating capacity, but it only happens on Tuesdays during the hour before the adult reading club convenes." Another useful statistic notes that "the three seats at the microform machines are never used concurrently. In fact, there is never more than one person in the microforms area at a time unless he or she is accompanied by a friend who is not using the microfilm or the readers."

Examples of Use Studies about Facilities

Use studies concerning facilities are commonly conducted on the adequacy of the space from the perspective of the library user. Is space adequately allocated for use for the varieties of ways users need to be able to work? For example, a study of academic library space examined how "soft spaces" that are not in the stacks and computer labs, but include carrels, tables, soft chairs, and study rooms, are used. Each physical area was observed over months, and data were entered into a database about the observation time (time of day, day of week, week of semester, and by semester); the observed numbers of users as individuals, in groups, and numbers of groups; and numbers of laptop users. The study found that soft spaces are used for studying, that studying increases throughout the semester, and that the most-preferred study space, popular with both individuals and groups, is a study room. Some of the areas with the lowest laptop use were those lacking electrical outlets, such as lounge seating and carrels.[1] A public library study found that young adults need spaces that reflect their identity and that they can call their own (symbolic ownership); spaces to be with friends (gathering places); spaces to be alone; spaces that are accessible; and spaces that are unsupervised yet safe.[2]

Another topic for facility use studies is to determine whether there is adequate square footage to support library functions. For example, "Is there enough floor space for the stacks needed for shelving materials?" and "Is there an area for displaying new books?" Another study might investigate whether appropriate seating options are available for the varieties of ways users want to be able to use the library, such as to read popular magazines and newspapers or to use personal laptops to take notes from reference materials or local archival sources.

A study might observe how users navigate the library. When they enter the facility, they are confronted by at least two information problems: the information problem one hopes to address using library resources and the spatial information problem of trying to locate those resources that will help solve the information problem. *Wayfinding* information systems contain the information necessary to make and execute decisions along a route, such as architectural cues, linearly arranged signage, and floor plans. Although most libraries depend on signage to help the user successfully navigate the facility, signage is only one component of a facility's spatial information system, and, in fact, signage cannot compensate for a confusing physical layout.[3]

A landmark facility study of new and renovated academic library facilities from 1995 to 2002 found that building improvements have a greater overall impact on basic facility use (gate count) than on circulation, reference transaction volume, and in-house collection use. Students use new and improved libraries at levels greater than their use of pre-construction/-renovation project library facilities. A high-quality building makes a difference, and students continue to use an improved facility even after the novelty of a new library has worn off. Harold B. Shill and Shawn Tonner identify a number of specific facility attributes associated with post-project usage gains, including the number of wired network ports; percentage of seats with wired network access; number and quality of public access computers; quality of the library instruction lab; quality of natural lighting; quality of user work spaces; quality of the layout (including location of service points); and quality of overall facility ambience. They conclude that, despite the anticipated decline in library facility use as libraries increase the availability of resources remotely through the Internet, students will use a comfortable, well-equipped library.[4]

SELECTED SERVICES USE

The facility enables users to access directly library services and resources that the library staff provide. Since the ubiquitous availability of the Internet as a communication means, access has also come to include the "around-the-clock-from-anywhere-on-the-planet" availability of electronic resources licensed or otherwise provided through the library.

The library's capacity to provide access to services through inputs depends on at least three factors. Direct access to services and resources available in the library facility depends on the facility being open so that users can enter. A closed library provides few, if any, face-to-face services. Another dependent factor is the availability of staff to offer and perform library functions and services for users. For users, the most visible staff are those at public service desks providing direct user services. Although not always as visible as staff in public services, staff in technical, technology, and administrative services also support library services and functions. The availability of virtual library services depends on the library's website and its integrated library system. Virtual services include searching library-licensed databases to find and retrieve content; renewing books; placing holds on items users wish to borrow; reviewing information about the library, such as hours open; and finding help available, such as answers to frequently asked questions or librarian-generated guides that help users navigate the virtual library and its content.

Librarians want to know how people use the library when it is open, the services provided through the library staff, and virtual library services. This section focuses on selected services and their use that are not addressed elsewhere in this chapter.

Library stakeholders want to know about the library's hours and visitors. Hours open and library entrances are two use metrics related to the availability of library services. How many hours is the library open during the week, and when is it open? It is assumed that, as long as the library is physically open, services are available. Box 9.1 depicts library visits use data. Granular data can also be applied to calculate the average number of visitors per hour, which helps managers plan when to staff public service desks and with what classification of staff.

Staff provide direct and indirect services. There are two important numbers to know. First is the total staff stated as full-time equivalents (FTE), tracked by the

BOX 9.1 LIBRARY VISITS USE DATA

The number of gate counts for a fiscal year

» Knowing this number can then yield the number of library visits per capita of the service population, which can be graphed on a trend line over time (e.g., ten years) to review changes in library visits per capita.

If possible, the number of gate counts by

» Hour of the day	» Week of the month
» Day of the week	» Month of the year

Apply the granular data from gate counts to determine the busiest

» Hour of the day	» Week of the month
» Day of the week	» Month of the year

month and then summed for the fiscal year. Second is the number of hours that public service desks are staffed during each week and by whom, such as professional librarians or support staff, summed monthly and for the fiscal year. (Chapter 5 discusses library staffing.)

Selected services provided by staff and consumed by library users include reference transactions, programs, presentations, and library instruction sessions. Reference transactions include the number of questions and the number answered as well as the means by which the questions were asked and answered:

» Face-to-face
» Mail (physical)
» Telephone
» Electronic, further delineated by chat, text message, and e-mail

Tracking the means by which users ask a question and the means used to answer can provide a ratio of electronic reference transactions to total reference transactions. Tracking the number of questions asked and answered can also yield the number of reference questions asked per capita of the service population as well as the number answered. If the reference questions asked and answered are captured daily and summed weekly and monthly, managers learn the number of questions asked and answered in a typical week or month, and they can calculate the number by week or month per capita of the service population. Such use data would be easy to graph for identifying and reviewing trends.

If possible, libraries should try to keep track of how long it takes to answer a reference question. Tracking might be done as part of two ranges: it took less than (or longer than) twenty minutes. Those taking longer than twenty minutes might be characterized as research consultations.

Library services include programs, presentations, and library instruction. Programs and presentations should exclude library instruction and may involve informative, educational, or entertainment events for which an audience is invited and attends. Another type is presentations to groups, such as orientations or tours of the library that are not a performance, lecture, or speech. The data collected for programs and presentations, and for presentations to groups, are the same, but the two types of programs/presentations should be separated for analysis and reporting:

» Programs and presentations (excluding library instruction) and
   presentations to groups (e.g., orientations, library tours)
   - Number of programs or presentations conducted
   - Number of attendees

In addition to the number of programs or presentations undertaken, the data collected can be used to provide the average number of attendees per program or presentation and the attendance per capita of the service population per program or presentation. These per capita figures may be graphed as a trend over time for review.

Although the basic use data collected for library instruction sessions are the same as those for programs and presentations, the data application differs if the library aligns learning objectives and outcomes to each session conducted. The library should collect the number of library instruction sessions conducted and the number of participants at each session. The description for each session should include the session's characteristics (e.g., demonstrated literature research methods for a chemistry course), learning objectives, and the learning outcomes if measured (e.g., use of a one-minute paper).[5] The ratio of the number of participants attending these instruction sessions can be calculated in relation to the population by academic semester and by fiscal year for reporting and for later graphing on a trend line to reveal changes over time.

The use of the library's virtual services may be increasing annually. Web-based virtual services depend on staff to provide locally relevant content, such as information about the library; to make certain that catalog information is accurate and that help information is available; and to manage and ensure reliable access to many of the vendor-licensed electronic resources made available. Use data to collect about and from the library's website include

- » Website visits
    - Time of day
    - Day of the week
    - Month of the year
    - Unique visitors
- » Number and use of library's web-based forms
- » Number of pages viewed
- » Number of library-created help guides, tutorials, and orientations viewed and downloaded

Knowing the number of website visits can yield the website visits per capita for the service population, which, over time, can be graphed as a trend line for analysis and reporting. Depending on the granularity of the use data collected about such visits, the library might identify and report on the average number of website visits per hour, day, week, and month.

Examples of Use Studies about Service

Librarians want to know about use of the library and its services and resources. One survey asked users about their frequency of library visits, their purpose for visiting the library, the information sources and services they frequently consulted and used, and their satisfaction level with the library collections and services. The findings reported how often users visited the library (8 percent surveyed visited the library monthly; 28 percent made daily visits), how much time they spent in the facility (40 percent of the visitors stayed longer than three hours), why users visited (to borrow or return books), what services they used (circulation, followed by the public computer workstations), and resources used (over 60 percent used reference sources).[6]

An academic library study found that the higher the gate count, the higher the number of reference transactions. The findings also indicated that spending more on electronic resources leads to an increase rather than a decrease in numbers of reference transactions in a typical week recorded.[7]

Libraries might also gauge the adequacy of access to the facility by surveying users about desired hours of operation. Unfortunately, many, if not most, respondents will state that the library should be open 24/7/365 as a matter of personal convenience because they pay for it. However, that expectation may be tempered by providing users with options for ranges of hours (e.g., Mondays from 9 a.m. to 9 p.m. or from 10 a.m. to 10 p.m.) each day for feedback. Another useful study would find the length of time spent by users in the library. Comments could lead to finding out why they leave; for example, time spent may be limited to the time available on a parking meter. A third study would measure average user wait time in lines. The user's perception of being in line too long may lead the library to introduce express lanes or other queuing considerations. Another study would determine the number of rings before a staff member answers a telephone or the time between an inquiry via chat or a text message and the library's response.

Several studies have examined public service staffing and staffing levels. Managers may want to determine the hours needed for staffing branch and central library facilities. A study reported that the number of hours of operation was the most important factor in determining staffing levels, followed by expected user traffic and historic usage figures, such as reference transactions.[8] Another set of studies analyzed the content of site-based reference questions recorded hourly and daily, and it found three categories of questions being asked (directional, reference, and technical) for queries made in-person, by telephone, and by e-mail.[9] Using these data better informs staffing of the reference desk, including how many staff are needed on the desk and the classification of staff—for example, when should professional librarians or support staff be on the desk, when are two public service staff members needed, and are there times when the reference desk can be unstaffed.

Applying the Examples

Taking one of the studies highlighted in the previous section,[10] we can explore whether the finding that the higher the gate count, the higher the number of reference transactions applies to a selected local academic library. Figure 9.1 graphs five years of compiled data of gate counts and reference transactions from the library's statistical management information system. This figure suggests that, while gate counts increased during three of the fiscal years represented in the graph, reference transactions decreased.

FIGURE 9.1 **COMPARISON OF GATE COUNTS TO THE NUMBER OF REFERENCE TRANSACTIONS**

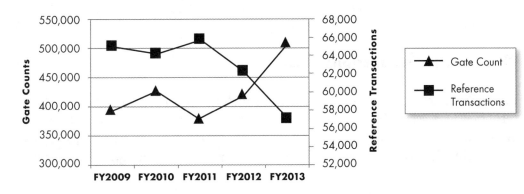

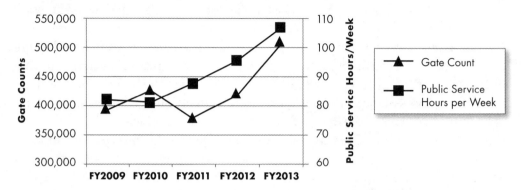

FIGURE 9.2 **COMPARISON OF GATE COUNTS TO PUBLIC SERVICE HOURS PER WEEK**

Figure 9.2 compares gate counts to public service hours open per week. Although this figure does not demonstrate a causal relationship, it is one means of reviewing readily available local usage data.

COLLECTIONS USE

Collections have been, and continue to be, the subject of numerous usage metrics, studies, and reports. Libraries now give collections closer attention as the multiplicity of information formats increases and the transition from print to electronic formats accelerates. Collections use formerly centered primarily on print materials—namely, on books and serials. Media were added with audio recordings (from long-playing albums and reel-to-reel tapes to 8-tracks to cassettes to CDs to MP3s), and print books and serials have been joined by microforms, visual media (from 8 mm to Beta to VHS to DVD to Blu-ray), e-books, and e-journals. Managers want to know what is being used and how much is being used and not being used. In addition to formats, they want to know about the local use of the types of collections, such as reference and special collections, and about subject collections, such as government documents and languages.

This section discusses the metrics of collection use through physical and virtual transactions. Several of the inputs concerning collections are straightforward: the collection as stated in size, by type, and by formats. One may state that a collection is strong in certain subject areas because of a high number of holdings. It is more difficult, however, to proclaim strength or make other assertions about the quality of the collections.

Physical Use Transactions

Physical use transactions about collections include circulation, reserves, and interlibrary loan. Many library use reports categorize these transactions as services. However, these borrowing data actually capture the counts of collections use by users. Libraries are encouraged to separate circulation transactions from reserve transactions. The data may be combined for reporting, but separating circulation from reserves improves use analysis. Box 9.2 summarizes circulation transactions counts. Possessing these transactions data helps managers to calculate

- » Circulation transactions per capita of the service population for each hour, day, and month (can be graphed over time as a trend line)
- » Number of times each item circulated (average number of transactions per item)
  - – Volumes circulated to total volumes available (collection turnover)
  - – Total number of circulations within a subject area divided by total number of holdings in that subject area
- » Ratio of new books purchased in a fiscal year and how often they are used (book use rate)
- » In-library information resources use as a percentage of total circulation

Box 9.3 covers the use of materials on reserve, which is similar to circulation transactions (many libraries combine the use counts). Possessing these transactions data helps the library to calculate

- » Reserves transactions per capita of the service population for each month (can be graphed over time as a trend line)
- » Number of times each reserve item circulated (average number of transactions per item)
  - – Volumes circulated to total volumes available (collection turnover)
  - – Total number of reserves transactions within a subject area divided by total number of holdings in that subject area

BOX 9.2 **CIRCULATION TRANSACTIONS COUNTS**

- » Total by the hour, day, and month
- » Total by calendar/academic/fiscal year (can be graphed over time as a trend line)
- » Average per hour open
- » Average per day open
- » Average per month
- » Initial transactions
- » Renewals
- » By format (e.g., print monograph, video, CD)

- » Books purchased that fiscal year
- » Total by user status (e.g., child, young adult, adult, senior citizen, undergraduate student, faculty, graduate student, and institutional staff)
- » Holds placed by users on items in circulation
- » In-library use of material (if counted)
  - – Books
  - – Journals
  - – Other

BOX 9.3 **USE OF MATERIALS ON RESERVE**

- » Total by the hour, day, and month
- » Total by calendar/academic/fiscal year (can be graphed over time as a trend line)
- » Average per hour open
- » Average per day open
- » Average per month

- » Initial transactions
- » Renewals
- » By format (e.g., print monograph, video, CD)
- » Total by user status (e.g., child, young adult, adult, senior citizen, undergraduate student, faculty, graduate student, and institutional staff)

EXAMPLE 9.1 **REVIEWING CIRCULATION TRANSACTIONS PER CAPITA–FIVE-YEAR TREND ANALYSIS**

STEP 1 Log on to PLA*metrics*.

STEP 2 Click on the Local tab and on the Report tab.

STEP 3 Click the Add button to create a new report.

STEP 4 Select "PLDS" as the Collection, and then type in a descriptive Report Name, and a description of the report. Add a Title if desired. Then, click the Save as New Report button.

STEP 5 Under Report Settings at the top, select the latest period for the report; in this case, we selected FY2011.

STEP 6 We want to run a trend. Therefore, as the Report Type, select "Trend/PI" for a trend line or "Graph/PI" for a bar chart presentation.

STEP 7 When Trend/PI or Graph/PI is selected, a Start Period box appears next to Period in the Report Settings. We want to look at five years and, therefore, select FY2007 as the start period.

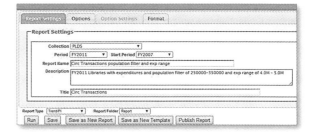

STEP 8 We can now select the indicators we want to include in the report. Return to the indicators box and select "Total Annual Circulation" and "Circulation Per Capita." To provide financial context to the circulation indicators, also select "Operating Expenditures Per Capita." This would be a good time to click on the Save button.

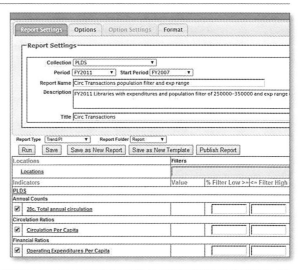

STEP 9a (Do either this step or step 9b.) Once you have selected one or more indicators, the Locations function appears. If you have saved a set of benchmarking partners, click Locations and select the filter you designated. If you have not set up the Locations filter, then go to Locations and select all of the libraries you wish to use as benchmarking partners. Provide a Filter Name (e.g., Benchmarking Partners), and click on the Apply button to save this group. Now this group of libraries will always be available for you to choose as a Locations filter.

STEP 9b   If you have not designated benchmarking partners, you may want to create a set now. For this example, we selected the indicators from the scrollable box at the bottom for "Population of legal service area" and "Total operating expenditures" to identify the partners. A filter was typed in for both indicators in order to limit the number of partners. For "Population of legal service area," a low filter of 250000 was typed in along with a high filter of 350000. We limited "Total operating expenditures" by applying a low filter of 4000000 ($4 million) and a high filter of 5000000 ($5 million). This would be a good time to click on the Save button.

STEP 10   We used the "Total operating expenditures" as a filter. We do not need the data as a reporting output because we will use "Operating Expenditures Per Capita" for context. Therefore, if you remove the checkmark to the left of the indicator, it will still be used in the calculation but will not appear in the report.

Report Type	Trend/PI ▼	Report Folder	Report ▼	
[Run] [Save] [Save as New Report] [Save as New Template] [Publish Report]				
Locations			Filters	
Locations				
Indicators			Value	% Filter Low >=	<= Filter High
PLDS				
A. GENERAL INFORMATION				
☑ 2.a Population of legal service area				250000	350000
Operating Expenditures				
☐ 24. Total operating expenditures (total of items 20-23)				4000000	5000000
Annual Counts				
☑ 28c. Total annual circulation					
Circulation Ratios				
☑ Circulation Per Capita					
Financial Ratios				
☑ Operating Expenditures Per Capita					

STEP 11   Run the report. The report returned is in table format.

2.a Population of legal service area ⊠	FY2007	FY2008	FY2009	FY2010	FY2011
GASTON-LINCOLN REGIONAL LIBRARY (NO DATA POST 2012)	262,372	272,696	278,447		287,599
MONT CO-NORRISTOWN PUB LIB	287,973	287,973	287,973	287,973	309,099
TULARE COUNTY FREE LIBRARY					332,495
WEST FLORIDA PUBLIC LIBRARY	306,407	306,407	306,407	303,343	303,343
HIGH	306,407	306,407	306,407	303,343	332,495
MEAN	285,584	289,025	290,942	295,658	308,134
MEDIAN	287,973	287,973	287,973	295,658	306,221
LOW	262,372	272,696	278,447	287,973	287,599
LIBRARIES REPORTING	3	3	3	2	4

28c. Total annual circulation ⊠	FY2007	FY2008	FY2009	FY2010	FY2011
GASTON-LINCOLN REGIONAL LIBRARY (NO DATA POST 2012)	1,305,313	1,363,539	1,375,836		1,260,665
MONT CO-NORRISTOWN PUB LIB	930,331	998,710	615,214	584,501	636,387
TULARE COUNTY FREE LIBRARY					555,100
WEST FLORIDA PUBLIC LIBRARY	680,577	747,294	778,052	820,091	
HIGH	1,305,313	1,363,539	1,375,836	820,091	1,260,665
MEAN	972,074	1,036,514	923,034	702,296	817,384
MEDIAN	930,331	998,710	778,052	702,296	636,387
LOW	680,577	747,294	615,214	584,501	555,100
LIBRARIES REPORTING	3	3	3	2	3

Circulation Per Capita ⊠	FY2007	FY2008	FY2009	FY2010	FY2011
GASTON-LINCOLN REGIONAL LIBRARY (NO DATA POST 2012)	4.98	5.00	4.94		4.38
MONT CO-NORRISTOWN PUB LIB	3.23	3.47	2.14	2.03	2.06
TULARE COUNTY FREE LIBRARY					1.67
WEST FLORIDA PUBLIC LIBRARY	2.22	2.44	2.54	2.70	
HIGH	4.98	5.00	4.94	2.70	4.38
MEAN	3.48	3.64	3.21	2.37	2.70
MEDIAN	3.23	3.47	2.54	2.37	2.06
LOW	2.22	2.44	2.14	2.03	1.67
LIBRARIES REPORTING	3	3	3	2	3

STEP 12   Clicking on the graph icon next to the name of the indicator will display a trend line graph. (Note: Trend line graphs are available when eight or fewer libraries are reported; to reduce line congestion, nine or more libraries produce another chart type that is easier to review.) In this chart Gaston-Lincoln Regional Library did not report circulation for FY2010, which disrupted its graph line when it reported for FY2011; Tulare County Free Library only reported circulation for FY2011; and the West Florida Public Library did not report circulation for FY2011.

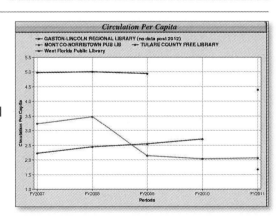

Example 9.1 shows how to review circulation transactions per capita with a public library's benchmarking partners. The example represents a five-year trend analysis.

Interlibrary loan/document delivery use data include the number of items borrowed from another library and the number of items lent to other libraries. The number of items borrowed from another library is an important collections data point as it may reveal weaknesses in the collections owned/leased by the borrowing library. The numbers of items lent to other libraries is an important collections use figure as well and may be a proxy of collection quality if there is a high volume of items lent on one or more subjects or genres.

Box 9.4 reports interlibrary loan totals. Analysis of interlibrary loan usage data includes the number of requests to borrow from other libraries as a percentage of the number of holdings in the specific subject area. If the ratio is high, then the library should consider further collection development through acquisitions in this subject area to reduce the number of interlibrary loan requests. A second interlibrary loan use calculation would be the number of items borrowed from other libraries per capita of the service population.

As an example of reviewing interlibrary loan borrowing and lending use by benchmarking with academic library peers, use ACRL*Metrics* to undertake a five-year trend analysis (see example 9.2).

BOX 9.4 INTERLIBRARY LOAN TOTALS

Items borrowed from other libraries (can be graphed over time as a trend line)
Items loaned to other libraries (can be graphed over time as a trend line)

Requests received from other libraries to borrow

» Total filled	» Total unfilled
– Returnable	– Returnable
– Nonreturnable	– Nonreturnable

Requests sent to other libraries to loan

» Total filled	» Total unfilled
– Returnable	– Returnable
– Nonreturnable	– Nonreturnable

Fill rate (requests filled)

» As lender	» As borrower

Commercial documents delivered

Turnaround time

» As lender	» As borrower

Cost per item to lend
Cost per item to borrow

EXAMPLE 9.2 **INTERLIBRARY LOAN BORROWING AND LENDING USE BY BENCHMARKING WITH ACADEMIC LIBRARY PEERS**

STEP 1   Log on to ACRL*Metrics*.

STEP 2   Click on the Local tab and then the Report tab.

STEP 3   Click the Add button to create a new report.

STEP 4   Select "ACRL" as the Collection, and then type in a descriptive Report Name and a description of the report. Add a Title if desired. Then, click the Save as New Report button.

STEP 5   Under Report Settings at the top, select the latest period for the report; in this case it was FY2012.

STEP 6   We want to run a trend. Therefore, as the Report Type, select "Trend/PI" for a trend line or "Graph/PI" for a bar chart presentation.

STEP 7   When Trend/PI or Graph/PI is selected, a Start Period box appears next to Period in the Report Settings. We want to look at five years and, therefore, select FY2008 as the start period.

STEP 8   We can now select the indicators we want to include in the report. Return to the Indicators box and select "Total Items Loaned (ILL)" and "Total Items Borrowed (ILL)." This would be a good time to click on the Save button.

STEP 9   Once you have selected one or more indicators, the Locations function appears. Most academic institutions already have a select list of peers and aspirants for benchmarking. If you have saved a set of benchmarking partners, click Locations and select the filter you designated. If you have not set up the Locations filter, then go to Locations and select all of the libraries you wish to use as benchmarking partners. Provide a Filter Name (such as Peers), and click on the Apply button to save this group. Now this group of libraries will always be available for you to choose as a Locations filter.

Virtual Use Transactions

A collections search tool is a mechanism used to search for items that may be housed in a library's collections. Many libraries employ two virtual collections search tools: an online catalog and a discovery service. Data are easier to collect

EXAMPLE 9.2 (continued)

STEP 10

The two selected indicators will provide summed data. To facilitate comparing the libraries, "add" the following indicators:

> » ILLs Provided per 1000 Enrolled FT Students
> » ILLs Received per 1000 Enrolled FT Students
> » ILL Loaned per Enrolled FT Students
> » ILL Borrowed per Enrolled FT Student
> » Ratio of Items Loaned to Items Borrowed

Now would be another good time to click on the Save button.

ACRL					
INTERLIBRARY LOANS					
☑	21. Total Items Loaned (ILL)				1	✕
☑	22. Total Items Borrowed (ILL)				2	✕
Output Measures					
☑	ILLs Provided per 1000 Enrolled FT Students				4	✕
☑	ILLs Received Per 1000 Enrolled FT Students				6	✕
Appendix M - Selected Metrics from Library Reports					
☑	Ratio of Items Loaned to Items Borrowed				3	✕
☑	ILL Loaned per Enrolled FT Students				5	✕
☑	ILL Borrowed per Enrolled FT Student				7	✕

STEP 11

Run the report. The report returned is in table format.

Ratio of Items Loaned to Items Borrowed ⊠	2008	2009	2010	2011	2012
East Tennessee State University	0.72	0.32	0.35	0.34	0.57
Indiana State University	1.02	1.36		0.00	1.35
Rowan University	2.88	1.15	0.90	0.97	1.22
Stephen F Austin State University	0.89	0.83	0.97	1.20	1.18
University of Arkansas at Little Rock	1.00	0.99	1.66	0.99	0.81
University of Massachusetts-Lowell	0.90	1.28	1.35	1.11	0.91
University of South Dakota	1.03	0.88	1.03	1.37	1.19
University of West Florida	3.23	2.12	2.02	2.39	2.25
University of West Georgia	1.90	2.54	3.64	4.37	2.08
Valdosta State University	1.04	1.58	0.94	1.07	0.72
Western Carolina University	0.45	1.24		0.57	0.78
Avg	1.37	1.30	1.43	1.31	1.19
Median	1.02	1.24	1.03	1.07	1.18

ILL Loaned per Enrolled FT Students ⊠	2008	2009	2010	2011	2012
East Tennessee State University	1.22	0.69	0.59	0.55	0.65
Indiana State University	0.98	1.34		0.00	0.90
Rowan University	0.52	0.54	0.48	0.39	0.56
Stephen F Austin State University	0.52	0.47	0.46	0.41	0.37
University of Arkansas at Little Rock	0.75	0.67	1.41	0.65	0.68
University of Massachusetts-Lowell	0.82	1.18	0.97	0.78	0.67
University of South Dakota	1.56	1.35	1.35	1.95	1.90
University of West Florida	0.72	1.09	1.32	1.52	1.57
University of West Georgia	0.47	0.00	0.00	0.82	0.49
Valdosta State University	0.57	0.56	0.48	0.31	0.26
Western Carolina University	0.34	1.65	0.00	0.31	1.13
Avg	0.77	0.87	0.71	0.70	0.83
Median	0.72	0.69	0.54	0.55	0.67

ILL Borrowed per Enrolled FT Student ⊠	2008	2009	2010	2011	2012
East Tennessee State University	1.70	2.17	1.67	1.59	1.13
Indiana State University	0.95	0.99		0.00	0.66
Rowan University	0.18	0.47	0.54	0.40	0.46
Stephen F Austin State University	0.58	0.56	0.48	0.34	0.31
University of Arkansas at Little Rock	0.75	0.68	0.85	0.66	0.83
University of Massachusetts-Lowell	0.92	0.92	0.72	0.70	0.75
University of South Dakota	1.52	1.53	1.31	1.43	1.60
University of West Florida	0.22	0.51	0.65	0.63	0.70
University of West Georgia	0.25	0.00	0.00	0.19	0.24
Valdosta State University	0.55	0.36	0.51	0.28	0.36
Western Carolina University	0.77	1.33	0.00	0.54	1.45
Avg	0.76	0.87	0.67	0.62	0.77
Median	0.75	0.68	0.60	0.54	0.70

STEP 12

By clicking on the graph icon next to the name of the indicator, a trend line graph is displayed. (Please note: Trend line graphs are available when eight or fewer libraries are being reported; to reduce line congestion, nine or more libraries produce another chart type, which is easier to review. The number of libraries was reduced for this example to produce a traditional line chart.) Several trend lines are incomplete in this example for those libraries that did not provide data for every fiscal year included in the period.

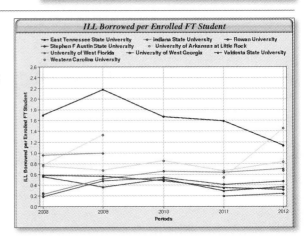

about online catalog use than about the use of its predecessor, the paper-based card catalog. Search data compiled could include the number of author, keyword, subject, and title searches by the hour, day, and month. These data can yield the average number of online catalog searches by the hour, day, and month. Another data point is the number of searches conducted remotely, which yields a ratio of searches conducted internally to searches conducted externally. A benefit of the online catalog is that data can be collected 24/7/365, which will help inform managers about searches when the library is physically closed.

Discovery services are a web scale tool, which creates one large, searchable index of all library databases and catalogs. A user searches the combined index through a simple search box that is coupled with a user interface designed for viewing and interacting with results. Box 9.5 indicates use data generated from discovery tools. Discovery data are usually compiled on a daily and monthly basis.

Measuring the use transactions of electronic resources is becoming increasingly important to public and academic library managers and their library's stakeholders. Public libraries are experiencing an increasing demand for e-books; many

BOX 9.5 **USE DATA GENERATED FROM DISCOVERY TOOLS**

Number of

- » Sessions
- » Searches (there can be multiple searches during each session)
- » Full-text requests
- » PDF full-text document downloads
- » HTML full-text document downloads

- » Image/video requests
- » Audio requests
- » Abstract requests
- » Searches from journal citations to the online catalog for link resolving

BOX 9.6 **USE OUTPUT DATA**

Number of

- » Log-ins to, or sessions with, e-resources (e.g., databases, e-books, and e-journals)
  - – From within the library
  - – From outside the library (remote)
  - – Turnaways

- » Proxy server log-ins to, or sessions with, e-resources
  - – From within the library
  - – From outside the library (remote)
  - – Turnaways

Database use by

» Hour   » Day   » Month

Databases (Number of)

- » Searches conducted (by hour, day, and month if available)
- » Abstracts viewed or downloaded
- » Full-text documents (PDF or HTML) viewed or downloaded

- » Journal titles if available
- » Images viewed or downloaded
- » Audio listened to or downloaded

E-books (Number of)

- » Searches conducted (by hour, day, and month if available)

- » Viewed or downloaded
- » Turnaways

academic libraries expend more funds for electronic resources than for print. Use data are important to explain user needs as well as to justify expenditures. It is important for the library to quantify its electronic inputs, such as the number of databases, and the number of owned or leased e-books and e-journals. Box 9.6 notes use output data of these electronic sources.

Analysis of use data about e-resources could yield

» Log-ins or sessions per capita
» Proxy server log-ins or sessions per capita
» Averages for database use per hour, day, and month
» Averages for full-text documents (PDF or HTML) / images / audio viewed or downloaded per hour, day, and month

Because much of the electronic content is housed outside the library, collecting use data for this content depends on the e-resource providers. Vendors, however, have varying definitions for log-ins, sessions, searches, and content retrieval, which complicates the application of use numbers among providers: one vendor's log-in is another's session. Improving the definitions of use metrics for electronic sources has been an ongoing effort. Fortunately, use data collection is being addressed as COUNTER (Counting Online Usage of Networked Electronic Resources) and SUSHI (Standardized Usage Statistics Harvesting Initiative), which are adopted by e-content providers. COUNTER provides an international, extendible Code of Practice covering journals, databases, books, reference works, and multimedia e-resources that allows the use of online information products and services to be measured in a consistent and compatible way using vendor-generated data. The Code of Practice dictates the exact format for the use reports, sets out expectations for terminology, provides a common set of rules for interpreting use logs, and certifies a content provider's compliance by requiring a formal audit. SUSHI came about after several librarians found that they were spending too much time obtaining COUNTER use data, leaving too little time for the analysis of what was collected. SUSHI enables COUNTER reports to be harvested automatically via a web service. Software running on the library's site (the SUSHI client) can request a COUNTER report from a program running on the content provider's site (SUSHI server).[11]

Examples of Use Studies about Collections

An evaluation of a library's collections can be a useful piece of collections development as it helps library managers understand whether the collections are adequate or what specific subject areas need attention. A range of methods are available to evaluate a library collection, three of them being quantitative (whether a library has *enough* books), qualitative (the *right* books), and use-based. A materials availability survey may be directly associated with collection use. Availability studies learn if the information content that users need is available in any format in their library. Are the books needed owned and available? Is the e-content available in the library's collections, and can the resources be accessed by searching the online catalog or the discovery tool, or both?

Use-based collection evaluation is focused on demand as measured by use. For this type of study, circulation and interlibrary loan statistics are considered collection use statistics. While circulation data reveal the ways in which the library meets users' needs, interlibrary loan data illustrate what else users need that their library does not have. Circulation use data can be applied to collection management, including weeding print book sections or relocating the books with a low number of checkouts to compact or off-site storage, and to collection development, in which a low number of checkouts in a subject may result in fewer books being purchased.[12]

Another common study involves the use of specific collections or formats. For instance, managers might want to understand better e-book use as a result of the increase in availability of e-books. One study performed a circulation analysis for a book title in print and accesses to the same title as an e-book. The use data found that the e-book titles receive 11 percent more use than their print equivalents. Additionally, findings suggest some approaches to e-book collection development. Attention should be paid to titles that particularly benefit from additional functionality offered by an electronic format, such as reference books. E-books are excellent candidates for additional copy purchases when print copies of titles are receiving heavy use.[13] Another study found that the size of the e-book collection exhibited the strongest association to use levels, suggesting how important the size and content of a collection can be to patron acceptance and utilization.[14] A use study of e-book content found that higher education students do not read e-books for extended periods in order to grasp their overall argument and point of view, but, rather, use them as convenient sources from which to extract information for course or project work.[15]

Studies about e-journal use are possible. An academic library study covering eleven years of e-journal use found that the size of an e-journal collection has an impact on its level of use; there is a relatively strong linear relationship between the number of e-journals and the number of articles downloaded. Alain R. Lamothe also found that there appears to be a critical mass that, once reached, slows or stops any further increase in use. When the author's university hit this critical mass, the number of articles downloaded failed to continue to increase as the e-journal collection continued to grow. As a result, the e-journal collection may no longer need substantial growth but, rather, a revision of its current contents.[16]

The application of collection use data is sometimes included as part of a library's collection development fund allocation formula. One study found that the most frequently used factors in collection allocation formulas were enrollment/number of students, cost/price of materials, use as measured by circulation, and the number of faculty.[17]

TECHNOLOGY USE

The availability and accessibility of technologies are increasingly important for library users. Although smartphones and tablets may eventually replace desktop workstations and laptops, many users still depend on library technologies for research, learning, and personal productivity, including the use of e-mail and social networking. And, we may need to be occasionally reminded that libraries acquire and maintain technologies in addition to computers, including photocopiers, microform readers, printers, and audiovisual playback units. Many libraries also lend technologies, including e-book readers, laptops, tablets, graphing calculators, digital cameras, camcorders, image projectors, and even telescopes. Additionally, libraries support communications means, including wired and wireless technology networks.

To measure use, one must first inventory the availability of technologies as inputs, accessible in-library and available for loan. This would include the number of public computer workstations, dedicated online catalog workstations, printers, microform reader/printers, and network printers for users. It would also be

BOX 9.7 **USE METRICS FOR TECHNOLOGIES**

Number of transactions for

» In-library devices
- By type (e.g., desktop workstation, microform reader)
- By purpose (e.g., personal productivity, online catalog)
- By location (e.g., reference area)
» Devices loaned, by type (e.g., laptop, e-reader, digital still camera)
» Use of information/learning commons
- Gate count (if possible)
  › Month of the year
  › Day of the week
  › Time of day
- Services used (academic)
  › Writing tutor
  › Reference service
  › IT support
» Pages printed in the library via computers
» Pages printed in the library via photocopiers
» Microform readers/printers
- Times used
- Pages printed

BOX 9.8 **RATIOS FOR USE TRANSACTIONS COUNTS**

» Devices (by type) available per capita of the service population (can be graphed over time on a trend line)
- For use in the library
- To borrow from the library
» Use of devices in the library per capita of the service population (can be graphed over time on a trend line)
» Average use of devices (can be graphed over time on a trend line)
- Per hour open
- Per week
- Per month
» Number of pages printed per capita (can be graphed over time on a trend line)
» Percentage of uptime (can be graphed over time on a trend line)
- For devices in the library (e.g., desktop computer workstation)
- Integrated library system
- Library's home page

beneficial to identify every public area in which the technology is installed, such as reference, children's, instruction, information/learning commons, and computer labs. The inventory would also include counts of the number and type of technologies loaned to users for in-library use and those devices that may leave the library facility.

Unlike measuring collections use, particularly in electronic formats, usage metrics for technologies are fairly straightforward. The most basic metric counts how many times each device was used and, if possible, when and for how long. Box 9.7 points out assorted metrics, while box 9.8 illustrates ratios that result from compiling use transactions.

Examples of Use Studies about Technologies

Many of the studies on technology use focus on adequacy: is there adequate access to the technologies, is the technology meeting the needs of the users, and is the technology up-to-date and applications current? One study designed to develop a profile of the users of public computer workstations in public libraries, for instance, found that library customers access a mix of recreational and work-related applications when using a library computer. The top four applications accessed were e-mail, social networking, job searches, and news. Additionally, more than half of the respondents used the library computers as their primary means of accessing the Internet.[18] Another public library study looked at alternatives to decrease the wait time that frustrated users of public computer workstations when the queue was based on first-come-first-served. The study found that dedicating one computer workstation as a fifteen-minute station was a poor strategy that, in some cases, nearly doubled the wait time for the other users. However, experimenting with alternative queuing strategies, such as "shortest job first," could reduce user waiting times.[19]

OUTREACH USE

Outreach to library users and nonusers through marketing and public relations is, in part, an effort to increase use of library services and resources. Libraries take a variety of approaches in these efforts to increase awareness and use, including print and electronic flyers, newsletters, e-mails, RSS feeds, and social media (e.g., Facebook and Pinterest). Outreach inputs include an outreach/marketing plan or strategy and the number of outreach efforts planned (e.g., a monthly newsletter). If focused on user segments (e.g., families with children under seven years of age), the library may have created a user profile of information, including

» Approximate age, usually in ranges
» Work location or where they live
» Frequency of library use
» Day or time of library use, or both
» Subject interests
» Desired information delivery mechanism (e.g., e-mail, text message, or telephone)

There are basically two metrics for libraries to collect concerning outreach. One is the number of outreach efforts made and the type of effort. The second is the use counts collected that have been identified in the other sections of this chapter, such as services and collections. A useful output metric is the percentage of the service population that has received newsletters or other content that is part of the library's outreach/marketing plan and strategies.

Example of a Use Study about Outreach

Planned outreach efforts guided by a marketing plan or strategies are intended to result in changes in library use. The number of outreach efforts made and the type of effort should be collected. For example, let us assume the library issued a newsletter ten times during the fiscal year in print (one thousand copies were distributed) and electronic forms (e-mailed to three thousand people; it was also mounted on the website and viewed three hundred times). A second metric would identify any changes in use that were part of the strategy to increase awareness through the outreach effort. As an example, the library publicized in the newsletters and then conducted two poetry readings during the fiscal year. People attended, and this program attendance would be counted under services (see that section earlier in this chapter). Circulation use figures are collected and are compiled by call numbers. Review of transactions found that the circulation of poetry books from the general collection increased each month when the poetry readings were conducted; checkouts for poetry books then returned to their expected use level during the months in which there were no poetry readings, based upon trends-over-time analysis. The library could reasonably link the poetry program attendance and the increased circulation of poetry books to the planned outreach effort when reporting to stakeholders.

VALUES AND USE: A CUSTOMER PERSPECTIVE

Library use literally depends on customers. The library's perspective concerning them involves outcomes: we want to learn how user interactions with the library change their skills, knowledge, and attitudes—how the library affects their lives (see chapter 8). The customer perspective is similar, but different: How does the library add value to my life? Although an incomplete picture, a customer's use of the library provides clues about the impact of library services and resources. In decades past, the library was a primary information source with few competitors. However, for customers today, there are increasing numbers of information sources in addition to a library. The library must provide wanted services and resources for it to be valuable to its customers.

The inputs concerning value are the services and resources the library provides through its infrastructure. The library also applies tools, such as surveys and serious reviews of customer-submitted complaints, to learn about customer needs and about how the library is used. These means may also help discover the changes in customers caused by their interaction with the library. Outputs as values can be grouped into three attributes from the customer perspective: accessibility, availability, and affordability.

Accessibility inputs include the number of hours and times during the day when the library is open. It also includes the availability of virtual resources (e.g., e-books and serials) and services (e.g., an online catalog to search for books and to renew a borrowed item) through the library's website and integrated library system. Use has a role in accessibility as an output; it includes the number of times the library is visited physically and virtually, and the types and numbers of services used.

Availability inputs are focused on the offerings of the library. Examples include the following:

» The books that users want are owned and on the shelf or can be downloaded onto e-readers.
» Programs are offered that are interesting, informative, and relevant.
» A variety of public areas and seating options encourage users to browse, linger, and be productive.
» An adequate number of public workstations, printers, and scanners are functioning and their hardware and applications are up-to-date.
» The library supports other technologies as needed, such as microform readers/printers and wireless networks.
» There is an adequate number of qualified staff to manage and perform library functions and to help when needed.

Availability as an output is often measured by use. Categories could include the number of books borrowed in print or as e-books; the number of attendees at conducted programs; the number of times users are observed in spaces throughout the library or browsing the shelves; how often queues form as customers wait for their turn to use the computers; and whether staff are responsive to user needs, are known by name to users, and are complimented for their services by customers rather than frustrating them.

Affordability as an input is exclusively a library perspective supported in part by efficiencies and economies of scale. A customer's perspective of affordability is focused on use as an output. Customers understand and appreciate the economic value of using the library; it saves them money and time. It is economically more advantageous to borrow books, music, and movies from the library than to purchase them. Reference librarians can provide quality answers to questions faster than customers can find the information themselves. Broadband technology may not be available or affordable at home, so the customer takes advantage of the technologies provided by the library for e-mail, job searching, the news, or watching popular YouTube videos. User perception of affordability as an output is also directly related to availability of inputs: Do customers want library services and resources? Libraries may not have all of the titles or enough copies of books to meet customer needs; it is difficult for a library to have all of the movies for loan that are available through the cloud, especially from those services requiring a subscription.

Accountability is an internal perspective the library brings to the values discussion framed by accessibility, availability, and affordability. How, and how well, is the library meeting the goals and objectives as stated in the institutional mission, guided by the library's mission and strategic plan? For example, academic libraries employ evaluation and assessment processes to understand and report better the value they provide to students, faculty, and other stakeholders. Academic libraries document their contributions to recruitment, retention, and graduation as well as to student success and learning outcomes. Libraries have a role in recruiting students by describing library services from a customer's perspective when conducting tours for prospective students and their families. Libraries' efforts to retain students include accessibility (number of hours open, virtual library services), availability (print and e-resources to support course requirements, remote access to e-resources, technologies to use and borrow, a helpful and informed staff, and a facility that is inviting as well as productive with a mix of comfortable furnishings and a variety of social and study areas), and affordability (reserves and interlibrary loan). Student learning outcomes are enhanced through library-led or -facilitated personal and group instruction. The library adds value for faculty by developing help guides they can use for teaching and helping their students and by acquiring information resources or borrowing necessary resources through interlibrary loan to support faculty research and scholarly work.

Examples of Use Studies about Values

Value studies can be undertaken to learn about customer satisfaction. A multiplicity of on-site and remote print and online surveys can be conducted to measure either satisfaction or service quality. The library can study and review the volume of complaints, suggestions, and compliments received via e-mail and suggestion boxes and compare the results over time as a percentage per capita of the service population. The extent to which library use is conducted by repeat customers may also serve as a proxy for satisfaction.

Return on investment is another measure of value. Use may help the library document how it contributes to affordability by calculating the estimated savings to users from using the library. For example, users save their personal funds when borrowing items from the general and reserve collections or when borrowing laptops. The library can calculate the costs for answering a reference question and borrowing an interlibrary loan item, which may help to demonstrate the value of these services when the sum value of service transactions exceeds the costs incurred to provide the services.

There is also value in community goodwill. Studies could document the availability of the online catalog for all to search for desired resources, the use of the library's collections and programs by users external to the service population, and the number of community organization contacts concerning library services.

As covered in chapter 1 (in the sections "Going Beyond Just Library Metrics" and "Relevant Studies"), academic libraries are increasingly interested in demonstrating their contribution to recruitment, retention, and student success, including learning outcomes and graduation. A study that measured academic library use with log-ins into authenticated resources and interlibrary loans of physical items suggested that higher levels of library use are coupled with retention.[20] However, it is important to remember that retention is a complex issue, and other variables are likely involved.

Concerning student learning, one academic library study investigated whether a statistical correlation existed between student cumulative grade point average (GPA) and students' borrowing of books and audiovisual materials. A positive relationship between GPA and checkouts was found, leading to a conclusion that students who have higher GPAs use (or like to use) more monographs and multimedia resources that are provided by the library.[21] Another study on GPAs investigated the relationship between students' use of information resources held in their university library and their academic achievement indicated by their grade point averages (GPAs). Correlation of the individual student responses about their library use with their personal GPA scores revealed that academic achievement had a significant relationship to their use of books, whereas their use of periodicals, reference materials, electronic resources, and other types of information resources had no significant relationship with their academic achievement.[22] Still, it is important to remember that GPA is an imperfect measure given the extent of grade inflation and questions about what grades really indicate.

Libraries from eight institutions of higher education explored student completion by examining whether there is a statistically significant correlation between library activity data and student attainment of a degree. Usage included book loans, e-resources as measured by web-based click-throughs, and use of the library building from statistics collected by the gate entry system. The findings indicated that there is a statistically significant relationship between student degree attainment and two of the indicators—e-resources use and book borrowing statistics—and that this relationship exists across all of the institutions.[23] However, such a study does not consider the impact of student learning outcomes and customer satisfaction on student completion and retention.

CONCLUDING THOUGHTS

Use can be applied toward discovering and documenting the library's contribution to meeting the institutional and organizational mission, goals, and objectives as added value from the user's perspective. Use metrics may appear quaint or even unnecessary as libraries focus on user outcomes and impacts. And, in the current library services environment in which users may value ease of access to "e-everything," there appear to be questions about the future of library use. Are reference services in decline as measured by the number of annual transactions? Will the availability of open source resources reduce the need for many academic libraries to expend more than 50 percent of the collections allocations on e-journals subscriptions, thereby reducing or even eliminating the role of generations of librarians as gatekeepers to quality scholarship? E-access is changing the use of library services, collections, and the library as place; it affects accessibility, availability, and affordability.

Libraries may need new use metrics. Do we really understand the extent to which users use e-journals despite COUNTER? Other use metrics need to be developed and applied; examples include unit costs that help to state a library's return on investment. Library use is one indicator of the value users place on the library. We have to refine our measures to reflect the users' perspectives better so that we can improve reporting about library use as a value to stakeholders.

EXERCISES

Answers to the following questions are in the "Appendix" at the back of the book. We encourage different members of a library staff to work on the exercises together and to discuss the results. Managers might also participate in that discussion.

QUESTION 1 Although a library's perspective looks at customer impact when analyzing use, a common customer perspective asks how the library adds value to his or her life. Return on investment is one measure of value. Which use indicators might a library consider when calculating a local return on investment from a customer perspective?

QUESTION 2 Managers of a public library want to know how their organization's collection turnover rate compares with that of other libraries. What can they do?

QUESTION 3 Managers of an academic library are interested in collection use as measured through circulation and interlibrary loan, and how the library compares with its institutional peer libraries. What can they do?

QUESTION 4 Managers of a public library surmise that circulation transactions are not as high as the library's busyness would suggest it should be. Staff have observed that many people seem to be using the library to read newspapers and periodicals, but do not check out books. They wonder if in-library use affects circulation. They also want to know how the findings compare with those of other libraries.

QUESTION 5 Managers of an academic library want to compare trends for use, including reference and circulation transactions and the number of filled full-text article requests, with those of institutional peer libraries. What can they do?

Notes

1. Rachel Applegate, "The Library Is for Studying: Student Preferences for Study Space," *Journal of Academic Librarianship* 35, no. 4 (July 2009): 341, 343–45.

2. Carolyn Bourke, "Library Youth Spaces vs Youth Friendly Libraries: How to Make the Most of What You Have," *Australasian Public Libraries and Information Services* 23, no. 3 (September 2010): 98.

3. Lauren H. Mandel, "Finding Their Way: How Public Library Users Wayfind," *Library & Information Science Research* 35, no. 4 (October 2013): 264–65.

4. Harold B. Shill and Shawn Tonner, "Does the Building Still Matter? Usage Patterns in New, Expanded, and Renovated Libraries, 1995–2002," *College and Research Libraries* 65, no. 2 (March 2004): 127, 148–49.

5. The one-minute paper focuses on a short question or two presented usually at the end of the session and provides real-time feedback to find out if students recognized the main points of a class session or were confused by them. The purpose is to enable the instructor to craft changes for the next class.

6. Suman Lata and Sanjeev Sharma, "Use and Usage of Information Sources and Services in T. S. Central State Library, Chandigarh: A User Study," *International Journal of Information Dissemination and Technology* 3, no. 2 (April–June 2013): 90–93.

7. Ana Dubnjakovic, "Electronic Resource Expenditure and the Decline in Reference Transaction Statistics in Academic Libraries," *Journal of Academic Librarianship* 38, no. 2 (March 2012): 99.

8. Jeanne Goodrich, "Staffing Public Libraries: Are There Models or Best Practices?" *Public Libraries* 44, no. 5 (September/October 2005): 277–78.

9. Bradley Wade Bishop and Jennifer A. Bartlett, "Where Do We Go from Here? Informing Academic Library Staffing through Reference Transaction Analysis," *College & Research Libraries* 74, no. 5 (September 2013): 499; Bella Karr Gerlich and Edward Whatley, "Using the READ Scale for Staffing Strategies: The Georgia College and State University Experience," *Library Leadership and Management* 23, no. 1 (Winter 2009): 26, 28; and Russell F. Dennison, "Usage-Based Staffing of the Reference Desk: A Statistical Approach," *Reference and User Services Quarterly* 39, no. 2 (Winter 1999): 158, 165.

10. Dubnjakovic, "Electronic Resource Expenditure and the Decline in Reference Transaction Statistics in Academic Libraries."

11. Oliver Pesch, "Standards That Impact the Gathering and Analysis of Usage," *Serials Librarian* 61, no. 1 (2011): 25, 27.

12. Karen C. Kohn, "Usage-Based Collection Evaluation with a Curricular Focus," *College & Research Libraries* 74, no. 1 (January 2013): 85, 87, 89, 94.

13. Justin Littman and Lynn Silipigni Connaway, "A Circulation Analysis of Print Books and E-books in an Academic Research Library," *Library Resources and Technical Services* 48, no. 4 (October 2004): 257, 260.

14. Alain R. Lamothe, "Factors Influencing the Usage of an Electronic Book Collection: Size of the E-book Collection, the Student Population, and the Faculty Population," *College & Research Libraries* 74, no. 1 (January 2013): 39, 50.

15. Jeff Stalger, "How E-books Are Used: A Literature Review of the E-book Studies Conducted from 2006 to 2011," *Reference and User Services Quarterly* 51, no. 4 (Summer 2012): 357.

16. Alain R. Lamothe, "Factors Influencing Usage of an Electronic Journal Collection at a Medium-Size University: An Eleven-Year Study," *Partnership: The Canadian Journal of Library and Information Practice and Research* 7, no. 1 (2012): 6, 17.

17. Kitti Canepi, "Fund Allocation Formula Analysis: Determining Elements for Best Practices in Libraries," *Library Collections, Acquisitions, and Technical Services* 31, no. 1 (March 2007): 21.

18. Kurt DeMaagd, Han Ei Chew, Guanxiong Huang, M. Laeeq Khan, Akshaya Sreenivasan, and Robert LaRose, "The Use of Public Computing Facilities by Library Patrons: Demography, Motivations, and Barriers," *Government Information Quarterly* 30, no. 1 (January 2013): 112, 113, 115.

19. Stuart Williamson, "Public Library Computer Waiting Queues: Alternatives to the First-Come-First-Served Strategy," *Information Technology and Libraries* 31, no. 2 (June 2012): 72, 74, 77, 81.

20. Gaby Haddow, "Academic Library Use and Student Retention: A Quantitative Analysis," *Library & Information Science Research* 35, no. 2 (April 2013): 132, 134.

21. Shun Han Rebekah Wong and T. D. Webb, "Uncovering Meaningful Correlation between Student Academic Performance and Library Material Usage," *College & Research Libraries* 74, no. 2 (July 2011): 361, 366, 368.

22. Atif Yousef Odeh, "Use of Information Resources by Undergraduate Students and Its Relationship with Academic Achievement," *Libri* 62, no. 3 (September 2012): 222, 230.

23. Graham Stone and Bryony Ramsden, "Library Impact Data Project: Looking for the Link between Library Usage and Student Attainment," *College & Research Libraries* 74, no. 6 (November 2013): 548, 556.

Presenting the Findings

LIBRARIES HAVE HISTORICALLY DONE little to create a proactive communications program that informs various stakeholders about the value of the library. For past decades library managers have relied on a range of performance metrics, typically consisting of input and output metrics, to communicate value. Not surprisingly, however, what has significance and relevance to them is not necessarily important (or even understandable or meaningful) to various stakeholders.[1] The communications process with the library's stakeholders focuses on what they value and how they want the information presented. Further, how does the message presented convey an interesting or important part of the library's story to them?

Libraries communicate with their stakeholders for a variety of reasons, such as to inform and persuade them, to demonstrate accountability, to prevent misunderstandings, to present a point of view, and to reduce barriers that may range from information overload to suspicion and prejudice. Effectively communicating the benefits from the use of the library's infrastructure (facilities; technology; staff; and collections, services, and programs) must start with a clear understanding of the library's mission and goals as set forth in a strategic plan. The goal is to align the library's mission, goals, and objectives with those of the institution or larger organization. In an academic setting, the college's or university's goals might be focused on student success as defined by surrogate metrics, such as the percentage of students graduating in five and six years, first-year to second-year student retention, and so forth. In a public library, a city or county might focus, in part, on the quality of the education provided to the community. In such an instance, the library might seek to demonstrate that a majority of its programs and services assist community members of all ages in excelling in school or in their daily lives.

A communications plan is a means of monitoring what messages are conveyed and the impact of those messages. The plan identifies ways to communicate the value of the library to stakeholders and how that value is integrated into daily operations. The plan, which adheres to the strategic plan, addresses the following:

» The organizational and institutional mission
» Goals and objectives
» Strategy, which identifies the ways in which the objectives can be accomplished
» The audience for the means of communication and those stakeholders who will be informed
» Tactics, or the tools to accomplish the objectives
» The message to deliver (what needs to be said)
» Timing (the time frame for the communications)
» Evaluation, or the measurement of the strategies, tactics, and effectiveness of the message
» Linkage of the findings back to the mission, goals, and objectives

Many stakeholders would become lost in the forest of facts and figures without being presented with a clear path toward the significance of the metrics displayed and the statistics presented. Developing a multipronged approach to communicating the value of the library, according to Glen Holt,[2] has several advantages, which include

» Encouraging library customers to consider using additional services
» Alerting nonusers about the availability and value of library services
» Informing the community (whether on a campus or in a city or county) about the value of the library
» Informing the library's stakeholders about the value of the library

UNDERSTAND THE AUDIENCE

Communication that works well is based on a clear understanding of the intended audience. Funding decision makers, for instance, have a set of experiences and perspectives that must first be understood and acknowledged before the library can begin to consider how to best communicate with them. Aside from the obvious concerns about operating the library in an efficient and transparent manner, stakeholders increasingly want to understand the library's value proposition.

A nationwide survey of public officials and library directors found a wide gap in perceptions when comparing library services to other community services: police, fire, streets, sewage, parks and recreation, and so forth.[3] Three-fourths of the responding library directors believed they initiated interactions with the stakeholders, whereas the public officials disagreed; only about half of them considered the library to be proactive. Interestingly, there was general agreement among all respondents about the goals, importance, and overall quality of the public library in their community.

Given the variety of ways in which people learn (some are auditory, others are visual, and still others prefer to absorb information by reading), it is important for library managers to visit the library's stakeholders on their turf—that is, in their offices, at community social gatherings, and even having lunch or dinner with them. However, before the meeting, managers should have some prior knowledge about their stakeholders and should view face-to-face contact times as a means of relationship building and of delivering information that will be of value to them.

Once the managers have developed an ongoing relationship with the library's stakeholders, they should carefully select (1) the performance metrics that will reflect the value of the library from the stakeholders' perspectives, and (2) the manner in which the information will be conveyed. It is important to remember that the only perspective that really counts is that of the stakeholder. Obviously, the information being conveyed must be free of library jargon and terminology; in other words, managers must remember that they are not speaking to other librarians and that stakeholders expect to view the library in accordance with their priorities. Because of this, managers should practice the message and their presentations on nonlibrarians, and they should ask these listeners to interrupt every time there is a word or phrase they do not understand.

FOCUS ON BENEFITS

When communicating with stakeholders, staff members, and other interested parties, managers should focus on the benefits and impacts that result from the use of the library, rather than merely reporting use metrics. These groups may not see use metrics as synonymous with value. For them, value in terms of academic libraries centers on:

- » **Saving time:** Students and faculty members save a significant amount of time when accessing the library's high-quality collections and downloading e-resources.
- » **Saving money:** The library's customers need not purchase materials or access to materials if they use the library (as the library has purchased or licensed access to content).
- » **Contributing to student success:** Several recent studies have demonstrated that students who use library collections and download e-resources do better academically, as evidenced by achieving better grades and staying in school (student retention).[4] Still, before accepting the validity of these claims, library managers should review the "Relevant Studies" section in chapter 1.
- » **Contributing to faculty productivity:** Gaining access to library resources, especially desktop access, significantly increases faculty members' productivity, as measured by the quantity of publications produced and research grants awarded.[5]

For public libraries, value focuses on:

- » **Saving money:** Library customers need not purchase the materials that they borrow from the library. For many customers, this can amount to a sizable annual savings. In addition, customers can visit the library and use the latest technology for a wide variety of purposes.

» **Saving time:** Reference librarians save customer time because of their skills and experience when searching for information.
» **Programs for increasing literacy:** From preschool-age children up to and including senior citizens, libraries offer a variety of ways in which people can improve their literacy skills and become more productive.
» **Economic development programs:** Many libraries offer programs, collections, and other services to assist people in improving their employment skills, applying for jobs, and pursuing job training, as well as encouraging entrepreneurs in starting up new businesses.

Imagine a communications plan for a public library that addresses value in terms of applying for and gaining employment, undertaking job training, and dealing with a myriad of issues associated with starting a small business. For an academic library, the communications plan might address *data curation* for the individual data sets that researchers generate (the activity of managing and promoting the use of data from its point of creation, to ensure it is available for discovery and reuse), and the development of data management plans that researchers can submit to the National Science Foundation and other government agencies to document how the research data they generate will be described, accessed, archived, shared, reused, and redistributed for the duration of the funded project and beyond.

PROVIDE CONTEXT

Providing some context or comparison about a particular statistic or performance metric will obviously improve the communication process. Comparing the monthly attendance (gate count) at the library to attendance at a sporting event or local movie theaters may make a more meaningful impression about how frequently the library is being used. Managers should try to develop some memorable one-liners, such as "the entire student body visits the library every x days." Or, "although a student's tuition is xx,xxx per semester, the library only receives yyy out of that and yet provides zzz of value to the student." And, what really resonates with stakeholders is the clear statement that the library contributes to student success and retention (and having the data to support the claim).

BE CREDIBLE

Engagement is the process of exchanging information, listening to, and learning from stakeholders. By engaging stakeholders, library managers seek to gain stakeholder trust, which "can be a significant competitive advantage for organizations. By understanding what influences and drives stakeholder trust, firms can identify risks, focus their strategies for maximum benefit, and develop initiatives to help them weather erosions of trust."[6] The goal is to build understanding and trust on issues of mutual interest. Library directors gain credibility based on their knowledge of the literature, experience, understanding of assorted issues (e.g., scholarly communication), and trustworthiness. By regularly engaging with campus or community stakeholders, they build trust and are better received when making presentations about the library and its value.

When managers present information about a set of performance metrics or the findings of a survey, it is important for them to

» ensure that the results of the survey are accurately portrayed and any limitations (and every survey has limitations, be they sample size, sample bias, and so forth) are clearly articulated and acknowledged;

» compare the results with those of other comparable libraries (acknowledging that selecting a set of peer libraries can take many paths);

» clearly document the process used to gather the data and the statistical tools that were used to analyze the resulting data; and

» contrast the results with those found in the literature, especially if the results differ.

IMPROVE COMMUNICATION SKILLS

Before managers develop a presentation, they should be sure the message conveys what they intend. They also need to consider the most effective manner in which to deliver the message. As shown in figure 10.1 in *Getting Started with Evaluation*, a wide variety of channels exists, and managers might select a combination of them.[7] You might review the list of channels listed in the figure and experiment with different ones, focusing on how to make any use of them effective. The impact should be quickly seen.[8]

The popularity of using graphical methods (remember the old saying, "A picture is worth a thousand words"?) must be tempered with the reality that too much of one thing can be bad. The popularity of PowerPoint (and its various offshoots) means that many presentations turn out to be dull or boring. Some suggestions for improving a graphical presentation include the following:

» Make sure the graphic (chart, table, or figure) can stand on its own.

» Make sure the graphic is simple enough and large enough to be seen by most people in the room.

» Minimize the number of words per line (no more than five to six words per line).

» Do not read your slides (each slide should be a prop upon which to base comments).

» Remember that the combination of stories plus statistics is an effective duo.

» Be informative, not boring.

» Test each slide and test the entire presentation. (Is it too long? Is library jargon being used? Are the graphics clear? Should each graphic be used? Are all of the slides really necessary?)[9]

STAGE THE RELEASE OF INFORMATION

Rather than being a one-time event (e.g., during a budget presentation), the process of communicating the value of the library is much more effective if done throughout the year. A combination of written and oral messages needs to be conveyed to the library's stakeholders, including library customers and other members of the community. A range of written materials can be produced to assist in communicating the value message. The library might consider

» looking for and capturing human-interest stories about the effectiveness of the library and its services.

» using the library's newsletter to focus on the progress being made to achieve the goals set by the library.

» preparing an executive summary of the library's annual report that has real visual appeal—use colorful charts, graphs, and so forth. By using tools on the Internet, it is possible to prepare quickly an infographic of the library's accomplishments and its contributions for its customers.

» maintaining an effective presence in social media: Twitter, Facebook, Flickr, Pinterest, and so forth.[10]

Storytelling is an effective way to put information into context and some life into dull and staid statistics that are often found in a report or presentation. Stories are one way people make sense of things. Managers might ask staff to collect and share stories of how the library has a real impact in the life of a student, faculty member, or community member. Stories allow a library to put a face on its services and demonstrate how the customer values the library. A memorable story will often be retained by a stakeholder and sometimes shared with other stakeholders. When the opportunity presents itself, managers might begin a conversation or presentation by saying, "Let me tell you a story."

In addition to delivering prepared presentations, it is important that the library management team, not just the director, prepare, rehearse, and be ready to deliver short and informative elevator speeches that provide a quick synopsis of the value of the library. A one-minute, two-minute, and five-minute version of the speech should be ready to go whenever the opportunity arises.

ASK FOR FEEDBACK

Managers should always seek to improve their presentation skills. As part of this, they should objectively critique their own presentation skills and compare their skills with those of their counterparts (other managers throughout the organization and in other settings). Do they find themselves comparable, or do they need to sharpen their skills? Perhaps they should consider joining Toastmasters in order to develop and refine their presentation skills better as well as watch others give presentations at conferences. Why are some presentations successful and others not so much? They might also ask for feedback from the library stakeholders and others about the library's communication strategy and the effectiveness of the library's message. Are the managers clearly demonstrating how the library affects the institution's or larger organization's mission and goals? It is important to remember that the goal of asking for feedback is to change the way in which someone presents the library's message in order to make it better. By acknowledging that people have different ways of learning and absorbing information, managers can tailor the library's message in ways that the stakeholders prefer.

Regardless of the specific metrics (output, return on investment, or outcome) selected by library managers to assist in communicating the value of the library, it is important to show trends over time (trend data over the last five years will usually be more than sufficient) and to make comparisons to capture audience attention (review the section "Provide Context" earlier in this chapter). Examples include:

- » "For every $6,448 spent on public libraries from public funding sources (federal, state, and local) in Florida, one job is created."
- » "For every dollar of public support spent on public libraries in Florida, income (wages) increases by $12.66."[11]

CONCLUDING THOUGHTS

As a library puts together its communications plan, everyone on the management team should practice delivering an elevator pitch of no more than thirty seconds, a short five- to ten-minute presentation, or a longer and more comprehensive message. It is important to tailor the library's message to fit the preferences of the stakeholders. The library's message will be strengthened if managers remember to do the following:

- » Develop personal relationships with each of the library's stakeholders so that they see the library director more than once a year at the budget presentation.
- » Avoid *overselling* the library's services—instead, *over-deliver*. Look for ways to add more value in the customers' lives.
- » Convey the message that the library provides real value to customers in unique and compelling ways.
- » Invite library stakeholders to visit the library and to see the high quality and diversity of services being delivered.
- » Provide some context for the statistics that are presented so that the message is more understandable and meaningful.
- » If managers need to use jargon, they should use that of the stakeholders.
- » One of the most important jobs for any library director is to communicate the value of the library effectively to the stakeholders. As a consequence, all managers should make sure they have devoted the time and energy needed to be prepared so that when opportunity arises, they are ready to take center stage.

EXERCISES

Answers to the following questions are in the "Appendix" at the back of the book. We encourage different members of a library staff to work on the exercises together and to discuss the results. Managers might also participate in that discussion.

QUESTION 1 Using either ALA*Metrics* or PLA*metrics*, display graphically for any library the relative ratio of expenses for collections, personnel, and other operating expenses. What type of visual would you consider using?

QUESTION 2 For the same library compare the ratios in question 1 to a set of library peers. What type of visual would you consider using?

QUESTION 3 Using the same data service, display graphically for that library e-book circulation over some period of time. How long did you select, and what type of visual would you consider using?

QUESTION 4 On what input and output metrics would the library's stakeholders want to be informed? What type of visual would you consider using? (This question cannot be quickly answered as there might be variations in expectations among stakeholders.)

QUESTION 5 For the same library and data service, what data might be meaningfully presented in the form of a bar chart? (A bar chart is a graph using rectangular bars to show how large each value is. The bars can be horizontal or vertical.)

Notes

1. See Peter Hernon, Robert E. Dugan, and Joseph R. Matthews, *Getting Started with Evaluation* (Chicago: American Library Association, 2014), chapter 10. That chapter, which highlights different stakeholders and effective ways to communicate with them, complements coverage in the present text.

2. Glen Holt, "Balancing Buildings, Books, Bytes, and Bucks: Steps to Secure the Public Library Future in the Internet Age," *Library Trends* 46, no. 1 (Summer 1997): 92–116.

3. Library Research Center, "A Survey of Public Libraries and Local Government," *Illinois State Library Special Report Series* 4, no. 1 (1997): 1–62.

4. Graham Stone and Bryony Ramsden, "Library Impact Data Project: Looking for the Link between Library Usage and Student Attainment," *College & Research Libraries* 74, no. 6 (November 2013): 546–59; Brian Cox and Margie Jantti, "Discovering the Impact of Library Use and Student Performance," *EDUCAUSE Review Online* (July 18, 2012), www.educause .edu/ero/article/discovering-impact-library-use-and-student-performance; Krista Soria, Jan Fransen, and Shane Nackerud, "Library Use and Undergraduate Student Outcomes: New Evidence for Students' Retention and Academic Success," *portal: Libraries and the Academy* 13, no. 2 (2013): 147–64.

5. See Association of College and Research Libraries, *Value of Academic Libraries: A Comprehensive Research Review and Report*, researched by Megan Oakleaf (Chicago: Association of College and Research Libraries, 2010), www.ala.org/acrl/sites/ala.org.acrl/ files/content/issues/value/val_report.pdf.

6. Conference Board of Canada, *Stakeholder Trust: A Competitive Strategy*, report by Michael Bassett (Ottawa, ON: Conference Board of Canada, 2008), www.conferenceboard.ca/e-library/abstract.aspx?did=2798.

7. Hernon, Dugan, and Matthews, *Getting Started with Evaluation*, 178.

8. See Geoffrey James, "Fix Your Presentations: 21 Quick Tips" (2012), www.inc.com/geoffrey-james/how-to-fix-your-presentations-21-tips.html.

9. See Hernon, Dugan, and Matthews, *Getting Started with Evaluation*, 180–82.

10. See Peter Hernon and Joseph R. Matthews, *Listening to the Customer* (Santa Barbara, CA: Libraries Unlimited, 2011).

11. José-Marie Griffiths, Donald W. King, Christinger Tomer, Thomas Lynch, and Julie Harrington, *Taxpayer Return on Investment in Florida Public Libraries: Summary Report* (Tallahassee: State Library and Archives of Florida, September 2004), http://dlis.dos.state.fl.us/bld/roi/pdfs/ROISummaryReport.pdf.

Managing with Data (Evidence)

EVER SINCE DAVID LETTERMAN introduced his top-ten lists, others have created their own lists, some of which address becoming a librarian. For example, one set of reasons includes, among others, learning something new every day and engaging in different activities so that work becomes less of a routine (number 10); obtaining a useful skill set, one based on the traditional values of librarianship (number 8); "liberal vacations" (number 6); "a job with scope," meaning doing "dozens of different things every day" (number 5, which complements number 10); "it pays the rent" (number 4); "good working conditions" (number 3); "co-workers who are intelligent, cultured, well-read people who bring a myriad of skills, backgrounds, and interests to the job" (number 2); and honoring the values of librarianship—for example, the freedom to read (number 1).[1] Other lists might be directed at those thinking about entering the profession, but these lists may not total ten reasons. On one such list, the first item, the "responsibilities of a librarian," might be seen as part of numbers 5 and 10 in the preceding list. Those responsibilities include the following:

> You'd assist library patrons in finding and using books, periodicals, audiovisual materials and digital resources. You could find work in various settings. . . . Your responsibilities would range from assisting patrons with research to developing reading and technology training programs and organizing collection materials. Additionally, you'd maintain a library's collection and decide what to purchase or discard.[2]

With many libraries losing significant funding because of the recent economic recession and its aftermath, some directors see the present not as "a time for retrenchment and timidity but for expansion and boldness."[3] For these libraries, transformative change is associated not with a bleak financial situation, but with a significant shift in where the institution or broader organization is going. As a result, the managerial leaders in the libraries at these places, most likely, find any traditional characterizations of a librarian, the work performed, and even portrayals of what comprises a library outdated and not reflecting the types of service roles they are developing to meet the ever-changing expectations and information needs of those within the communities they serve. They might also see the future staff as consisting of those with a master's degree from a program accredited by the American Library Association as well as those with assorted other graduate degrees, knowledge, abilities, and skill sets.

Increasingly relevant questions for libraries engaged in "expansion and boldness" focus on what vision will guide the organization into the future, how well that vision fits within the one set by the institution or broader organization, how leaders create staff and stakeholder buy-in to that vision, and how well members of the organization work together and accept new roles and responsibilities. Such questions refocus attention on issues of management (i.e., change management, leadership, planning, evaluation, and assessment) and on topics such as the library's value and relevance to the mission of the institution or broader organization, the need to question "our traditions in light of the needs of our users in the digital age,"[4] and to meet stakeholder expectations of accountability (associated with customer satisfaction, relevance, and value).

ACCOUNTABILITY

Accountability, a cornerstone of good management, links management to planning, meeting stakeholder expectations, and fulfilling the institutional or broader organizational mission. In this context, accountability examines performance and the inputs behind that performance. Accountability exists when the relationship between an organization and its members, and what the organization accomplishes as well as the effective and efficient performance of the tasks and duties performed, is subject to the oversight, direction, or requests of key stakeholders. The organization and its members must provide information or justification for their actions and, in some cases, the library's very existence. Accountability, therefore, involves two stages: *answerability* and *enforcement*. Answerability refers to the obligation of the organization and its members to provide information reporting their inputs, outputs, and outcomes and to connect this information to their planning process, decisions, and actions and how well they can justify what they are doing to those engaged in oversight. Enforcement suggests that a stakeholder responsible for accountability can sanction the organization or remedy a questionable behavior.

One approach to accountability, known as social accountability, focuses on civic engagement—namely, a situation in which some stakeholders participate, either directly or indirectly, in exacting accountability. Such accountability provides direct answerability from key stakeholders (e.g., government and accreditation organizations) to the public and other stakeholders with an oversight function; however, some stakeholders might also engage in enforcement.[5]

Accountability extends to libraries as library managers increasingly need to document and articulate the value and relevance of the organizations in which they work and their contribution to the overall institutional mission and strategic and other plans. Accountability is not the only reason to engage in data collection. Libraries should also focus on service improvement, which means creating relevant, new services while replacing those that are outdated and fine-tuning those most relevant to helping the library to achieve its mission. Consequently, librarians should not assume libraries are valuable; instead, they should provide evidence that validates value. The purpose is to show realistically what the actual value is and not make unsupported assertions. At the same time, as Meredith Farkas explains, "service-oriented organizations . . . should also be learning organizations, focused on learning not only what we are doing right, but also what we could be doing better."[6] To this we add, "And then making the necessary improvements and determining how well they worked out and what needs further improvement or refinement." Clearly, planned change relates to the planning process and engagement in an ongoing cycle of planning through evaluation and assessment.

RELEVANCE AND VALUE

Increasingly, relevance and value are linked to a library's contribution to its institution or broader organization. That contribution may be defined in terms of meeting changing service roles and expectations as well as having libraries position themselves better to demonstrate their relevance and value, or, more precisely, to help the institution or broader organization demonstrate its value and show the ongoing relevance of the library to the overall mission. Simply stated, relevance and value address questions such as the following:

» How are we doing?
» Where are we going?
» How will we get there?
» Are we doing what the parent institution or broader organization expects and needs us to do?
» Are we performing in a cost-effective way?
» Are we making a difference and changing people's lives?

Central to most of these questions is the need for academic and public libraries to measure and demonstrate customer satisfaction and service quality, as well as the return on investment for their customers and the institution or broader organization. Return on investment, a traditional business measure, shows the worth of a library and its services to individuals or communities in terms of dollars and cents. Some of the preceding questions relate to effectiveness and efficiency, but they all should be considered within the context of the organizational and institutional mission and vision. A vision addresses where the organization is going and whether that direction matches the one set for the institution or broader organization.

The question, "How will we get there?" involves planning and the setting of short-term goals and objectives and includes monitoring progress in achieving those objectives and goals. While managers monitor progress, they may find the organization did not accomplish what it set out to achieve. In such instances, do they reallocate resources to accomplish the goal, or do they decide to move in another direction? The latter choice should be used sparingly, otherwise the strategic or other plans in place will not be accomplished.

The final question, "Are we making a difference and changing people's lives?" is the hardest to address because it involves outcomes assessment, as described in chapter 8. That question is also the hardest to measure as it requires a methodological tool chest for which many organizations do not have staff sufficiently trained in research as an inquiry process (see note 7) to determine the impact of their services on those they serve.

EVIDENCE-BASED DECISION MAKING

Evidence-based management, which originated in the health sciences and has been used in education and the social sciences, among other fields and disciplines, involves aligning evidence (in the context of customer needs, expectations, and preferences) with an identifiable problem, applying the evidence, evaluating the change, and looping back to the problem and its redefinition. Evaluation, however, may not be limited to the production and use of data that can be inserted into the type of metrics highlighted in this book. It might be linked to the investigation of a problem associated with the steps of research as an inquiry process. However, such a discussion is beyond the scope of this book.[7]

Although evidence-based management is essentially the same as evidence-based practice, the inclusion of the word management is a reminder that the results generated should apply to planning and service improvement. In effect, the goal is to make managerial decisions based on the best available evidence and to link the evidence to the planning process, goals, and objectives.[8] Evidence-based management involves the use of benchmarking and supports the adoption of guidelines and standards—best practices—to place problems in context and to make comparisons *across an industry*. A type of evidence is trend data, which place some occurrence in a broader perspective so that the occurrence can be better understood. In fact, the event or occurrence might represent a blip on the radar screen, and having trend data is intended to avoid misreading the importance of a blip; is the occurrence relevant or not, or can what is seen be reversed or accentuated?

Managing with Data

It is common in the literature of library and information science for authors to refer to a culture of assessment,[9] which we broaden to include a culture of evaluation and assessment. Regardless of the term used, the goal is for

> [s]taff and [library] leadership . . . to understand changing customer [and institutional or
> broader organization] expectations and values. In this context, collecting and analyzing
> data are understood as crucial aspects of [creating and] delivering the right services, at the

right time, to a well-understood customer base. In such an environment, continuous analysis of changing customer expectations is internalized in the institution's vision, mission, processes, and impact.[10]

More succinctly, the culture "is integrally connected to the notion of systemic organizational change."[11]

As Richard Boss notes, "Public libraries have been keeping voluminous library statistics for many decades to focus their resources on needed services, demonstrate the value of their services, aid library directors in the administration of their libraries, and to satisfy the needs of governmental planning bodies." "Historically," he continues,

> the emphasis has been on profiling communities and library users, collection sizes and growth, and circulation. Only recently have state library agencies . . . begun to gather data about the availability of patron access to the Internet, the number of PCs available to patrons, and the electronic resources available. An examination of public library data posted on the Web by a dozen states selected at random suggests that as useful as the data might be for state and federal planning . . . and to assure the equitable distribution of grant funds [especially LSTA funds], the data are not adequate for libraries seeking to respond to the needs and expectations of their constituencies and adjust to changing patterns of library use.[12]

Turning to the present, Boss points out the "dramatic increase in access to a library's electronic resources from homes, offices, and schools," while mentioning that "many directors have not been able to demonstrate conclusively that their libraries' total activity levels have increased."[13]

The keeping of "voluminous library statistics" is not confined to public libraries. Any library might keep and report statistics, but a relevant question is, "How do libraries use the data collected for service improvement linked to a planning process and helping the parent institution or organization with its accountability?" As this book illustrates, library managers should carefully think about what data and metrics they want to gather and how they can best use those data and metrics. In this way, they can seek to avoid data and metric overload; "too much data overwhelms, reduces clarity, and inhibits informed decision making."[14] Further, without engaging in research as an inquiry process, what other data and metrics do managers really need? If libraries collect unused data and metrics, why do they continue to do so? Are such data and metrics truly needed, valued, and linked to planning? Perhaps more important, "if data (evidence) and metrics are not valued, why not?" The answer to this question has implications for accountability, service improvement, and the demonstration of both relevance and value—all of which are important to stakeholders and the communities the library serves. Clearly, a library has choices about which data to collect and metrics to use. Undoubtedly, the list grows given the expectations of different stakeholders, but libraries should resist not collecting data simply because they cannot use them immediately, and, at the same time, they should avoid the collection of data that will never be used or are temporal in nature. Two critical questions for the data needed are these: "How often should they be collected?" and "How do they relate to the planning process?"

PLANNED ORGANIZATIONAL CHANGE

Evidence-based management might be associated with *positive (or planned) organizational change,* which focuses on positive results, processes, and attributes of organizations and their staff and on making the organizations excellent conveyors of outstanding service. Such organizations thrive in a competitive environment, and their institutions or broader organizations see them as resilient and vital. Furthermore, the staffs of these organizations should find deeper meaning in their work and react favorably to change and new opportunities as individuals and their managers craft and redefine positions to address where the organization is heading.[15]

The following ten tidbits are organized around ideas that can be quickly reviewed and understood. Those that seem irrelevant may be skipped, while those that are more interesting and relevant to you may be explored elsewhere in this book and beyond. In short, the tidbits may be read as a summary or an introduction to your journey into evaluation, accountability, data use and management, and continuous improvement of services. The tidbits could be reviewed from the context of the library's infrastructure (the collections and services, physical facilities, staff, and technology) and how it is used to serve the community better.

Tidbit 1: Data and statistics are not necessarily synonymous.

Some people refer to data as statistics. However, with this tidbit, we view statistics in terms of the formal collection, organization, analysis, interpretation, and presentation of data. We do not expect librarians to become statisticians. We have heard numerous librarians say, "I did not go to library school to become a statistician and deal with accountability." Nonetheless, we see value in taking statistics courses, but we do not regard them as a necessity. The type of statistics pertinent to the data services highlighted in this book comprises descriptive statistics, which describe or summarize patterns in the data. In contrast, with inferential statistics, researchers want to draw inferences that extend beyond the immediate data; such statistics are not relevant to the data services. Descriptive statistics, such as those reported in the two data services, focus on measures of central tendency—the average (the mode, median, and mean) and dispersion, the spread of the values around the central tendency. Two common measures of dispersion are the range (high to low values) and the standard deviation, which refers to how closely the scores cluster around the mean in a data set. Descriptive statistics lend themselves to graphical display; sometimes patterns are easier to see in a graph than a table. Clearly, librarians serving in managerial positions need some familiarity with descriptive statistics, but they might gain this from a workshop.

Tidbit 2: Managers should look for patterns among the data and present the results in a manner most meaningful to stakeholders.

The key part of this tidbit is "most meaningful." Not all stakeholders will want patterns reported in the same way. Instead of receiving a series of numbers, they might prefer a type of graph or the use of a graphical dashboard, a tool to communicate the health or performance of the organization and the organization's progress toward achieving stated goals and objectives as identified in the strategic plan.[16] One example is the Texas Tracking Postsecondary Outcomes Dashboard, an interactive display of data about Texas public high school graduates who enroll in higher education in the state in the fall immediately following graduation from high school. The dashboard (www.txhighereddata.org/index.cfm?objectid =8333C053-F6FC-03E9-E466C89A7C4EA74A), among other things, includes enrollment and demographic summaries, persistence patterns, and college readiness statistics. It also enables comparisons across the state, districts, and time periods. Some libraries apparently use dashboards but only to display their energy efficiency.[17] However, the concept of a dashboard might be expanded to include, for instance, the extent of customer satisfaction reported in the form of a net promoter score, a perspective that divides into three categories: (1) *promoters*, loyal enthusiasts who keep using the library and urging their friends to do the same; (2) *passives*, satisfied but unenthusiastic customers who can be easily wooed by the competition; and (3) *detractors*, unhappy customers trapped in a bad relationship.[18]

Tidbit 3: Management information systems are a necessity, not a luxury.

Undoubtedly, at one time this tidbit was not true. Today, Counting Opinions is an example of a company that lets academic and public libraries create and maintain a management information system through the company's subscription-based online service, which enables subscribers to add data to monitor performance and to make informed decisions about customer satisfaction, use, and return on investment. Depending on how a library defines quality, this concept might also be tracked through the system, and managers can correlate metrics with operational, customer, and competitive changes, thus enabling them to respond to new realities as they occur. With a management information system, managers can monitor the infrastructure from a customer's perspective and take corrective action as needed. They can also provide stakeholders with whatever inputs and outputs they require at the moment of demand and produce an updated return on investment quickly.

Tidbit 4: Effective managers avoid data overload.

As previously discussed, managers could be overwhelmed with the amount of data at their disposal. To be effective, they need to focus on the data elements and metrics with the greatest value to the organization, given its ability and need to improve service and demonstrate accountability. This book offers guidance in the selection of appropriate metrics. The key questions, in turn, become these:

» What are the data sources for those metrics?
» What is the quality of those data sources?
» How current are the data sources?
» Is it possible to compare data sources over time and produce trend data?

Tidbit 5: It is becoming easier to store, share, and reuse management data.

Storing refers to management information systems or the holding of the types of data services discussed in this book. *Sharing* means that management data (inputs and outputs) for one library are available for other libraries or that a library has access to trend data about its performance and budget distribution. Libraries can also reuse the management data over time, assuming the definitions of terms remain consistent. *Reuse* enables managers to compile the same metrics over time or to use the data in new contexts—create new metrics, ones meaningful to future planning processes.

Tidbit 6: Comparisons over time require maintaining consistent time series.

This tidbit, which stems from the previous one, does not prevent recalculations due to methodological changes and refinements. The development of new and different data sets, or redefinitions of terms, often drives methodological changes. However, any changes should be carefully considered, in part, to minimize the inability to make valid comparisons over time.

Tidbit 7: Libraries should take care in the compilation and reporting of data for inclusion in national data services.

This tidbit, which is the most basic one on the list, underscores that managers in the library producing the data, as well as those elsewhere, intend to use the data for identifying trends, reporting performance to stakeholders, engaging in benchmarking, creating and participating in best practices, and making decisions that align with existing planning processes. Because of this, care should be taken in the collection and reporting of the data. Managers should review both processes and occasionally check on the accuracy of the data. If they have questions about either process, they should raise them and take steps to ensure reliability (accuracy) and validity (measures what it purports to measure). After all, why would they want to report on performance or make decisions based on distorted data? Because the intent is not to mislead, anomalous results should be appropriately footnoted.

Tidbit 8: To be effective, managers need relevant data for decision making.

This tidbit does not mean that managers cannot make any decisions without data; rather, it refers to data-driven, or data-informed, decisions, which include strategic decisions, which advance the long-term direction of the organization; tactical decisions, which involve implementation of strategic decisions and involve responses to unforeseen events and operational decisions (e.g., fiscal year budget adjustments); and operational decisions, which are short-term decisions involving tasks required to implement tactical decisions. Further, with relevant data, managers address accountability and stakeholders' expectations while seeking to avoid making decisions based on whims, speculations, and assumptions.

Tidbit 9: Libraries need to develop a culture in which they learn from the evidence gathered.

Organizational culture refers to group norms of behavior and the underlying values that help keep those norms in place. As a result, it is insufficient for managers to embrace evidence-based management while not instilling evidence-based practices throughout the organization. Undoubtedly managerial leaders who view libraries as learning organizations that facilitate the learning of their members and continuously transform themselves appreciate more data-driven decision making and the importance of planning, evaluation and assessment, accountability, and service improvement based on the collection and use of evidence. Organizational leaders need to encourage knowledge creation and sharing as well as motivational strategies that lead to a new culture that embraces evidence-based management as members of the organization work to shape their future role and services.

Tidbit 10: The skill set of those working in academic and public libraries will continue to evolve.

Much has been written on this topic. One of these sources notes that "[t]he research library of today and tomorrow is a dynamic, service-oriented organization, supporting a diverse clientele with a wide range of sophisticated information, learning, and teaching needs." As such, the library will need professional staff who are intellectually curious, flexible, adaptable, persistent, and able to be enterprising. These individuals must also "possess excellent communication skills" and be "committed to life-long learning and personal career development."[19] This list of attributes actually extends beyond research libraries, and it could easily be expanded. One attribute often overlooked is the ability to engage in evaluation and assessment and to link the results to evidence-based management.

Other Tidbits?

Perhaps we could have added tidbits about the development, use, and interpretation of figures—graphs and other illustrative matter.[20] Both ACRL*Metrics* and PLA-*metrics* include assorted figures that library managers can download and include in their reports. Managers might even want to create their own figures as they recast the data.[21] Further, the University of Texas System, for instance, provides an online productivity dashboard to increase transparency and accountability, as well as to demonstrate the productivity, efficiency, and impact of each campus (www.utsystem.edu/offices/strategic-initiatives/productivity-dashboard). The dashboard provides a wealth of data from several perspectives: student success (access, engagement, and outcomes), faculty productivity, research and technology transfer, and finance and productivity.

As calls for accountability increase, it is not surprising that campus administrators are asking each department, including the library, to demonstrate the value provided to students, faculty, and researchers. There seems to be increased interest in presenting data in graphic form via dashboards. However, libraries infrequently replicate dashboards such as the Minnesota State Colleges and Universities Board of Trustees Accountability Dashboard (www.mnscu.edu/board/accountability/). Perhaps dashboards should be more common as they enable libraries and other organizations to communicate effectively and efficiently with stakeholders.

ANOTHER MAJOR DATA SET

The Association of Research Libraries (ARL) maintains its own data service that includes data collected and published annually for association members since 1961–1962. Before then, James Gerould compiled annual statistics for university libraries dating back to 1907–1908; this data set is known as the Gerould statistics. The ARL Statistics data series, which includes the Gerould statistics, describes the collections, expenditures, staffing, and service activities of these libraries (see www.arlstatistics.org/home). The series is included as a subscription-based service for nonmember libraries, vendors, commercial parties, and others. ACRL*Metrics* covers ALA university libraries, but this data series provides more trend data and detailed coverage of these university libraries. Subscribers can, for instance, pro-

FIGURE 11.1 **SERVICE TRENDS IN ARL LIBRARIES, 1991–2012**

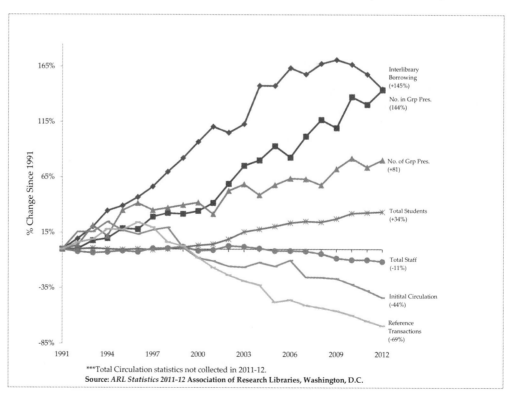

***Total Circulation statistics not collected in 2011-12.
Source: *ARL Statistics 2011-12* **Association of Research Libraries, Washington, D.C.**

duce institutional rankings by selected criteria, create data graphs, and download the data by year in spreadsheet format. Figures 11.1 and 11.2 are examples of the graphs that can be produced from the data set.

FIGURE 11.2 **MONOGRAPH AND SERIAL COSTS IN ARL LIBRARIES, 1986–2011***

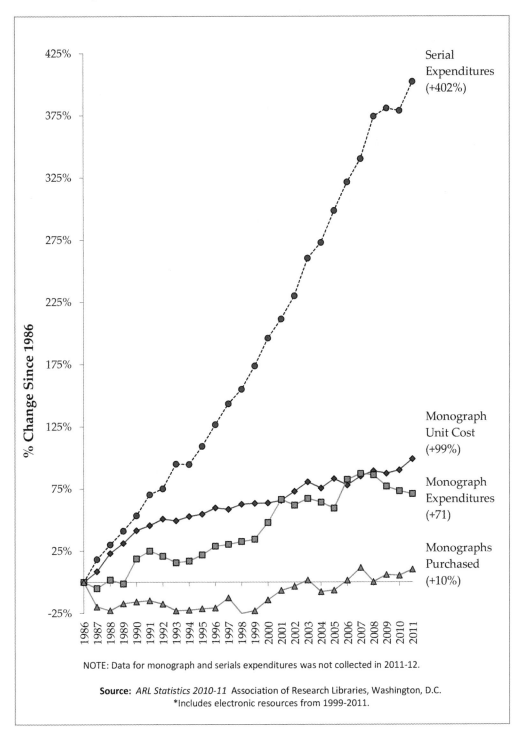

NOTE: Data for monograph and serials expenditures was not collected in 2011-12.

Source: *ARL Statistics 2010-11* Association of Research Libraries, Washington, D.C.
*Includes electronic resources from 1999-2011.

INSTITUTIONAL REPUTATION

Writing in the *Chronicle of Higher Education*, Eric Hoover notes that increased enrollment for a college correlates with that institution's reputation and annual ranking in such sources as the *Princeton Review* or *U.S. News & World Report*. Some of the academics quoted in his article argue that reputation relates explicitly to the strength of an institution's academic programs, the quality of student life, and the beauty of the campus, assuming students do not receive their education through online courses.[22] Sharon Weiner adds another component to the discussion of reputation—the role of libraries, in this case those associated with research universities. She examined institutional variables (grants received; instruction, research, and student services expenditures; and alumni, foundation, and corporate giving) and library variables (amount of library expenditures and the number of reference transactions, library presentations and attendees at those presentations, and professional staff). The only significant library variable was library expenditures.[23] Missing from her analysis are variables reflecting customers' expectations and experiences; the role of special collections in teaching, learning, and research; and the impact of facilities, such as information (and other types of) commons, on customers. Facilities might add a social dimension to reputation.

Reputation might also be viewed independently of institutional context. Units on campus, such as libraries, might have their own reputation. That reputation might even be negative. Undoubtedly for a library, such a label is probably associated with the perceived quality of its collections or customer encounters with staff or the services provided. For this reason, we encourage you to complement any use of the metrics contained in ACRL*Metrics* and PLA*metrics* with the methodologies outlined in *Listening to the Customer*.[24]

CONCLUDING THOUGHTS

With the involvement of research university libraries in the management of e-research data and increased expectations for academic librarians to become research data managers, the services that these libraries offer continue to expand. At the same time, these and other libraries are staking out new roles in scholarly communication[25] and the opportunities arising from the fact that more disciplines are becoming more collaborative, data-intensive, and computational. With so much attention in the literature of library and information science devoted to these topics, we should not forget that data management also includes the types of data included in the data services detailed in this book. In other words, data management is not confined to one type of library, and it expands the role of the library across the institution and globally but also internally in its ability to document its services and take corrective actions as necessary. Further, the data collected are useful to, among others, policy makers, the public, professional associations, and local practitioners for policy making, planning, and accountability.

EXERCISES

Answers to the following questions are in the "Appendix" at the back of the book. We encourage different members of a library staff to work on the exercises together and to discuss the results. Managers might also participate in that discussion.

QUESTION 1   Review ACRLMetrics (including the IPEDS data) or PLAmetrics. Are there any variables or metrics that might be relevant to institutional or organizational reputation? Thinking beyond those data services, are there other input metrics (e.g., those related to facilities and technology) and outputs that might better capture customer expectations and experiences and be useful for relating those expectations and experiences to reputation? If you think of additional metrics, how would you collect them (see note 22)?

QUESTION 2   The chapter discussed accountability as it links management to planning, meeting stakeholder expectations, and fulfilling the institutional or broader organizational mission. In this context, accountability examines performance and the inputs behind that performance. Discuss how a library might address accountability by linking its planning with inputs and outputs.

QUESTION 3   Evidence-based management involves the use of benchmarking and the adoption of best practices to place problems in context and to make comparisons across an industry. How might a library demonstrate that it practices evidence-based management?

QUESTION 4   Describe one model for implementing and maintaining an internal management information system (MIS).

QUESTION 5   Identify at least three sources of internal data.

QUESTION 6   How does *data-informed* relate to evidence-based management?

Notes

1. Martha J. Spear, "The Top 10 Reasons to Be a Librarian (with Apologies to David Letterman)," *American Libraries* 39, no. 9 (October 2002): 54–55.

2. DegreeDirectory.org, "How to Become a Librarian in 5 Steps," http://degreedirectory.org/colleges/how-to-become-a-librarian .html?eg=fe67b4b2beff62dc908aea8350598df9&rcntxt=aws&crt=26786497139&kwd =how%20to%20become%20a%20librarian.

3. Rush Miller, "Damn the Recession, Full Speed Ahead," *Journal of Library Administration* 52, no. 1 (2012): 3.

4. Miller, "Damn the Recession, Full Speed Ahead," 17.

5. Rick Stapenhurst and Mitchell O'Brien, *Accountability in Governance*, http://siteresources.worldbank.org/PUBLICSECTORANDGOVERNANCE/ Resources/AccountabilityGovernance.pdf.

6. Meredith Farkas, "Accountability vs. Improvement: Seeking Balance in the Value of Academic Libraries Initiative," *OLA Quarterly* 19, no. 1 (2013): 6.

7. See Peter Hernon, Robert E. Dugan, and Danuta A. Nitecki, *Engaging in Evaluation and Assessment Research* (Santa Barbara, CA: Libraries Unlimited, 2011).

8. For the steps associated with evidence-based practice and management, see Peter Hernon, Robert E. Dugan, and Joseph R. Matthews, *Getting Started with Evaluation* (Chicago: American Library Association, 2014).

9. Amos Lakos, "Evidence-Based Library Management: The Leadership Challenge," *portal: Libraries and the Academy* 7, no. 4 (2007): 431–50.

10. Lakos, "Evidence-Based Library Management," 432.

11. Lakos, "Evidence-Based Library Management," 432.

12. Richard W. Boss, *Rethinking Library Statistics in a Changing Environment* (Chicago: Public Library Association, 2006), www.ala.org/pla/tools/technotes/rethinkinglibrary.

13. Boss, *Rethinking Library Statistics in a Changing Environment*.

14. J. Eric Davies, "Editorial: What Gets Measured, Gets Managed: Statistics and Performance Indicators for Evidence Based Management," *Journal of Librarianship and Information Science* 34, no. 3 (2002): 132.

15. See Hernon, Dugan, and Matthews, *Getting Started with Evaluation*, 187–91.

16. See Elazar C. Harel and Toby D. Sitko, "Digital Dashboards: Driving Higher Education Decisions," *Research Bulletin*, issue 19 (Boulder, CO: EDUCAUSE Center for Applied Research, 2003), https://net.educause.edu/ir/library/pdf/ERB0319.pdf.

17. See, for instance, Drake Community Library, "Drake Community Library Shows Energy Efficiencies with Dashboard," www.prweb.com/releases/green-library/library-kiosk/prweb8822398.htm.

18. See Hernon, Dugan, and Matthews, *Getting Started with Evaluation*, 114–15.

19. Association of Southeastern Research Libraries, "Shaping the Future: ASERL's Competencies for Research Librarians" (Durham, NC: ASERL, 2000), www.aserl.org/programs/competencies/.

20. See Edward R. Tufte, *The Visual Display of Quantitative Information*, 2nd ed. (Cheshire, CT: Graphics Press, 2001); Edward R. Tufte, *Envisioning Information* (Cheshire, CT: Graphics Press, 1990); Edward R. Tufte, *Visual Explanations: Images and Quantities, Evidence and Narrative* (Cheshire, CT: Graphics Press, 1997); and Edward R. Tufte, *Beautiful Evidence* (Cheshire, CT: Graphics Press, 2006).

21. See Hernon, Dugan, and Matthews, *Getting Started with Evaluation*, 173–86; and Hernon, Dugan, and Nitecki, *Engaging in Evaluation and Assessment Research*, 179–99.

22. Eric Hoover, "Your College's Reputation Matters in Measurable Ways," *Chronicle of Higher Education* 60, no. 19 (January 24, 2014): A14.

23. Sharon Weiner, "The Contribution of the Library to the Reputation of a University," *Journal of Academic Librarianship* 35, no. 1 (January 2009): 3–13. See also Primary Research Group, *Academic Library Reputation Management Practices*, http://primaryresearch.com/view_product.php?report_id=440; and Association of College and Research Libraries, *Value of Academic Libraries: A Comprehensive Research Review and Report*, researched by Megan Oakleaf (Chicago: Association of College and Research Libraries, 2010).

24. Peter Hernon and Joseph R. Matthews, *Listening to the Customer* (Santa Barbara, CA: Libraries Unlimited, 2011).

25. Peter Hernon and Joseph R. Matthews, *Reflecting on the Future of Academic and Public Libraries* (Chicago: American Library Association, 2013).

APPENDIX
ANSWERS TO CHAPTER EXERCISES

CHAPTER ONE

These questions are ones for discussion as no single or simple answer applies to all libraries. Any additional variables and metrics should be relevant to the local planning process and accountability to the library's stakeholders. As you answer the questions, you should review a list of the library's key stakeholders and what their expectations are. What are the similarities and differences?

Note that chapter 6, which covers benchmarking, will provide insight into the answer for question 3, while chapter 7, which addresses best practices, will help shape the response to question 4.

CHAPTER TWO

1. To answer this question use ACRL*Metrics*.

STEP 1   Log on to the data service.

STEP 2   Click on the Local tab and the Report tab.

STEP 3   Click the Add button to create a new report.

STEP 4   Completing this report demonstrates the capabilities of ACRL*Metrics*. As the Collection, highlight "Select IPEDS Metrics for Libraries." This is the collection where the institutional information will reside. Type in a descriptive Report Name, a description of the report, and a Title if desired. Then, click the Save as New Report button.

STEP 5   We want to create a trend report, so under Report Type, select "Trend/PI." Once this is selected, a Start Period will appear. Because the IPEDS 2012 information was not complete when this exercise was created, use 2011 for the Period. Because we are looking for a five-year report, set the Start Period to 2007. This would be a good time to click on the Save button.

STEP 6   We can now select the indicators we want to include in the report. Going down the list of indicators, you will see "Total Expenses" under Finance. This is the operating expenditures for the institution, which includes academic support, student services, and the like. Highlight it, and click the Add button. Then, find "Total Library Expenditures (7+8+9)" further down the list of indicators. Highlight this indicator and click the Add button. Then, click on the Save button.

STEP 7   Once you have selected one or more indicators, the Locations function appears. We want just one library. Click on the Locations link, find and check the box for the library, and then click the Apply button. Then, click on the Save button.

STEP 8   Run the report. (The report returned is in a table format. Click on the trend line graph image to see a trend report.)

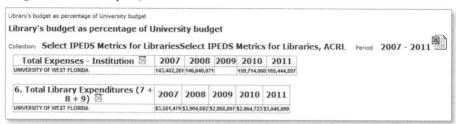

STEP 9   The question was to determine the library's budget as a percentage of a college's or university's annual operating budget for the past five years. To make this calculation, download the table as a spreadsheet by clicking on the Excel icon. Then, use Excel to create the percentage.

2. This becomes a metrics-based planning process that will help a library prepare to explain to stakeholders what it intends to do, how it will do it, and how they will know if it is successful.

     A. Input metrics (resources that will go into the program)
- » Amount of funding for staff time expected to prepare and implement the summer reading program
- » Amount of funding for supplies
- » Amount of funding for refreshments for program attendees and their parents/guardians
- » Amount of funding for books if not already acquired
- » Amount of funding to support publicity and public relations materials, such as posters and handouts announcing the program
- » Reading levels of second graders during their last quarter in school
- » A means of measuring the reading levels of second graders at the end of the summer program

     B. Activities (ones to be undertaken)
- » Planned for programs in the library for eight consecutive weeks
- » Parents/guardians are separated from their children for half of the time during each weekly program and may attend an information session with librarians about services, browse the library, or read (they cannot leave the library)
- » Every other week a community leader meets with the children; the person may be a city official or a sports figure to talk about the importance of reading
- » Measuring the reading levels of second graders at the end of the summer who attended at least five of the eight weekly programs

     C. Output (how much is the program/service used)
- » Counts of the number of programs implemented
- » Counts of the number of program participants and the number of adults attending

» Counts of the number of times community leaders actually showed up
» Counts of the number of books checked out to children
» Counts of the number of books the children or their parents/guardians self-reported that were read
» Number of second graders at the end of the summer who attended at least five of the eight weekly programs
» Measured reading levels of second graders at the end of the summer who attended at least five of the eight weekly programs
» Cost per attendee of the program (the sum of costs as inputs)

D. Outcome/Impact
» Number of second graders who had their reading level measured at the end of the summer and who improved one reading level
» Ratio of the number of second graders who had their reading level measured at the end of the summer and who improved one reading level and those who were also measured but did not improve by one grade level

CHAPTER THREE

1. To answer the question use ACRL*Metrics*.

STEP 1   Log on to the data service.

STEP 2   Click on the Local tab and the Report tab.

STEP 3   Click the Add button to create a new report.

STEP 4   Select "ACRL" as the Collection, then type in a descriptive Report Name and a description of the report. Add a Title if desired. Then, click the Save as New Report button.

STEP 5   Under Report Settings at the top, select the latest period for the report. In this case it was FY2012.

STEP 6   We want to create a table, so under Report Type, select "Table."

STEP 7   We can now select the indicators we want to include in the report. Go to the indicators box and select those indicators related to the size of the collection, including:
» Titles Held
» Volumes Held (as of June 30 reporting year)
» Number of Electronic Books Held
» Titles Held per Enrolled FT Student
» Volumes Held per Enrolled FT Student

Use of the collection may be measured by circulation transactions. Including ILL transactions will help the library to learn about the quality of its collection as well as serving as a transaction metric. Select these indicators to include:
» Initial Circulation Transactions
» Circulation per Enrolled Students
» Total Items Borrowed (ILL)
» Total Items Loaned (ILL)
» ILL Borrowed per Enrolled FT Student
» ILL Loaned per Enrolled FT Students

This would be a good time to click on the Save button.

STEP 8 Once you have selected one or more indicators, the Locations function appears. Most academic institutions already have a select list of peers and aspirants for benchmarking. If you have saved a set of benchmarking partners, click Locations and select the filter you designated. If you have not set up the Locations filter, then go to Locations and select all of the libraries you wish to use as benchmarking partners. Type in a Filter Name (such as Peers), and click on the Apply button to save this group. Now this group of libraries will always be available for you to choose as a Locations filter.

STEP 9 Run the report. (The report returned is in a table format. It may be downloaded as a spreadsheet by clicking on the Excel icon.)

Collections Size and Use

Collection: **ACRL**   Period: **2012, Start 2011-07**   Months: **12**

Locations (11) ▲	1. Titles Held	2. Volumes held (as of June 30 reporting year)	4. Number of electronic books held	Titles Held per Enrolled FT Student	Volumes Held per Enrolled FT Student	17. Initial Circulation Transactions	Circulation Per Enrolled Students	22. Total Items Borrowed (ILL)	21. Total Items Loaned (ILL)	ILL Borrowed per Enrolled FT Student	ILL Loaned per Enrolled FT Students
East Tennessee State University	866,505	889,753	79,932	73	75	118,519	8.08	13,407	7,673	1.13	0.65
Indiana State University	1,384,378	1,213,878	155,000	146	128	120,149	11.07	6,312	8,528	0.66	0.90
Rowan University	366,009	407,891	50,686	40	44	27,161	2.30	4,236	5,170	0.46	0.56
Stephen F Austin State University	1,713,193	2,002,825	29,581	168	196	48,956	3.79	3,173	3,738	0.31	0.37
University of Arkansas at Little Rock	516,173	660,229	29,686	74	95	25,729	2.23	5,772	4,698	0.83	0.68
University of Massachusetts-Lowell	215,983	273,391	1,791	24	30	12,514	0.83	6,758	6,117	0.75	0.67
University of South Dakota	695,865	1,082,263	13,789	120	186	23,340	2.34	9,306	11,030	1.60	1.90
University of West Florida	528,729	1,086,562	148,653	70	143	217,758	18.17	5,312	11,938	0.70	1.57
University of West Georgia	339,435	456,807	102,200	39	52	78,713	6.69	2,075	4,313	0.24	0.49
Valdosta State University	547,694	555,667	76,949	54	55	58,562	4.47	3,615	2,618	0.36	0.26
Western Carolina University	914,368	1,064,200	437,282	129	150	32,234	3.45	10,314	8,035	1.45	1.13

2.   To answer the question use ACRL*Metrics*.

STEP 1 Log on to the data service.

STEP 2 Click on the Local tab and then the Report tab.

STEP 3 Click the Add button to create a new report.

STEP 4 Select "ACRL" as the Collection, and then type in a descriptive Report Name and a description of the report. Add a Title if desired. Then, click the Save as New Report button.

STEP 5 Under Report Settings at the top, select the latest period for the report. In this case it was FY2012.

STEP 6 We want to create a table, so under Report Type, select "Table."

STEP 7 We can now select the indicators we want to include in the report. Go to the indicators box and select this indicator related to e-book holdings:
   » Number of electronic books held
      Although this is the metric we are looking for, three more indicators may be included to provide some context and to create a few ratios later when the library is reviewing the data:
   » Total Library Materials (7a + 7b + 7c) [expended]
   » Total Library Materials Expenditures per Enrolled Student FTE
   » Total Students, Full-Time and Part-Time
This would be a good time to click on the Save button.

STEP 8   Once you have selected one or more indicators, the Locations function appears. Most academic institutions already have a select list of peers and aspirants for benchmarking. If you have saved a set of benchmarking partners, click Locations and select the filter you designated. If you have not set up the Locations filter, then go to Locations and select all of the libraries you wish to use as benchmarking partners. Type in a Filter Name (such as Peers), and click on the Apply button to save this group. Now this group of libraries will always be available for you to choose as a Locations filter.

STEP 9   Run the report. (The report returned is in a table format. It may be downloaded as a spreadsheet by clicking on the Excel icon.)

E-Book Holdings

Collection: **ACRL**   Period: **2012, Start 2011-07**   Months: **12**

Locations (11) ▲	4. Number of ▼ electronic books held	7. Total Library ▼ Materials (7a + 7b + 7c)	Tot Library Materials Expenditures / ▼ Enrolled Student FTE	Total students, full- ⬍ time and part-time
▲	COLLECTIONS ▼	MATERIALS EXPENDITURES ▼	Expenditures Ratios ▼	ENROLLMENT - FALL ⬍
East Tennessee State University	79,932	$1,370,214	$115.84	14,662
Indiana State University	155,000	$2,402,111	$252.80	10,857
Rowan University	50,686	$1,732,447	$188.56	11,816
Stephen F Austin State University	29,581	$1,477,554	$144.62	12,903
University of Arkansas at Little Rock	29,688	$1,702,798	$245.29	11,533
University of Massachusetts-Lowell	1,791	$2,057,543	$226.98	15,045
University of South Dakota	13,789	$1,373,440	$236.31	9,970
University of West Florida	148,653	$1,052,630	$138.76	11,982
University of West Georgia	102,200	$1,084,088	$123.00	11,769
Valdosta State University	76,949	$1,378,041	$137.12	13,089
Western Carolina University	437,282	$2,152,955	$302.64	9,352
Mean	102,323	$1,616,711	$191.99	12,089
Median	76,949	$1,477,554	$188.56	11,816

3.   To answer this question use PLA*metrics*.

STEP 1   Log on to the data service.

STEP 2   Click on the Local tab and the Report tab.

STEP 3   Click the Add button to create a new report.

STEP 4   Select "PLDS" as the Collection, then type in a descriptive Report Name and a description of the report. Add a Title if desired. Then, click the Save as New Report button.

STEP 5   Under Report Settings at the top, select the latest period for the report. In this case it was FY2012.

STEP 6   Because the information request is for a five-year trend, for the Report Type select "Trend/PI."

STEP 7   Once Trend/PI is selected for the report type, a Start Period box appears next to Period. To create a five-year report, set Start Period to FY2008.

STEP 8   A report about "total budget" actually means "operating expenditures" as budgets can be revised during the fiscal year. We also want to learn about total operating expenditures per capita. From the list of indicators select

»   Total Operating Expenditures

»   Operating Expenditures per Capita

This is a good time to click the Save button.

STEP 9 To limit the results to our benchmarking group, use the Locations filter to find the benchmarking partners or apply the Locations filter if you have identified the benchmarking group and have saved the list as a filter. For this report, we will add the indicator for "Population of legal service area" to help limit the libraries in our benchmarking group.

STEP 10 After adding all of the indicators, use the filters associated with the indicators to designate desired ranges. For population, we will use a low of 250,000 and a high of 500,000. For operating expenditures, we will use a low of $4 million and a high of $5.5 million. This is another good time to click the Save button.

STEP 11 Run the report. The results are displayed in a table format. In this example, information from seven libraries is available in three reports.

Total budget and per capita funding: trend

Collection: **PLDS**   Period   **FY2008 - FY2012**

24. Total operating expenditures (total of items 20-23)	FY2008	FY2009	FY2010	FY2011	FY2012
ERIE COUNTY PUBLIC LIBRARY	$6,199,246	$6,050,106	$6,293,403	$6,301,114	$4,794,082
FIRST REGIONAL LIBRARY	$4,736,400	$5,167,842	$4,884,649	$5,538,124	$5,338,102
FLINT RIVER REGIONAL LIBRARY SYSTEM					$4,003,874
GASTON-LINCOLN REGIONAL LIBRARY (NO DATA POST 2012)	$4,512,635	$4,616,436		$4,660,155	$4,468,235
MONT CO-NORRISTOWN PUB LIB	$5,201,993	$5,015,313	$4,522,169	$4,231,376	$4,393,998
PORTLAND PUBLIC LIBRARY	$3,826,396	$3,704,646	$3,668,146	$3,861,396	$4,206,527
SANTA ANA PUBLIC LIBRARY	$3,338,909				$4,056,480
AVG	$4,635,930	$4,910,869	$4,842,092	$4,918,433	$4,465,900
MEDIAN	$4,624,518	$5,015,313	$4,703,409	$4,660,155	$4,393,998

Operating Expenditures Per Capita	FY2008	FY2009	FY2010	FY2011	FY2012
ERIE COUNTY PUBLIC LIBRARY	$25.27	$21.59	$22.46	$22.46	$17.09
FIRST REGIONAL LIBRARY	$17.88	$19.51	$17.72	$19.57	$18.63
FLINT RIVER REGIONAL LIBRARY SYSTEM					$14.15
GASTON-LINCOLN REGIONAL LIBRARY (NO DATA POST 2012)	$16.55	$16.58		$16.20	$15.73
MONT CO-NORRISTOWN PUB LIB	$18.06	$17.42	$15.70	$13.69	$14.22
PORTLAND PUBLIC LIBRARY	$8.46	$8.19	$7.64	$7.92	$8.62
SANTA ANA PUBLIC LIBRARY	$9.45				$12.38
AVG	$15.95	$16.66	$15.88	$15.97	$14.40
MEDIAN	$17.21	$17.42	$16.71	$16.20	$14.22

2.a Population of legal service area	FY2008	FY2009	FY2010	FY2011	FY2012
ERIE COUNTY PUBLIC LIBRARY	245,275	280,243	280,243	280,566	280,566
FIRST REGIONAL LIBRARY	264,880	264,880	275,712	282,974	286,474
FLINT RIVER REGIONAL LIBRARY SYSTEM					282,945
GASTON-LINCOLN REGIONAL LIBRARY (NO DATA POST 2012)	272,696	278,447		287,599	284,012
MONT CO-NORRISTOWN PUB LIB	287,973	287,973	287,973	309,099	309,099
PORTLAND PUBLIC LIBRARY	452,354	452,354	480,435	487,759	487,759
SANTA ANA PUBLIC LIBRARY	353,184				327,731
AVG	312,727	312,779	331,091	329,599	322,655
MEDIAN	280,335	280,243	284,108	287,599	286,474

FILTERS	VALUES	
	MIN / %	MAX
POPULATION OF LEGAL SERVICE AREA	250,000	500,000
TOTAL OPERATING EXPENDITURES (TOTAL OF ITEMS 20-23)	4,000,000	5,500,000

STEP 12 To view a trend line graph, click on the graph icon for one of the three indicators, which will produce a graph as follows:

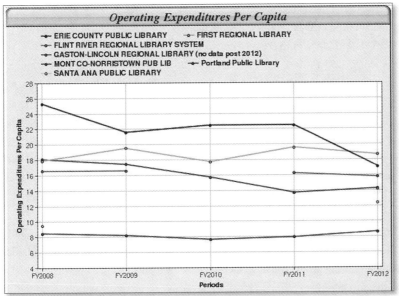

STEP 13 You may save the data to an Excel spreadsheet by clicking on the Excel icon on the Results page.

CHAPTER FOUR

These questions are ones for discussion as no single or simple answer applies to all libraries. As you answer the questions, you might include some customers in the discussion. At the same time, it is important to remember that libraries have both internal (their own staff) and external customers.

CHAPTER FIVE

1. A stacked bar chart would be one means to report staff type classifications. The staff chart from table 5.1 has been revised to include data for the last five years.

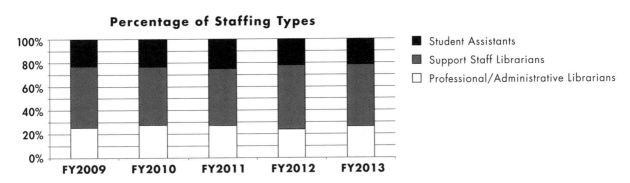

2. Use the data from PLA*metrics* to find the data.

STEP 1   Log on to the data service.

STEP 2   Click on the Local tab and the Report tab.

STEP 3   Click the Add button to create a new report.

STEP 4   Select "PLDS" as the Collection, then type in a descriptive Report Name and a description of the report. Add a Title if desired. Then, click the Save as New Report button.

STEP 5   Under Report Settings at the top, select the latest period for the report. In this case it was FY2012.

STEP 6   We want to create a report about the staff FTEs per transaction for circulation, reference, and library visits. Review the indicators available in the groups. A good set found are FTEs Per 1,000 for Circulation, Reference Transactions, and Visits. Include these three by adding them to the report. This is a good time to click the Save button.

STEP 7   To limit the results to our benchmarking group, use the Locations filter to find the benchmarking partners or apply the Locations filter if you have identified the benchmarking group and have saved the list as a filter. For this report, we will add indicators for "Population of legal service area" and "Total operating expenditures" to help limit the libraries in the benchmarking group.

STEP 8   After adding all of the indicators, use the filters associated with the indicators to designate desired ranges. For population, we will use a low of 250,000 and a high of 350,000. For operating expenditures, we will use a low of $4 million and a high of $5.5 million. This is another good time to click the Save button.

STEP 9   Run the report and the results are displayed. In this example, data from six libraries are available.

STEP 10   The table report includes columns for population and expenditures. These are not needed for this report—they were used for finding benchmarking partners. Return to Report Template, and uncheck the boxes to the left of the indicators. Do not remove these two indicators. Save, and then run the report again.

STEP 11   Once you have the report results as you want them, you may save the data to an Excel spreadsheet by clicking on the Excel icon on the Results page.

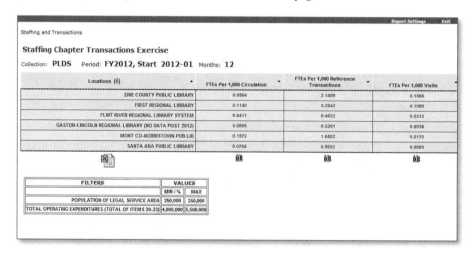

Staffing and Transactions

Staffing Chapter Transactions Exercise

Collection: **PLDS**   Period: **FY2012, Start 2012-01**   Months: **12**

Locations (6)	FTEs Per 1,000 Circulation	FTEs Per 1,000 Reference Transactions	FTEs Per 1,000 Visits
ERIE COUNTY PUBLIC LIBRARY	0.0564	2.1499	0.1966
FIRST REGIONAL LIBRARY	0.1140	0.2942	0.1089
FLINT RIVER REGIONAL LIBRARY SYSTEM	0.0411	0.4632	0.0313
GASTON-LINCOLN REGIONAL LIBRARY (NO DATA POST 2012)	0.0595	0.3301	0.0938
MONT CO-NORRISTOWN PUB LIB	0.1572	1.6802	0.5170
SANTA ANA PUBLIC LIBRARY	0.0766	0.5692	0.0869

FILTERS	VALUES	
	MIN / %	MAX
POPULATION OF LEGAL SERVICE AREA	250,000	350,000
TOTAL OPERATING EXPENDITURES (TOTAL OF ITEMS 20-23)	4,000,000	5,500,000

3. Use ACRL*Metrics* to find the data.

STEP 1 Log on to the data service.

STEP 2 Click on the Local tab and the Report tab.

STEP 3 Click the Add button to create a new report.

STEP 4 Select "ACRL" as the Collection, then type in a descriptive Report Name and a description of the report. Add a Title if desired. Then, click the Save as New Report button.

STEP 5 Under Report Settings at the top, select the latest period for the report. In this case it was FY2012.

STEP 6 We want to create a table, so under Report Type, select "Table."

STEP 7 We can now select the indicators we want to include in the report. Go to the indicators box and select those indicators related to staff and reference:

  » Reference Transactions per Professional Staff
  » Reference Transactions per Support Staff
  » Reference Transactions per Student Assistants
  » Reference Transactions per Staff FTE
  » Staff FTEs per 1000 Reference Transactions
  » Professional Staff per 1000 Reference Transactions
  » Total Staff Expenditures per Reference Transaction

This would be a good time to click on the Save button.

STEP 8 Once you have selected one or more indicators, the Locations function appears. Most academic institutions already have a select list of peers and aspirants for benchmarking. If you have saved a set of benchmarking partners, click Locations and select the filter you designated. If you have not set up the Locations filter, then go to Locations and select all of the libraries you wish to use as benchmarking partners. Type in a Filter Name (such as Peers), and click on the Apply button to save this group. Now this group of libraries will always be available for you to choose as a Locations filter.

STEP 9 Run the report. The report returned is in a table format. (It may be downloaded as a spreadsheet by clicking on the Excel icon.)

Collection: **ACRL**   Period: **2012, Start** 2011-07   Months: **12**

Locations (11)	Reference Transactions Per Professional Staff	Reference Transactions Per Support Staff	Reference Transactions Per Student Assistants	Reference Transactions Per Staff FTE	Staff FTEs Per 1000 Reference Transactions	Professional Staff Per 1000 Reference Transactions	Total Staff Expenditures per Reference Transaction
East Tennessee State University	2,928	2,157	4,554	976	1.02	0.34	$28.27
Indiana State University	609	373	538	162	6.16	1.64	$214.72
Rowan University	147	126	553	61	16.51	6.80	$1,074.14
Stephen F Austin State University	192	305	324	86	11.58	5.21	$409.55
University of Arkansas at Little Rock	459	565	565	175	5.71	2.18	$186.14
University of Massachusetts-Lowell	167	439	140	65	15.38	5.98	$769.25
University of South Dakota	441	294	587	136	7.38	2.27	$303.71
University of West Florida	3,672	1,683	4,488	918	1.09	0.27	$33.00
University of West Georgia	616	580	379	167	5.98	1.62	$190.72
Valdosta State University	559	664	1,003	233	4.29	1.79	$128.06
Western Carolina University	746	608	2,735	298	3.35	1.34	$119.71
Avg	958	709	1,442	298	7.14	2.68	$314.30
Median	559	565	565	167	5.98	1.79	$190.72

4. Use PLA*metrics* to find the data.

STEP 1   Log on to Counting Opinions.

STEP 2   Click on the Local tab and the Report tab.

STEP 3   Click the Add button to create a new report.

STEP 4   Select "PLDS" as the Collection, then type in a descriptive Report Name and a description of the report. Add a Title if desired. Then, click the Save as New Report button.

STEP 5   Under Report Settings at the top, select the latest period for the report. In this case it was FY2012.

STEP 6   We want to create a report about the staff expenditures per transaction for circulation, reference, and library visits. Review the indicators available in the groups. A good set found are Total Staff Expenditures per Circulation, Reference Transaction, and Visit. Include these three indicators by adding them to the report. This is a good time to click the Save button.

STEP 7   To limit the results to our benchmarking group, use the Locations filter to find the benchmarking partners or apply the Locations filter if you have identified the benchmarking group and have saved the list as a filter. For this report, we will add indicators for "Population of Legal Service Area" and "Total Operating Expenditures" to help limit the libraries in our benchmarking group.

STEP 8   After adding all of the indicators, use the filters associated with the indicators to designate desired ranges. For population, we will use a low of 250,000 and a high of 350,000. For operating expenditures, we will use a low of $4 million and a high of $5.5 million. This is another good time to click the Save button.

STEP 9   Run the report and the results are displayed. In this example, data from six libraries are available.

STEP 10   The table report includes columns for population and expenditures. These are not needed for this report—they were used for finding benchmarking partners. Return to Report Template and uncheck the boxes to the left of the indicators. Do not remove these two indicators. Save, and then run again.

STEP 11   Once you have the report results as you want them, you may save the data to an Excel spreadsheet by clicking on the Excel icon on the Results page.

Collection: **PLDS**   Period: **FY2012, Start 2012-01**   Months: **12**

Locations (6)	Total Staff Expenditures per Circulation	Total Staff Expenditures per Reference Transaction	Total Staff Expenditures per Visit
ERIE COUNTY PUBLIC LIBRARY	$3.00	$114.29	$10.45
FIRST REGIONAL LIBRARY	$2.67	$6.89	$2.55
FLINT RIVER REGIONAL LIBRARY SYSTEM	$2.22	$25.05	$1.69
GASTON-LINCOLN REGIONAL LIBRARY (NO DATA POST 2012)	$2.67	$14.61	$4.21
MONT CO-NORRISTOWN PUB LIB	$5.06	$54.03	$16.63
SANTA ANA PUBLIC LIBRARY	$5.65	$41.96	$6.41
Avg	$3.54	$42.84	$6.99
Median	$2.83	$33.51	$5.31

FILTERS	VALUES	
	MIN / %	MAX
POPULATION OF LEGAL SERVICE AREA	250,000	350,000
TOTAL OPERATING EXPENDITURES (TOTAL OF ITEMS 20-23)	4,000,000	5,500,000

5. Use ACRL*Metrics* to find the data.

STEP 1 Log on to the data service.

STEP 2 Click on the Local tab and the Report tab.

STEP 3 Click the Add button to create a new report.

STEP 4 Select "ACRL" as the Collection, then type in a descriptive Report Name and a description of the report. Add a Title if desired. Then, click the Save as New Report button.

STEP 5 Under Report Settings at the top, select the latest period for the report. In this case it was FY2012.

STEP 6 We want to create a table, so under Report Type, select "Table."

STEP 7 We can now select the indicators we want to include in the report. Go to the indicators box and select those indicators related to staff expenditures; however, for this answer do not include fringe benefits:

>> Salaries & Wages Professional Staff

>> Salaries & Wages Support Staff

>> Total Salaries & Wages

>> Total Staff Expenditures per Enrolled FT [full-time] Students

>> % of Staff Expenditures Spent on Professional Staff

>> % of Staff Expenditures Spent on Student Assistants

>> % of Staff Expenditures Spent on Support Staff

This would be a good time to click on the Save button.

STEP 8 Once you have selected one or more indicators, the Locations function appears. Most academic institutions already have a select list of peers and aspirants for benchmarking. If you have saved a set of benchmarking partners, click Locations and select the filter you designated. If you have not set up the Locations filter, then go to Locations and select all of the libraries you wish to use as benchmarking partners. Provide a Filter Name (such as Peers), and click on the Apply button to save this group. Now this group of libraries will always be available for you to choose as a Locations filter. This would be another good time to click on the Save button.

STEP 9 Run the report. The report returned is in a table format. (It may be downloaded as a spreadsheet by clicking on the Excel icon.)

Collection: **ACRL** Period: **2012, Start 2011-07** Months: **12**

Locations (11)	8a. Salaries & Wages Professional Staff	8b. Salaries & Wages Support Staff	8c. Salaries & Wages Student Assistants	8. Total Salaries & Wages	Total Staff Expenditures per Enrolled FT Students	% of Staff Expenditures spent on Professional Staff	% of Staff Expenditures spent on Support Staff	% of Staff Expeditures spent on Student Assistants
East Tennessee State University	$639,540	$480,480	$38,590	$1,158,610	$97.95	55.20%	41.47%	3.33%
Indiana State University	$1,513,038	$730,607	$240,232	$2,483,877	$261.41	60.91%	29.41%	9.67%
Rowan University	$1,814,333	$1,146,250	$69,564	$3,030,147	$329.79	59.88%	37.83%	2.30%
Stephen F Austin State University	$1,384,501	$471,171	$256,211	$2,121,883	$207.68	65.72%	22.21%	12.07%
University of Arkansas at Little Rock	$912,961	$364,693	$90,760	$1,368,314	$197.11	66.71%	26.65%	6.63%
University of Massachusetts-Lowell	$1,824,036	$385,060	$490,961	$2,700,057	$297.86	67.56%	14.26%	18.18%
University of South Dakota	$778,655	$675,750	$151,031	$1,605,436	$276.23	48.50%	42.09%	9.41%
University of West Florida	$617,851	$549,957	$165,041	$1,332,849	$175.70	46.36%	41.26%	12.38%
University of West Georgia	$1,464,277	$233,423	$183,227	$1,880,927	$213.40	77.85%	12.41%	9.74%
Valdosta State University	$1,185,392	$457,481	$218,951	$1,861,824	$185.26	63.67%	24.57%	11.76%
Western Carolina University	$1,124,592	$805,366	$34,651	$1,964,609	$276.16	57.24%	40.99%	1.76%
Avg	$1,206,280	$572,749	$176,293	$1,955,321	$228.96	60.87%	30.29%	8.84%
Median	$1,185,392	$480,480	$165,041	$1,880,927	$213.40	60.91%	29.41%	9.67%

CHAPTER SIX

1. Benchmarking as a managerial learning process enables librarians to learn from one another by looking at why there are differences in performance results among organizations undertaking similar functions. Although measuring service use from one year to the next in a single library is useful for tracking internal progress, it is a limited evaluative tool. The discovery of methods deployed by other libraries to attain successful processes, services, and outcomes can help the library improve its own performance by duplicating the best practices of these successful libraries. However, one must first discover these libraries.

2. Use PLA*metrics* to find the data.

STEP 1 Log on to the data service.

STEP 2 Click on the Local tab and the Report tab.

STEP 3 Click the Add button to create a new report.

STEP 4 Select "PLDS" as the Collection, then type in a descriptive Report Name and a description of the report. Add a Title if desired. Then, click the Save as New Report button.

STEP 5 Under Report Settings at the top, select the latest period for the report. In this case it was FY2012.

STEP 6 To create a report about operating expenditures, we want to know about the expenditures for staff, library materials, and other operating expenses, and the total reported. To place this comparison in context, we can also benchmark total operating expenditures per capita. The indicators include

» Operating Expenditures–Staff

» Total expenditures for Library Materials

» Expenditures on All Other Items

» Total Operating Expenditures

» Operating Expenditures per Capita

This is a good time to click the Save button.

STEP 7 To limit the results to our benchmarking group, use the Locations filter to find the benchmarking partners or apply the Locations filter if you have identified the benchmarking group and have saved the list as a filter. For this report, we will add the indicator for "Population of legal service area" to help limit the libraries in the benchmarking group.

STEP 8 After adding all of the indicators, use the filters associated with the indicators to designate desired ranges. For population, we will use a low of 250,000 and a high of 500,000. For operating expenditures, we will use a low of $4 million and a high of $5.5 million. This is another good time to click the Save button.

STEP 9 Run the report and the results are displayed. In this example, data from the seven libraries are available.

STEP 10   Once you have the report results, you might save the data to an Excel spreadsheet by clicking on the Excel icon on the Results page.

Benchmarking Expenditures

Collection: **PLDS** Period: **FY2012, Start 2012-01** Months: **12**

Locations (7)	Operating Expenditures – Staff	22.e Total expenditures for library materials	23. Expenditures on all other items	24. Total operating expenditures (total of items 20-23)	Operating Expenditures Per Capita	2.a Population of legal service area
ERIE COUNTY PUBLIC LIBRARY	$4,093,273	$700,809		$4,794,082	$17.09	200,566
FIRST REGIONAL LIBRARY	$3,490,313	$440,910	$1,398,279	$5,330,102	$15.63	296,474
FLINT RIVER REGIONAL LIBRARY SYSTEM	$2,704,424	$494,512	$894,938	$4,003,874	$14.15	232,946
GASTON-LINCOLN REGIONAL LIBRARY (NO DATA POST 2012)	$3,094,671	$618,900	$754,658	$4,465,335	$15.73	284,012
MONT CO-NORRISTOWN PUB LIB	$3,151,366	$624,128	$610,511	$4,393,898	$14.72	300,093
PORTLAND PUBLIC LIBRARY	$2,764,650	$369,540	$1,073,293	$4,204,527	$8.62	437,759
SANTA ANA PUBLIC LIBRARY	$2,053,900	$316,250	$1,084,291	$4,066,436	$12.36	327,731
Avg	$3,136,096	$497,909	$970,860	$4,465,900	$14.40	322,656
Median	$3,094,677	$449,540	$904,111	$4,393,998	$14.22	286,474

FILTERS	VALUES	
	MIN / %	MAX
POPULATION OF LEGAL SERVICE AREA	250,000	500,000
TOTAL OPERATING EXPENDITURES (TOTAL OF ITEMS 20-23)	4,000,000	5,500,000

3.   Use ACRL*Metrics* to find the data.

STEP 1   Log on to the data service.

STEP 2   Click on the Local tab and the Report tab.

STEP 3   Click the Add button to create a new report.

STEP 4   Select "ACRL" as the Collection, then type in a descriptive Report Name and a description of the report. Add a Title if desired. Then, click the Save as New Report button.

STEP 5   Under Report Settings at the top, select the latest period for the report. In this case it was FY2012.

STEP 6   We want to create a table, so under Report Type, select "Table."

STEP 7   We can now select the indicators we want to include in the report. Go to the indicators box and select those indicators related to holdings:

    » Titles Held

    » Volumes Held (as of June 30 reporting year)

    » Number of Electronic Books Held

    This would be a good time to click on the Save button.

STEP 8   Once you have selected one or more indicators, the Locations function appears. Most academic institutions already have a select list of peers and aspirants for benchmarking. If you have saved a set of benchmarking partners, click Locations and select the filter you designated. If you have not set up the Locations filter, then go to Locations and select all of the libraries you wish to use as benchmarking partners. Type in a Filter Name (such as Peers), and click on the Apply button to save this group. Now this group of libraries will always be available for you to choose as a Locations filter.

STEP 9   Run the report. The report returned is in a table format. (It may be downloaded as a spreadsheet by clicking on the Excel icon.)

Benchmarking Holdings

Collection: **ACRL** Period: **2012, Start 2011-07** Months: **12**

Locations (11)	1. Titles Held	2. Volumes held (as of June 30 reporting year)	4. Number of electronic books held
	COLLECTIONS	COLLECTIONS	COLLECTIONS
East Tennessee State University	966,905	888,763	78,912
Indiana State University	1,384,378	1,213,878	165,000
Rowan University	365,008	407,891	50,586
Stephen F Austin State University	1,713,193	2,002,826	29,591
University of Arkansas at Little Rock	516,173	868,229	29,688
University of Massachusetts-Lowell	215,963	273,391	1,791
University of South Dakota	695,865	1,062,263	13,789
University of West Florida	529,729	1,006,562	148,653
University of West Georgia	339,435	456,807	102,200
Valdosta State University	547,694	655,667	76,949
Western Carolina University	514,365	1,064,200	437,282
Mean	735,303	881,224	102,323
Median	547,694	889,753	76,949

4. Use PLA*metrics* to find the data.

STEP 1   Log on to the data service.

STEP 2   Click on the Local tab and the Report tab.

STEP 3   Click the Add button to create a new report.

STEP 4   Select "PLDS" as the Collection, then type in a descriptive Report Name and a description of the report. Add a Title if desired. Then, click the Save as New Report button.

STEP 5   Under Report Settings at the top, select the latest period for the report. In this case it was FY2012.

STEP 6   We want to create a report about ILL lending and receiving transactions. The indicators include

» Interlibrary Loan to Other Libraries

» Interlibrary Loan from Other Libraries

» ILL Lending per Week

» ILLs Received per Week

» ILL Lending per 1,000 Served

» ILLs Received per 1,000 Served

» This is a good time to click the Save button.

STEP 7   To limit the results to our benchmarking group, use the Locations filter to find the benchmarking partners or apply the Locations filter if you have identified the benchmarking group and have saved the list as a filter. For this report, we will add indicators for "Population of legal service area" and "Total operating expenditures" to help limit the libraries in our benchmarking group.

STEP 8   After adding all of the indicators, use the filters associated with the indicators to designate desired ranges. For population, we will use a low of 250,000 and a high of 500,000. For operating expenditures, we will use a low of $4 million and a high of $5.5 million. This is another good time to click the Save button.

STEP 9   Run the report and the results are displayed. In this example, data from seven libraries are available.

STEP 10 The table report includes columns for population and expenditures. These are not needed for this report. They were used for finding benchmarking partners. Return to Report Template and uncheck the boxes to the left of the indicators. Do not remove these two indicators. Save, and then run the report again.

STEP 11 Once you have the report results as you want them, you may save the data to an Excel spreadsheet by clicking on the Excel icon on the Results page.

Benchmarking ILL

Collection: **PLDS**   Period: **FY2012, Start 2012-01** Months: **12**

Locations (7)	Interlibrary loan to other libraries	Interlibrary loan from other libraries	ILL Lending Per Week	ILLs Received Per Week	ILL Lending Per 1,000 Served	ILLs Received Per 1,000 Served
ERIE COUNTY PUBLIC LIBRARY	39,829	30,077	766	578	320.43	241.97
FIRST REGIONAL LIBRARY	5,241	1,751	101	34	34.72	11.60
FLINT RIVER REGIONAL LIBRARY SYSTEM	89,479	78,309	1,144	1,506	367.31	483.59
GASTON-LINCOLN REGIONAL LIBRARY (NO DATA POST 2012)	522	1,499	10	29	4.30	12.36
MONT CO-NORRISTOWN PUB LIB	95,945	85,888	1,845	1,652	0.00	0.00
PORTLAND PUBLIC LIBRARY	20,581	21,429	396	412	294.01	306.13
SANTA ANA PUBLIC LIBRARY	173	10	3	0	1.30	0.08
Avg	31,681	31,280	609	602	146.01	150.82
Median	20,581	21,429	396	412	34.72	12.36

FILTERS	VALUES	
	MIN / %	MAX
POPULATION OF LEGAL SERVICE AREA	250,000	500,000
TOTAL OPERATING EXPENDITURES (TOTAL OF ITEMS 20-23)	4,000,000	5,500,000

5. Use ACRL*Metrics* to find the data.

STEP 1   Log on to the data service.

STEP 2   Click on the Local tab and the Report tab.

STEP 3   Click the Add button to create a new report.

STEP 4   Select "ACRL" as the Collection, then type in a descriptive Report Name and a description of the report. Add a Title if desired. Then, click the Save as New Report button.

STEP 5   Under Report Settings at the top, select the latest period for the report. In this case it was FY2012.

STEP 6   We want to create a table, so under Report Type, select "Table."

STEP 7   We can now select the indicators we want to include in the report. Go to the indicators box and select those indicators related to group presentations (instruction sessions), group participants (instruction attendees), and, for context, an indicator about the number of students:

» Presentations to Groups

» Participants in Group Presentations

» Average Participants per Group Presentation

» Total Students, Full-Time and Part-Time

» Presentations to Groups per Enrolled Students

» Participants in Group Presentations per Enrolled Student

This would be a good time to click on the Save button.

STEP 8   Once you have selected one or more indicators, the Locations function appears. Most academic institutions already have a select list of peers and aspirants for benchmarking. If you have saved a set of benchmarking partners, click Locations and select the filter you designated. If you have not set up the Locations filter, then go to Locations and select all of the libraries you wish to use as benchmarking partners. Provide a Filter Name (such as Peers), and click on the Apply button to save this group. Now this group of libraries will always be available for you to choose as a Locations filter. This would be another good time to click on the Save button.

STEP 9   Run the report. The report returned is in a table format. (It may be downloaded as a spreadsheet by clicking on the Excel icon.)

Benchmarking Presentations

Collection: **ACRL**   Period: **2012, Start 2011-07**   Months: **12**

Locations (11)	14. Presentations to Groups	15. Participants in Group Presentations	Average Participants Per Group Presentation	Total students, full-time and part-time	Presentations to Groups Per Enrolled Students	Participants in Group Presentations per Enrolled Student
East Tennessee State University	130	4,633	35.64	14,662	0.01	0.32
Indiana State University	260	4,555	17.52	10,857	0.02	0.42
Rowan University	103	2,060	20.00	11,816	0.01	0.17
Stephen F Austin State University	144	3,082	21.40	12,903	0.01	0.24
University of Arkansas at Little Rock	222	3,837	17.28	11,533	0.02	0.33
University of Massachusetts-Lowell	356	7,036	19.82	15,045	0.02	0.47
University of South Dakota	419	7,144	17.05	9,970	0.04	0.72
University of West Florida	232	4,088	17.62	11,982	0.02	0.34
University of West Georgia	854	23,086	27.03	11,769	0.07	1.96
Valdosta State University	210	5,250	25.00	13,089	0.02	0.40
Western Carolina University	292	6,836	23.41	9,352	0.03	0.73
Avg	293	6,510	21.98	12,089	0.03	0.55
Median	232	4,633	20.00	11,816	0.02	0.40

CHAPTER SEVEN

1. This question is one for discussion as there is no set answer.

2. A library need not limit its best practices search to its peers. Reviewing the peers or benchmarking partners should be considered, but the purpose of best practices is to find one or more libraries that have implemented an activity or procedure that has produced outstanding results in a situation that could be adopted through local replication to improve effectiveness or efficiency, or both, in a similar situation. The library's peers or benchmarking partners, however, may be experiencing the same unresolved problem or issue.

3. The library might search for other libraries that are circulating e-books at a high level and those that provide customers with access to downloadable media. You can use PLA*metrics* to answer the question.

STEP 1	Log on to the data service.
STEP 2	Click on the Local tab and the Report tab.
STEP 3	Click the Add button to create a new report.
STEP 4	Select "PLDS" as the Collection, then type in a descriptive Report Name and a description of the report. Add a Title if desired. Then, click the Save as New Report button.
STEP 5	Under Report Settings at the top, select the latest period for the report. In this case it was FY2012.
STEP 6	We want to create a report about the circulation of e-books and downloadable audio and visual media. Reviewing the indicators available in the data service, the public library chooses the following:

> » Expenditures for e-books
> » Expenditures for Downloadable Audio Books, Music, Video, and Other Multimedia
> » % of Library Materials Expenditures on e-books
> » % of Library Materials Expenditures on Downloadable Audio Books, Music, Video, and Other Multimedia

These expenditure figures will provide the financial context the library needs for its review. And, for circulation data:

> » Total Circulation for e-books, Downloadable Audio Books, Music, and Video
> » % of Total Circulation to Electronic Circulation
> » Electronic Circulation per Registered Borrower
> » Electronic Circulation per Capita

This is a good time to click the Save button.

STEP 7	To see what this all looks like, run the report. More than 2,200 libraries are listed. That is far too many; we will set some filters to narrow the results.

The library has a limited budget with which to purchase these electronic materials. It was decided that the library could expend 10 to 15 percent of its library materials on e-books and 5 to 10 percent on downloadable media. Enter these into the respective indicators' filters. Save the report and run it again. The report generates seven libraries.

Best Practices E-books and Downloadables

Collection: **PLDS**   Period: **FY2012, Start 2012-01**   Months: **12**

Locations {7}	Electronic circulation	% of Total Circ to Electronic Circulation	Electronic Circulation per Registered Borrower	Electronic Circulation per Capita	22.c.i Expenditures for eBooks	Expenditures for multimedia	% of Library Materials expenditures on Ebooks	% of Library Materials expenditures on Downloadable audio books, music, video, and other multimedia
ALLEN COUNTY PUBLIC LIBRARY	3,674,538	38.80%	12.00	10.34	$369,653	$217,892	11.12%	6.55%
ARLINGTON PUBLIC LIBRARY SYSTEM	117,588	5.54%	0.60	0.32	$115,447	$66,487	10.43%	6.01%
CALCASIEU PARISH PUBLIC LIBRARY	85,671	7.70%	1.07	0.44	$100,000	$78,000	11.64%	8.40%
CALHOUN COUNTY PUBLIC LIBRARY	7,486	6.01%	0.80	0.35	$6,415	$3,000	13.29%	6.21%
GREENSBORO PUBLIC LIBRARY	80,290	4.71%	0.34	0.20	$150,000	$85,284	14.21%	8.00%
HOOVER PUBLIC LIBRARY	47,884	3.04%	0.72	0.59	$80,758	$38,435	13.22%	6.29%
KENT DISTRICT LIBRARY	370,914	5.68%	1.90	0.94	$243,405	$174,544	10.33%	7.41%

FILTERS	VALUES	
	MIN / %	MAX
% OF LIBRARY MATERIALS EXPENDITURES ON EBOOKS	10	15
% OF LIBRARY MATERIALS EXPENDITURES ON DOWNLOADABLE AUDIO BOOKS, MUSIC, VIDEO, AND OTHER MULTIMEDIA	5	10

STEP 8   The results are for libraries expending a low of $6,415 for e-books and $3,000 for downloadable media to a high of $369,653 for e-books and $217,892 for media. The public library could not come close to the high expenditures, but was already expending above the low. Adjust the filters, eliminating the percentage of expenditures in favor of actual dollar amounts and placing a range of $10,000 to $20,000 for e-books and $5,000 to $10,000 for media. Because we are interested in circulation data, set that indicator's low filter to 1 to ensure the target libraries reported circulation. Save the report and run it again.

Report Settings **Options** **Option Settings** **Format**

Report Settings

Collection: PLDS
Period: FY2012
Report Name: Best Practices E-books and Downloadables
Description: E-books and Downloadables
Title: E-books and Downloadables

Report Type: Table   Report Folder: Report

[Run] [Save] [Save as New Report] [Save as New Template] [Publish Report]

Locations		Filters		
Locations				
Indicators		Value	% Filter Low >=	<= Filter High

PLDS

Operating Expenditures

☑	22.c.i Expenditures for eBooks		10000	20000
☑	22.c.ii Expenditures for downloadable audio books, music, video, and other multimedia		5000	10000

Annual Counts

☑	30. Total circulation for e-books, downloadable audio books, music, and video		1	

Circulation Ratios

☑	% of Total Circ to Electronic Circulation			
☑	Electronic Circulation per Registered Borrower			
☑	Electronic Circulation per Capita			

Financial Ratios

☑	% of Library Materials expenditures on Ebooks			
☑	% of Library Materials expenditures on Downloadable audio books, music, video, and other multimedia			

STEP 9 The results display fifteen libraries, which provides adequate data for the library to review and analyze, and to determine which libraries to contact to learn about their e-book and downloadable media services. (The report may be downloaded as a spreadsheet by clicking on the Excel icon.)

4. Library managers might search for other academic libraries that have a lower cost per reference transaction. We can use ACRL*Metrics* to find these libraries.

STEP 1 Log on to the data service.

STEP 2 Click on the Local tab and the Report tab.

STEP 3 Click the Add button to create a new report.

STEP 4 Select "ACRL" as the Collection, then type in a descriptive Report Name and a description of the report. Add a Title if desired. Then, click the Save as New Report button.

STEP 5 Under Report Settings at the top, select the latest period for the report. In this case it was FY2012.

STEP 6 We want to create a table, so under Report Type, select "Table."

STEP 7 We can now select the indicators we want to include in the report. Go to the indicators box and select those indicators related to reference transactions and possible cost areas, including

- » Reference Transactions
- » Total Staff Expenditures per Reference Transaction
- » Total Operating Expenditures per Reference Transaction
- » Reference Transactions per Staff FTE
- » Reference Transactions per Week
- » Total Staff (FTE)
- » Professional Staff (FTE)
- » Support Staff (FTE)
- » Student Assistants (FTE)

This would be a good time to click on the Save button.

STEP 8 We need to add some filters to limit the results. Cost per reference transaction is largely based on staffing costs, including the mixture of staff type (e.g., professional, support) answering reference questions. Use Total Staff (FTE) with a low filter of 40 and a high filter of 50 because the library's FTE is in the middle of this range.

STEP 9 Save the report, and then run it. The result is 67 libraries, which is too many for an efficient review.

STEP 10 The library has twelve FTE professional staff. Filter this indicator with a low of 10 and a high of 14. Save and run the report. The result is seventeen libraries, which is a good start for this library's best practices review. (The report may be downloaded as a spreadsheet by clicking on the Excel icon.)

Best Practices Reference Transactions

Collection: **ACRL** Period: **2012, Start 2011-07** Months: **12**

Locations (17)	16. Reference Transactions	Total Staff Expenditures per Reference Transaction	Total Operating Expenditures per Reference Transaction	Reference Transactions Per Staff FTE	Reference Transactions Per Week	13. Total Staff (FTE)	13a. Professional Staff (FTE)	13b. Support Staff (FTE)	13c. Student Assistants (FTE)
Brigham Young University-Idaho	68,670	$25.63	$39.91	1,373	1,320.58	50.00	12.00	8.50	30.00
California State University, East Bay	23,816	$71.99	$120.55	594	458.00	40.75	11.00	16.25	13.50
California State University-San Marcos	7,984	$322.74	$444.86	179	153.54	44.50	13.00	22.50	9.00
Coastal Carolina University	5,150	$367.27	$479.21	126	99.04	41.00	11.00	15.00	15.00
College of New Rochelle	3,828	$403.14	$499.38	87	73.62	44.00	13.00	15.00	15.00
CUNY Bronx Community College	34,276	$47.31	$63.07	816	659.04	42.00	12.00	13.00	17.00
East Tennessee State University	40,988	$29.27	$63.83	976	788.17	42.00	14.00	19.00	9.00
Eastern Washington University	5,918	$306.48	$742.97	138	113.81	43.00	14.00	18.00	11.00
Furman University	2,291	$575.43	$1,424.19	57	44.06	40.00	14.00	15.00	11.00
Humboldt State University	3,690	$450.54	$707.46	88	70.96	42.00	13.50	19.50	9.00
Ithaca College	9,060	$172.98	$358.61	191	172.05	47.00	14.00	17.00	16.00
Lamar Institute of Technology	2,407	$628.55	$1,456.33	52	46.29	46.00	15.00	19.00	14.00
Louisiana Tech University	17,001	$69.86	$141.42	362	326.94	47.00	13.00	14.00	20.00
McNeese State University	2,825	$355.54	$598.13	58	54.25	49.00	12.00	9.00	28.00
Saint Mary's University	7,387	$356.91	$561.85	148	142.06	50.00	13.00	28.00	9.00
University of California-Merced	2,261	$661.58	$1,376.66	57	43.48	40.00	10.00	11.00	19.50
University of West Florida	40,391	$32.00	$65.11	518	776.79	44.00	11.00	24.00	9.00

1/1   20   Sort multiple columns by holding down the shift key and clicking another column header

Filters	Values	
	Min / %	Max
Total Staff (FTE)	40	50
Professional Staff (FTE)	10	14

5. The library might search for other libraries that have a high level of attendance per program to find out why they are successful, perhaps because they implemented a program marketing strategy. We can use PLA*metrics* to answer the question.

STEP 1 Log on to the data service.

STEP 2 Click on the Local tab and the Report tab.

STEP 3 Click the Add button to create a new report.

STEP 4 Select "PLDS" as the Collection, then type in a descriptive Report Name and a description of the report. Add a Title if desired. Then, click the Save as New Report button.

STEP 5 Under Report Settings at the top, select the latest period for the report. In this case it was FY2012.

STEP 6 We want to create a report about program attendance. Reviewing the indicators available in the data service, the public library chooses the following:
   » Total Annual Number of Programs
   » Total Annual Program Attendance
   » Program Attendance per Program
   » Program Attendance Per Capita
This is a good time to click the Save button.

STEP 7 To see what this all looks like, run the report; more than 2,200 libraries are listed. Because this number is so large, we can set some filters to narrow the results.

The library has limitations on the number of programs it can offer: a children's program twice a week and biweekly adult programs. Therefore, set the high filter on "Total annual number of programs" to 128. The library also expects to conduct at least weekly children's programs and a monthly adult program. Set the low filter to 64. Save the report and run it again. The report returns 195 libraries, which is still too many.

STEP 8 The library also has a limitation on attendees, although that number is currently unmet. It can accommodate a maximum of 35 children per program and 100 adults per program, for an annual total of 4,420. Enter that number into the "Total annual program attendance" indicator as the high filter. Save the report and run it again. The results are only reduced by eleven libraries.

STEP 9 Because the number of results is still too many, add the indicator for "Population of legal service area." Then set filters to reflect the library's service area: a low of 10,000 for the immediate geographic area and a high of 25,000 to include the surrounding areas. Save the report and then run it. The results return twenty-eight libraries, which is sufficient for the library to begin its review. (The report may be downloaded as a spreadsheet by clicking on the Excel icon.)

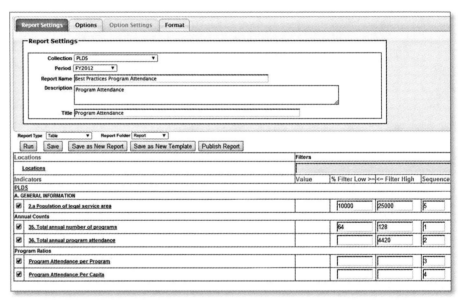

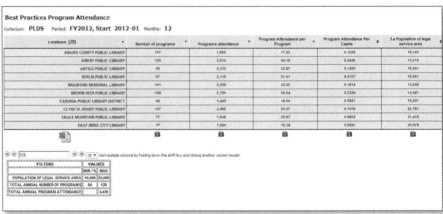

6. The library's managers could search for other academic libraries that have materials expenditures above 50 percent by using ACRL*Metrics*.

STEP 1 Log on to the data service.

STEP 2 Click on the Local tab and the Report tab.

STEP 3 Click the Add button to create a new report.

STEP 4 Select "ACRL" as the Collection, then type in a descriptive Report Name and a description of the report. Add a Title if desired. Then, click the Save as New Report button.

STEP 5 Under Report Settings at the top, select the latest period for the report. In this case it was FY2012.

STEP 6 We want to create a table, so under Report Type, select "Table."

STEP 7 We can now select the indicators we want to include in the report. Go to the indicators box and select those indicators related to staff expenditures; however, for this answer do not include fringe benefits:

> » % of Operating Expenditures on Staff Expenditures
> » % of Operating Expenditures on Collection Materials
> » % of Operating Expenditures on Other
> » Total Staff (FTE)
> » Professional Staff (FTE)
> » Support Staff (FTE)
> » Student Assistants (FTE)

This would be a good time to click on the Save button.

STEP 8 Filters will help to limit the results. The key indicator for this report is that the expenditures on collection materials exceed 50 percent of total operating expenditures. Insert the 50 percent as the indicator's low filter. Save and run the report. The results return 217 libraries, which exceeds the library's capacity to review and then contact the target libraries for information about staffing.

STEP 9 The other variable to examine is staffing FTE. Insert a low of 10 and a high of 14 as the filters for the Professional Staff (FTE) indicator, the range for this type of staff in the local library. Save and run the report.

STEP 10 The results display twenty-three libraries, which is a good starting point to review the target libraries and their mixture of staff to support collection materials expenditures of greater than 50 percent. (The report may be downloaded as a spreadsheet by clicking on the Excel icon.) Only the first page from the report has been captured because of the size of the report.

Best Practices Materials Expenditures

Collection: **ACRL**   Period: **2012, Start 2011-07**   Months: **12**

Locations (23)	% of Operating Expenditures on Staff Expenditures	% of Operating Expenditures on Collection Materials	% of Operating Expenditures on Other	13a. Professional Staff (FTE)	13b. Support Staff (FTE)	13c. Student Assistants (FTE)	13. Total Staff (FTE)
Bates College	39.41%	56.17%	4.42%	11.33	14.50	4.46	30.29
Creighton University	37.89%	55.77%	6.34%	10.00	10.50	4.50	25.00
East Tennessee State University	44.29%	52.38%	3.34%	14.00	19.00	9.00	42.00
Fayetteville State University	33.73%	61.57%	4.70%	12.00	18.00	4.00	34.00
Furman University	40.69%	59.31%	0.00%	14.00	15.00	11.00	40.00
Gettysburg College	40.50%	50.55%	8.95%	14.00	12.00	7.00	33.00
John Marshall Law School	44.77%	55.23%	0.00%	14.00	4.00	1.25	19.25
Kenyon College	48.91%	51.09%	0.00%	12.00	6.60	17.00	35.60
Lamar Institute of Technology	43.05%	52.67%	4.27%	13.00	19.00	14.00	46.00
Louisiana State University Health Sciences Center at New Orleans	35.48%	62.84%	1.68%	11.00	11.00	2.00	24.00

1/3   10 ▾   Sort multiple columns by holding down the shift key and clicking another column header

Filters	Values	
	Min / %	Max
Professional Staff (FTE)	10	14
% of Operating Expenditures on Collection Materials	50	

CHAPTER EIGHT

These questions are ones for discussion as no single or simple answer applies to all libraries. Any additional variables and metrics should be relevant to the local planning process and to accountability to the library's stakeholders. As you answer the questions, you should review a list of the library's key stakeholders and what their expectations are. What are the similarities and differences in those expectations?

CHAPTER NINE

1. Customers save personal funds when they borrow books and other resources from the library (circulation transactions, library visits). Receiving an answer to an information need from reference services saves the customer personal time (reference transactions). A customer may use the library's computers attached to a broadband Internet connection because it is not available or affordable to them at home (number of times public workstations are used). A parent bringing a child to a story hour or other library-sponsored educational programs may be an experience not locally available elsewhere (program attendance, library visits). Being able to access library resources and services remotely may save the customer time as well as the cost of traveling to the library (visits to library website, number of items downloaded). The ability to use the library's website to answer a question—what are today's hours?—may save customers time as well as increase their satisfaction with the library by being able to answer the question on their own and not arriving at a closed library (visits to library website, page visits to the FAQ). There are other local services and resources that customers find valuable. When calculating a return on investment, each library needs to identify and assign a dollar value to the services and resources customers use and consider beneficial from their perspective. (See, for instance, University of West Florida Libraries, Office of the Dean of Libraries, "Student Return on Investment [SROI]," http://libguides.uwf.edu/content.php?pid=188487&sid=2183215.)

2. Collection turnover rate is calculated by dividing the number of materials checked out by the size of the collection. The result of the calculation indicates how often each item in the collection was lent; it is a relevant metric about the use of the collection. Use PLA*metrics* to answer the question.

STEP 1	Log on to the data service.
STEP 2	Click on the Local tab and the Report tab.
STEP 3	Click the Add button to create a new report.
STEP 4	Select "PLDS" as the Collection, then type in a descriptive Report Name and a description of the report. Add a Title if desired. Then, click the Save as New Report button.
STEP 5	Under Report Settings at the top, select the latest period for the report. In this case it was FY2012.

STEP 6   We want to create a report about collection turnover. Because the turnover rate involves holdings and circulation, we want to also include circulation and holdings data for context. Reviewing the indicators available in the Counting Opinions PLDS data set, the public library chooses the following:

» Collection Turnover

» Total Annual Circulation

» Circulation per Capita

» Holdings

» Holdings per Capita

This is a good time to click the Save button.

STEP 7   To see what this all looks like, run the report. More than 1,808 libraries are listed. This is far too many; we can set some filters to narrow the results.

STEP 8   Add the "Population of legal service area" indicator. Then apply the filter associated with the indicator to designate a population range with a low of 250,000 and a high of 400,000; the library's population is about in the middle. Save the report and run it again.

STEP 9   The report lists sixty-one libraries. In reviewing the report table, we observe that not all libraries have a calculated collection turnover rate because they have failed to report holdings. To further refine the report, add a low filter of .1 for the Collection Turnover indicator to ensure all libraries listed in the table have a turnover rate. (Note: Counting Opinions displays this filter only in whole numbers and not decimals. Therefore, .1 shows as 0.) Save the report and run it again.

STEP 10   The results display fifty-seven libraries, which provides adequate information for the library to review and analyze. The report may be downloaded as a spreadsheet by clicking on the Excel icon. (Because of the size of the table, only the first ten libraries from the report are displayed.)

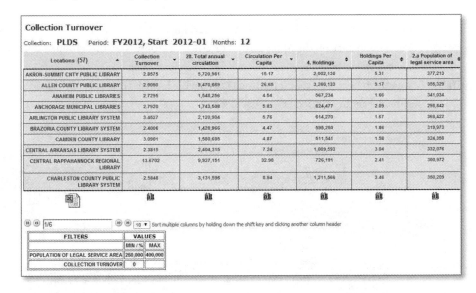

3. To answer the question, use ACRL*Metrics*.

STEP 1 Log on to the data service.

STEP 2 Click on the Local tab and the Report tab.

STEP 3 Click the Add button to create a new report.

STEP 4 Select "ACRL" as the Collection, then type in a descriptive Report Name and a description of the report. Add a Title if desired. Then, click the Save as New Report button.

STEP 5 Under Report Settings at the top, select the latest period for the report. In this case it was FY2012.

STEP 6 We want to create a table, so under Report Type, select "Table."

STEP 7 We can now select the indicators we want to include in the report. Go to the indicators box and select those indicators related to collection use, including

» Initial Circulation Transactions
» Circulation per Enrolled Students
» Total Items Borrowed (ILL)
» ILL Borrowed per Enrolled FT Student

To place circulation and interlibrary loan in context, we can include collection indicators:

» Titles Held
» Titles Held per Enrolled FT Student
» Volumes Held (as of June 30 reporting year)
» Volumes Held per Enrolled FT Student

This would be a good time to click on the Save button.

STEP 8 Once you have selected one or more indicators, the Locations function appears. Most academic institutions already have a select list of peers and aspirants for benchmarking. If you have saved a set of benchmarking partners, click Locations and select the filter you designated. If you have not set up the Locations filter, then go to Locations and select all of the libraries you wish to use as benchmarking partners. Type in a Filter Name (such as Peers), and click on the Apply button to save this group. Now this group of libraries will always be available for you to choose as a Locations filter.

STEP 9 Run the report. The report returned is in a table format. (It may be downloaded as a spreadsheet by clicking on the Excel icon.)

Circulation and ILLs

Collection: **ACRL**   Period: **2012, Start 2011-07**   Months: **12**

Locations (11)	17. Initial Circulation Transactions	Circulation Per Enrolled Students	22. Total Items Borrowed (ILL)	ILL Borrowed per Enrolled FT Student	1. Titles Held	Titles Held per Enrolled FT Student	2. Volumes held (as of June 30 reporting year)	Volumes Held per Enrolled FT Student
East Tennessee State University	118,519	8.08	13,497	1.13	866,595	73	899,753	76
Indiana State University	120,149	11.07	6,312	0.66	1,384,378	148	1,213,878	129
Rowan University	27,161	2.30	4,236	0.46	366,009	40	407,891	44
Stephen F Austin State University	48,956	3.79	3,173	0.31	1,713,193	168	2,002,825	196
University of Arkansas at Little Rock	25,729	2.23	5,772	0.83	516,173	74	660,229	95
University of Massachusetts-Lowell	12,514	0.83	6,788	0.75	215,983	24	273,391	30
University of South Dakota	23,340	2.34	9,306	1.60	695,865	120	1,082,263	186
University of West Florida	217,758	18.17	5,312	0.70	528,729	70	1,086,562	143
University of West Georgia	78,713	6.69	2,075	0.24	339,435	39	456,807	52
Valdosta State University	58,562	4.47	3,615	0.36	547,694	54	555,667	55
Western Carolina University	32,234	3.45	10,314	1.45	914,368	129	1,064,200	150

1/1   20 ▼   Sort multiple columns by holding down the shift key and clicking another column header

4. Managers may seek data concerning library visits, circulation, and in-library use. Use PLA*metrics* to answer the question.

STEP 1 Log on to the data service.

STEP 2 Click on the Local tab and the Report tab.

STEP 3 Click the Add button to create a new report.

STEP 4 Select "PLDS" as the Collection, then type in a descriptive Report Name and a description of the report. Add a Title if desired. Then, click the Save as New Report button.

STEP 5 Under Report Settings at the top, select the latest period for the report. In this case it was FY2012.

STEP 6 We want to create a report about in-library use, visits, and circulation. Reviewing the indicators available in the PLDS data set, we choose the following:

» In-Library Use per Visit

» In-Library Use per Capita

» Total Annual In-Library Materials Use

» Total Annual Number of Library Visits

» Visits per Capita

» Circulation per Capita

» Total Annual Circulation

This is a good time to click the Save button.

STEP 7 To see what this all looks like, run the report. More than 2,200 libraries are listed. This is far too many; we can set some filters to narrow the results.

We note that data for in-library use are missing for many libraries. To eliminate those libraries from the report, we can set the low filter for the "Total annual in-library materials use" indicator to 1 so that a library would have had to report in-library use to be listed on the table. Save the report and run it again. The results list 487 libraries.

STEP 8 Add the "Population of legal service area" indicator. Then apply the filter associated with the indicator to designate a population range with a low of 250,000 and a high of 400,000; the library's population is about in the middle. Save the report and run it again.

STEP 9 The results return twenty-five libraries, which is sufficient for the library to begin its review. (The report may be downloaded as a spreadsheet by clicking on the Excel icon. Because of the size of the table, only the first ten libraries from the report are displayed.)

In-Library use

Collection: **PLDS** Period: **FY2012, Start 2012-01** Months: **12**

Locations (25)	In-Library Use Per Visit	In-Library Use Per Capita	In-library use of materials	Library visits	Visits per Capita	Circulation Per Capita	28. Total annual circulation	2.a Population of legal service area
AKRON-SUMMIT CNTY PUBLIC LIBRARY	0.6272	4.9962	1,884,636	3,004,841	7.97	15.17	5,720,981	377,213
ALLEN COUNTY PUBLIC LIBRARY	0.1653	1.2879	457,615	2,768,804	7.79	26.65	9,470,669	355,329
BRAZORIA COUNTY LIBRARY SYSTEM	0.4206	0.8051	257,608	612,468	1.91	4.47	1,428,966	319,973
CAMDEN COUNTY LIBRARY	0.2774	0.7168	232,492	838,240	2.59	4.87	1,580,695	324,358
CENTRAL ARKANSAS LIBRARY SYSTEM	0.9465	6.4420	2,139,245	2,260,175	6.81	7.24	2,404,315	332,076
CENTRAL RAPPAHANNOCK REGIONAL LIBRARY	0.1793	1.7733	533,702	2,977,364	9.89	32.98	9,927,191	300,972
CHARLESTON COUNTY PUBLIC LIBRARY SYSTEM	0.4838	2.6814	939,941	1,940,896	5.54	8.94	3,131,596	350,209
FORSYTH COUNTY PUBLIC LIBRARY	0.4659	2.0224	711,458	1,526,949	4.34	5.45	1,915,971	351,790
GENESEE DISTRICT LIBRARY	0.0000	0.1469	48,561	N/A	0.00	11.32	3,741,783	330,562
HENRICO COUNTY PUBLIC LIBRARY	0.5000	3.2722	1,020,037	2,040,073	6.54	15.48	4,825,923	311,726

1/3   10 ▼ Sort multiple columns by holding down the shift key and clicking another column header

FILTERS	VALUES	
	MIN / %	MAX
POPULATION OF LEGAL SERVICE AREA	250,000	400,000
TOTAL ANNUAL IN-LIBRARY MATERIALS USE	1	

5. Use ACRL*Metrics* to answer the question.

STEP 1   Log on to the data service.

STEP 2   Click on the Local tab and the Report tab.

STEP 3   Click the Add button to create a new report.

STEP 4   Select "ACRL" as the Collection, then type in a descriptive Report Name and a description of the report. Add a Title if desired. Then, click the Save as New Report button.

STEP 5   Under Report Settings at the top, select the latest period for the report. In this case it was FY2012.

STEP 6   We want to create a trend report, so under Report Type, select "Trend/PI."

STEP 7   Selecting a trend report causes a Start Period box to appear in the Report Settings. Select the year for the trend's starting point. For this report 2010 was selected.

STEP 8   We can now select the indicators we want to include in the report. Go to the indicators box and select the indicators for

»   Initial Circulation Transactions

»   Reference Transactions

»   Number of Successful Full-Text Article Requests

This would be a good time to click on the Save button.

STEP 9   Once you have selected one or more indicators, the Locations function appears. Most academic institutions already have a select list of peers and aspirants for benchmarking. If you have saved a set of benchmarking partners, click Locations and select the filter you designated. If you have not set up the Locations filter, then go to Locations and select all of the libraries you wish to use as benchmarking partners. Type in a Filter Name (such as Peers), and click on the Apply button to save this group. Now this group of libraries will always be available for you to choose as a Locations filter.

STEP 10   To ensure that all indicators have data, set a low filter for each at 1. Save and run the report.

STEP 11   The report provides three tables of data. (The report may be downloaded as a spreadsheet by clicking on the Excel icon.)

17. Initial Circulation Transactions	2010	2011	2012
East Tennessee State University	86,075	68,092	118,519
Rowan University	25,581	25,308	27,161
University of Arkansas at Little Rock	25,251	26,834	25,729
University of Massachusetts-Lowell	8,425	11,529	12,514
University of South Dakota	27,376	25,173	23,340
University of West Florida	66,595	58,446	217,758
University of West Georgia	63,924	72,104	78,713
Valdosta State University	62,662	62,763	58,562
Western Carolina University		36,367	32,234

16. Reference Transactions	2010	2011	2012
East Tennessee State University	16,777	35,780	40,985
Rowan University	7,487	5,936	2,821
University of Arkansas at Little Rock	11,144	11,150	7,351
University of Massachusetts-Lowell	1,900	3,632	3,510
University of South Dakota	5,407	4,266	5,286
University of West Florida	63,864	65,732	40,391
University of West Georgia	4,635	3,223	9,862
Valdosta State University	9,694	11,311	14,539
Western Carolina University		21,550	16,411

18. Number of successful full-text article requests	2010	2011	2012
East Tennessee State University	300,000	500,000	259,521
Rowan University	NA/UA	0	65,124
University of Arkansas at Little Rock	991,304	222,790	241,976
University of Massachusetts-Lowell	657,687	1,049,396	1,110,904
University of South Dakota	491,947	625,853	616,776
University of West Florida	183,422	433,456	486,550
University of West Georgia	155,614	200,614	591,788
Valdosta State University	1,075,785	455,868	1,215,862
Western Carolina University		52,166	77,383

STEP 12   To view the trend lines, click on the trend line chart to the right of the indicator's name on the table report.

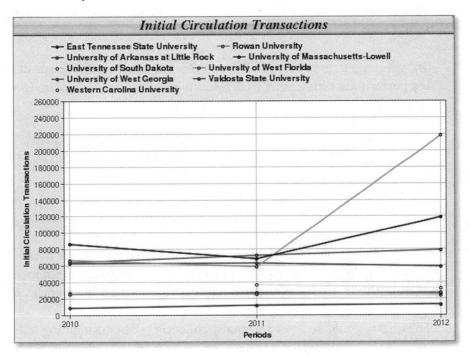

Initial Circulation Transactions

CHAPTER TEN

1. Construct a pie chart, which is a circular chart divided into sections; each section shows the relative size of each value. Note that if you want part of the pie chart to stand out (for instance, the portion on personnel or other operating expenses), an exploding pie chart might be used. In this chart, a slice of the pie—or even every slice—is pulled out, or separated, from the whole.

2. Construct a bar chart, which is a graph in which rectangular bars show the size of each value.

3. A common trend is for five years. A line chart illustrates trends. An alternative is to use bar charts, but with the addition of a trend line, which is a line on a chart showing the general direction that a group of points seems to be heading.

4. The first part of the question is for discussion. The visual might take the form of a dashboard (see chapter 11); a dashboard might also be labeled an assessment dashboard. Like the instrument panel in a car or airplane, a dashboard displays critical data in easy-to-read graphics. For an example, see University of Richmond, Boatwright Memorial Library, "Library Assessment Dashboard," http://library.richmond.edu/about/assessment/.

5. This is a discussion question. (The question might also be answered by considering a dashboard.)

CHAPTER ELEVEN

1. This question is one for discussion as no single or simple answer applies to all libraries.

2. One means is to measure and report to stakeholders on the status of meeting key performance indicators (KPIs) in the library's strategic plan. Here is an example:
   » The library has developed a five-year strategic plan.
   » The plan identifies several objectives; by definition, an objective is measurable. One objective states that the library will acquire and make available a user-relevant print collection.
   » Apply collection use as a proxy for the relevancy of the collection. Collection use indicators include circulation transactions, in-library use, interlibrary loan borrowing, and collection turnover.
   » The library could link those four indicators to demonstrate in its accountability report to stakeholders that it is meeting, or not meeting, the objective of acquiring and making available a user-relevant print collection.

3. The library could do so by internally collecting data, responding to library surveys to submit data, using data sets to benchmark indicators with peers, and seeking best practices. The starting point is to collect internal data

MANAGEMENT INFORMATION STATISTICS: DOCUMENT DELIVERY

	FY2004	FY2005	FY2006	FY2007	FY2008
INTERLIBRARY LOANS & DOCUMENTS PROVIDED TO OTHERS					
Returnable	3,426	2,428	4,841	4,712	4,818
Non-returnable	3,249	2,097	4,536	3,676	2,707
Uborrow (went public August 1, 2011)					
Total loaned	6,675	4,525	9,377	8,388	7,525
INTERLIBRARY LOANS & DOCUMENTS RECEIVED FROM OTHERS					
Returnable	3,250	2,181	2,088	1,761	1,398
Non-returnable	1,935	1,743	1,712	1,451	931
Uborrow (went public August 1, 2011)					
Documents received from commercial services	0	0	0	0	0
Total received	5,185	3,924	3,800	3,212	2,329
Net lending ("-" means we are net borrower)	1,490	601	5,577	5,176	5,196

revised: July 29, 2013

that can be used to respond to surveys from the divisions of the American Library Association or other responsible bodies. The local data submitted must be accurate and align with the survey question: one may not substitute circulation transactions for reference transactions. The bodies then compile the data and make them available as a data set. Once available, the library uses the data set to compare indicators with its peers or other comparison groups. It may also use a data set to identify libraries with best practices that meet or exceed one or more objectives set by the library but currently unmet. For example, the library's objective is to circulate 2.0 print books per capita. Using one or more data sets, the local library identifies other libraries that have achieved that objective and then seeks to learn from them, possibly adopting their procedures and practices so as to improve. Continuous implementation of these data activities would help to establish the library as a practitioner of evidence-based management.

4. A simple model uses an internal spreadsheet to organize the library's collected data. Additionally, using a spreadsheet enables the library to organize data representing years by columns and rows. The information can be organized by the library's infrastructure (collections, staffing, technologies, and facilities) and by functions (e.g., expenditures) or activities (e.g., circulation transactions). An example of an MIS spreadsheet about interlibrary loan (document delivery) is shown below.

	FY2009	FY2010	FY2011	FY2012	FY2013
INTERLIBRARY LOANS & DOCUMENTS PROVIDED TO OTHERS					
Returnable	4,997	3,518	3,446	2,741	2,206
Non-returnable	1,701	5,744	7,611	7,625	8,862
Uborrow (went public August 1, 2011)			212	1,572	1,540
Total loaned	6,698	9,262	11,269	11,938	12,608
INTERLIBRARY LOANS & DOCUMENTS RECEIVED FROM OTHERS					
Returnable	1,713	2,393	2,204	2,279	1,686
Non-returnable	1,398	2,190	2,402	2,175	2,634
Uborrow (went public August 1, 2011)			104	852	847
Documents received from commercial services	0	0	1	6	1
Total received	3,111	4,583	4,711	5,312	5,168
Net lending ("-" means we are net borrower)	3,587	4,679	6,558	6,626	7,440

The decade of data could be graphed as trends for visual presentations to stakeholders.

5. The sources include the following:
   » Transaction data gathered from the integrated library system
   » Gate/entrance counts
   » Data from the library's website, such as number of pages visited and number of unique users
   » Activity data from web-based library forms or documents, such as the number of times a library orientation video has been viewed
   » Forms used by the reference staff to compile information about the number and context of questions and answers
   » Database and other e-resources use data provided by third-party information providers
   » Surveys completed by users and nonusers
   » Sheets of paper with tally marks from library staff counting activities, such as program attendance

6. Data are applied as evidence to support decision making in the management of libraries. To qualify as evidence, the data must be reliable, valid, and relevant to the decision for which they are being applied. Data are also applied for reporting library inputs, processes, outcomes, and value to stakeholders supporting assessment and evaluation, both of which are processes of evidence-based management.

ABOUT THE AUTHORS

ROBERT E. DUGAN is the dean of libraries at the University of West Florida (Pensacola, Florida). Prior to assuming this position, he had been at Suffolk University, Boston; Wesley College, Dover, Delaware; and Georgetown University, Washington, D.C. He has also worked in state and public libraries during his more than forty-year career. He is the coauthor of twelve books, including the award-winning *Viewing Library Metrics from Different Perspectives* (2009).

PETER HERNON is a professor emeritus at Simmons College, Boston, and was the principal (and founding) faculty member for the doctoral program, Managerial Leadership in the Information Professions. He received his PhD degree from Indiana University, Bloomington, was the 2008 recipient of the Association of College and Research Libraries' award for Academic/Research Librarian of the Year, is the coeditor of *Library & Information Science Research*, and has taught, conducted workshops, and delivered addresses in ten countries outside the United States. He is the author or coauthor of fifty-six books, including the award-winning *Federal Information Policies in the 1980s* (1985), *Assessing Service Quality* (1998), and *Viewing Library Metrics from Different Perspectives* (2009).

JOSEPH R. MATTHEWS is a consultant specializing in strategic planning, assessment and evaluation of library services, customer service, use of performance metrics, and the balanced scorecard. He was an instructor at the San Jose State University School of Library and Information Science. He is the author of, among other books, *Research-Based Planning for Public Libraries* (2013), *The Customer-Focused Library* (2009), *The Evaluation and Measurement of Library Services* (2007), *Scorecards for Results* (2008), and *Strategic Planning and Management for Managers* (2005); the coauthor (with Peter Hernon) of *Reflecting on the Future of Academic and Public Libraries* (2013) and *Listening to the Customer* (2011); and the coauthor (with Peter Hernon and Robert E. Dugan) of *Getting Started with Evaluation* (2014).

INDEX

f denotes figures; *t* denotes tables; *b* denotes text boxes

A